C000178559

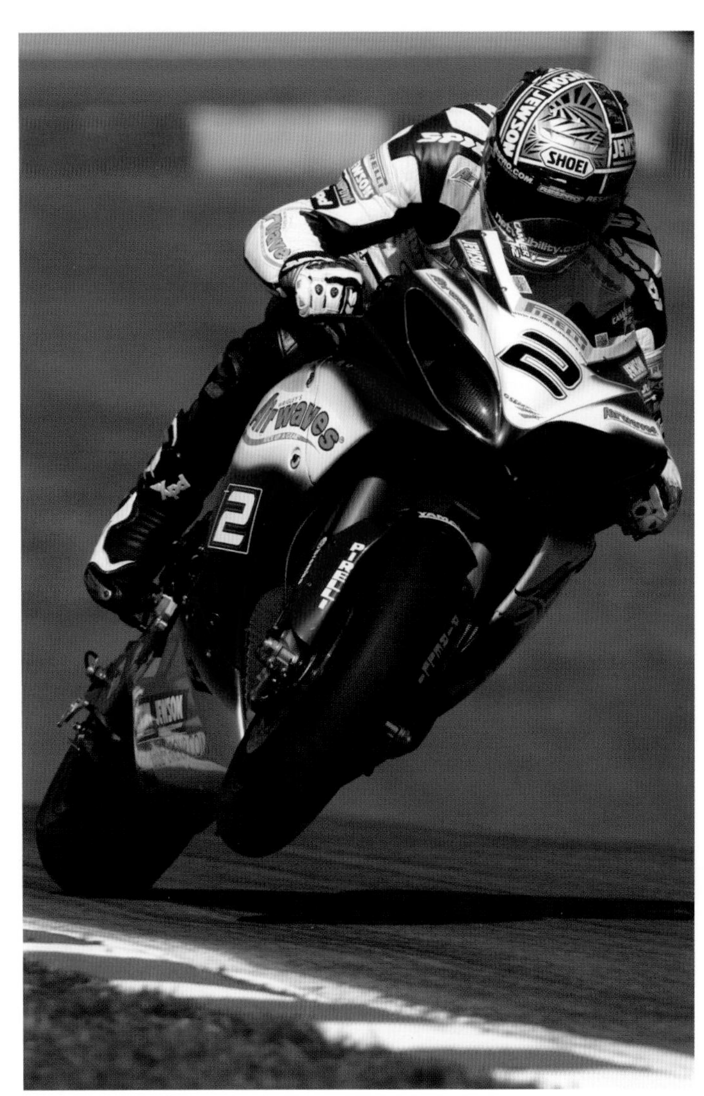
SHOEI

Published in 2009 by
The Original Double Red Ltd
4 Gateway Court
Dankerwood Road
South Hykeham
Lincoln LN6 9UL

Tel: +44 (0)1522 693 278
www.doublered.co.uk

ISBN 978-0-9534420-6-5

Photography and Copyright of all images
Double Red

Project Manager
Sue Ward

Picture Editors
James Wright
Sue Ward

Contributors
Dave Fern
Sue Jobling
Phil Wain

Contributing Editors
Larry Carter

Design and Layout
Katie Ward

Results and statistics
Timing Solutions Ltd. www.tsl-timing.com

Special Thanks to:
The organisers and sponsors involved in the MCE Insurance British Superbike Series, especially the team at MSVR, whose dedication and commitment makes the MCE British Insurance Superbike Championship the strongest domestic championship in the world. Every single person involved in the organisation and running of the championship whose often difficult jobs go unnoticed and unrewarded - they know who they are - the medics, physios, marshals, press officers, scrutineers, journalists, television crews, truck drivers, mechanics, chefs, cleaners, hospitality crews, commentators etc and last but not least the riders and teams, who seldom complain at 'just one more shot' and make the MCE Insurance British Superbike Championship the amazing spectacle it is.

Contents

"Champions aren't made in gyms, champions are made from something they have deep inside them - a desire, a dream, a vision."

- Muhammad Ali

Foreword
Seeing Red 2009

What a season!
I could never have even dreamed it would go so well, especially at the beginning of the year when we found out we weren't going to have the opportunity to test and that there was a good chance we might not even be at the first race! To be fair, on paper, we didn't even look like we were in for a shot at the title. But thankfully we don't race on paper and to finish the season with 19 race wins from 26 starts, most poles in a championship season and most points in a season is simply unbelievable.

Darrell Healey has played a massive part throughout my career, he got me started in 125s in 2000 and after my crash at Cadwell Park in 2007 (when I managed to wrap my leg around my head), I was told I didn't have a job for 2008, Darrell stepped in and gave me a massive opportunity to prove myself - first of all riding with Shakey and then this season on the brand new Airwaves Yamaha.

So many people have put effort into getting me where I am now and I can't thank everyone enough. Jewson have supported me since 2005 and stuck by me through the ups and downs. My Mum and Dad who sacrificed so much (including their house) for me to go racing. I owe everything to them, and it really has been such a team effort from all my friends and family.

My best mate and manager Andy Walker has been a massive influence, we raced together in 125s in 2000 and since then with his help we've won both Supersport and Superbike titles. Looking to the future... who knows, with a likely move to WSB in 2010 I am working for even more success.

Leon Camier
2009 MCE Insurance British Superbike Champion

British Superbike Championship Top Ten

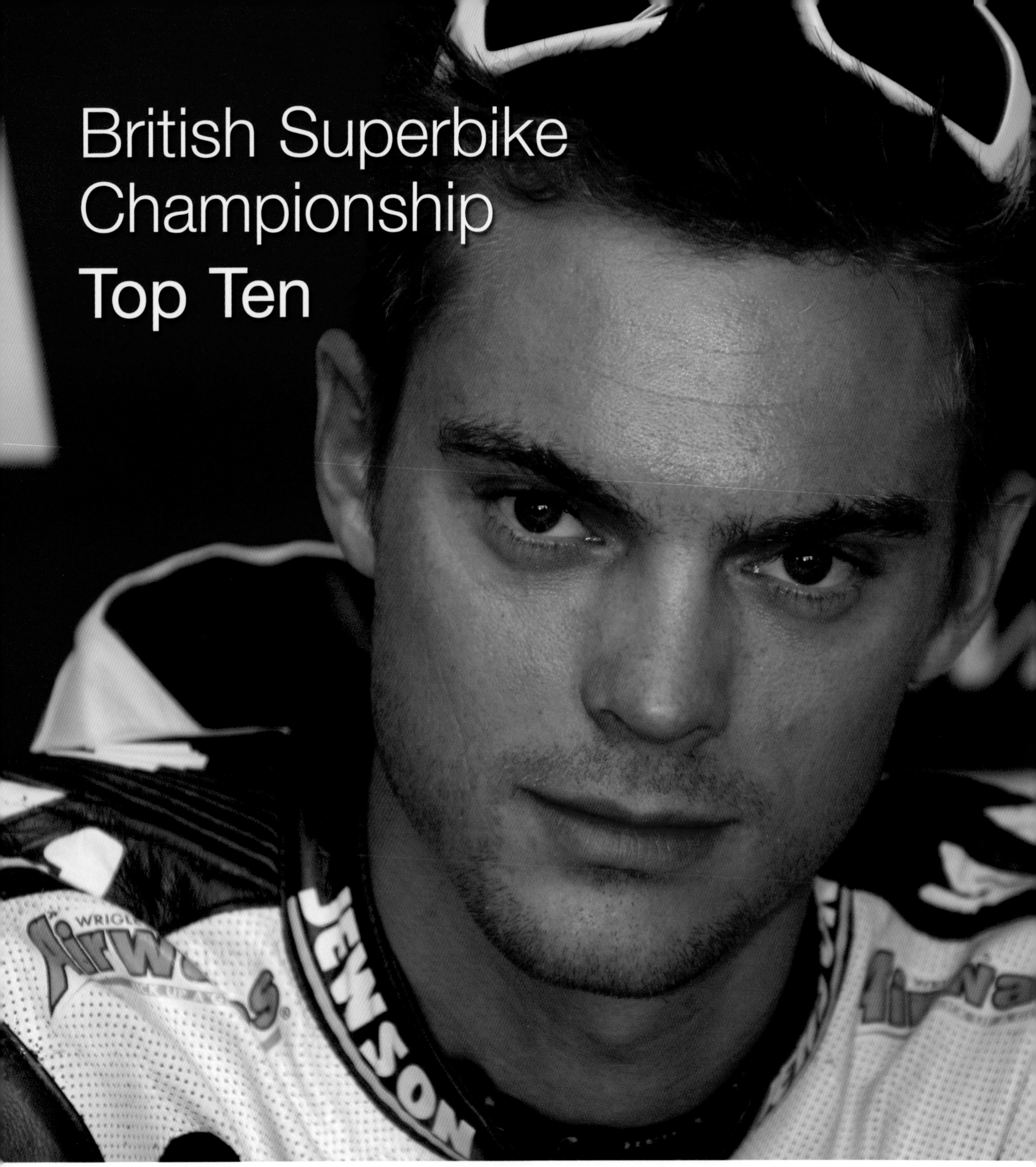

Results	
Position:	1
Points:	549.5
Poles:	9
Front Rows:	2
Best Grid:	Pole
Races:	26
Wins:	19
Podiums:	3
Best Result:	19 x 1st
Fastest Laps:	18

R1	Brands Hatch Indy:	4th + 1st
R2	Oulton:	1st + 1st
R3	Donington:	1st + 12th
R4	Thruxton:	1st + 1st
R5	Snetterton:	1st + 1st
R6	Knockhill:	1st + 1st
R7	Mallory:	2nd + 1st
R8	Brands Hatch GP:	1st + 1st + 1st
R9	Cadwell:	1st + DQ
R10	Croft:	6th + 1st
R11	Silverstone:	1st + 2nd
R12	Oulton:	2nd + 1st + 1st

Leon Camier

Airwaves Yamaha

What more can be said about King Leon the First after the most dominant performance in BSB history. Records not only broken, but smashed beyond recognition as quite simply, 'The Shafter' was a class above the rest. Most wins ever, most poles ever, most fastest laps ever, the highest points total ever and the only rider to do the 'triple double' and apart from some confusion over flag signals at Cadwell, would have had a perfect season. Some accused him of making the racing boring, such was his dominance, Camier was stunning and a deserved champion although wherever his destiny lies for 2010, it's doubtful he'll be back to defend his crown.

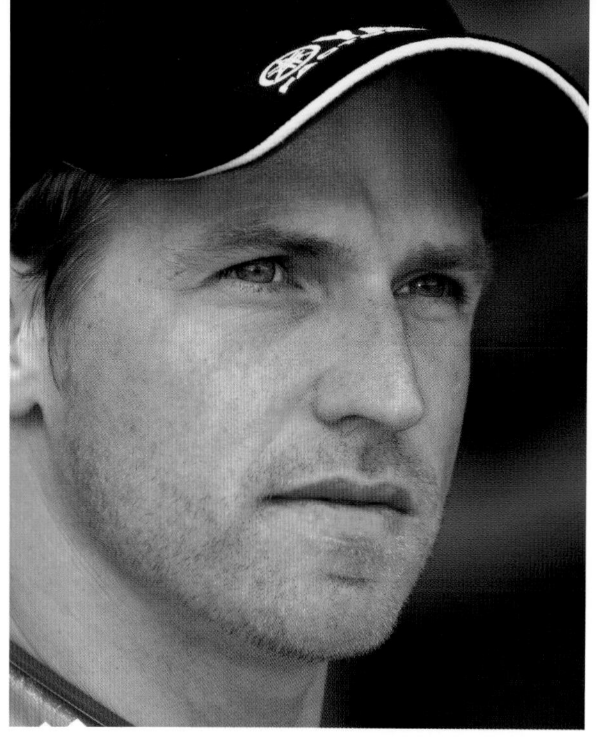

James Ellison

Airwaves Yamaha

Everyone had high hopes of Ellison after a superb return to BSB the previous season but for whatever reason, the amiable Cumbrian just couldn't match his team-mate Camier. Mechanical gremlins aboard the brand new and untested R1 hindered his start to the season and his first three victories, it has to be said, came only because Camier hit problems. However, James bounced back with some much needed aggression towards the end of the season and we saw a glimpse of the old Ellison in the final two rounds as he scrapped for his life (and perhaps another contract) but whilst runner-up is a fantastic achievement, and his best to date, James and his team were perhaps expecting better.

Results	
Position:	2
Points:	413
Poles:	0
Front Rows:	4
Best Grid:	2nd
Races:	26
Wins:	4
Podiums:	11
Best Result:	4 x 1st
Fastest Laps:	4

R1	Brands Hatch Indy:	5th + 7th
R2	Oulton:	5th + 4th
R3	Donington:	2nd + 1st
R4	Thruxton:	2nd + 2nd
R5	Snetterton:	4th + 2nd
R6	Knockhill:	5th + 3rd
R7	Mallory:	1st + 2nd
R8	Brands Hatch GP:	6th + 5th + 3rd
R9	Cadwell:	3rd + 1st
R10	Croft:	2nd + 4th
R11	Silverstone:	2nd + 1st
R12	Oulton:	4th + 3rd + 12th

Stuart Easton

Hydrex Honda

Results	
Position:	3
Points:	374
Poles:	1
Front Rows:	6
Best Grid:	Pole
Races:	26
Wins:	2
Podiums:	12
Best Result:	2 x 1st
Fastest Laps:	2

R1	Brands Hatch Indy:	3rd + 4th
R2	Oulton:	4th + R
R3	Donington:	3rd + 3rd
R4	Thruxton:	3rd + 4th
R5	Snetterton:	2nd + 4th
R6	Knockhill:	2nd + 4th
R7	Mallory:	R + R
R8	Brands Hatch GP:	3rd + 3rd + 4th
R9	Cadwell:	2nd + 2nd
R10	Croft:	1st + 2nd
R11	Silverstone:	4th + 4th
R12	Oulton:	1st + 2nd + C

2009 saw the quietly spoken Scot come of age in more ways than one as he continued to tick boxes in what is turning out to be an illustrious career. Hydrex Honda boss Shaun Muir only offered Easton a contract at the last minute and he was expected to play second fiddle to lead rider Karl Harris but it became immediately clear that Stuart had other intentions. After Harris started to fade, he took the race to the best of the rest behind Camier and was rewarded with his first BSB victory at Croft, just 24 hours before his son Finley was born. With just one crash all season, Stuart has confirmed he'll be back next season in his bid to hold the BSB crown, won previously by his hero and fellow Hawick townsman, Steve Hislop.

Josh Brookes

HM Plant Honda

From the very first meeting, Brookes' season has been swathed in controversy as the steely-eyed Aussie has made one hell of an impact in BSB. Because of Visa irregularities, he had to miss that opening round at Brands and, after a mediocre showing at Oulton, came the infamous sighting-lap smash which injured Guintoli. Blaming the bike in an un-Honda-like fashion, he then started to rack up the podiums, but it was at Mallory, where he actually took out only one rider (Simon Andrews) with the resulting melee inadvertently taking out another half dozen, that saw him banned for two meetings. Dubbed 'Bad Boy', he bounced back to take his podium tally to ten for the season but one wonders whether that's all been good enough for Honda.

Results	
Position:	4
Points:	188
Poles:	1
Front Rows:	3
Best Grid:	Pole
Races:	17
Wins:	0
Podiums:	10
Best Result:	2nd
Fastest Laps:	0

R1	Brands Hatch Indy:	NS + NS
R2	Oulton:	10th + R
R3	Donington:	NS + R
R4	Thruxton:	7th + 3rd
R5	Snetterton:	3rd + 3rd
R6	Knockhill:	3rd + 2nd
R7	Mallory:	F + NS
R8	Brands Hatch GP:	S
R9	Cadwell:	S
R10	Croft:	3rd + 3rd
R11	Silverstone:	3rd + 3rd
R12	Oulton:	R + 7th + 3rd

Key:

1	Finishing Position	S	Suspended	DQ	Disqualified
C	Crashed	Inj.	Injured	NS	Non Starter
R	Retired				

Ian Lowry

Relentless Suzuki by TAS

Results	
Position:	5
Points:	170
Poles:	0
Front Rows:	0
Best Grid:	5th
Races:	26
Wins:	0
Podiums:	0
Best Result:	2 x 4th
Fastest Laps:	0

R1	Brands Hatch Indy:	13th + 19th
R2	Oulton:	7th + 6th
R3	Donington:	8th + 6th
R4	Thruxton:	19th + 8th
R5	Snetterton:	5th + 7th
R6	Knockhill:	6th + R
R7	Mallory:	8th + 20th
R8	Brands Hatch GP:	12th + 12th + 9th
R9	Cadwell:	4th + C
R10	Croft:	5th + 7th
R11	Silverstone:	8th + 9th
R12	Oulton:	8th + R + 4th

It's easy to forget that up until the start of this season, the young Ulsterman hadn't ridden a Superbike in BSB so to claim a strong fifth in the standings is seriously impressive. His season didn't get off to a great start when he was injured at Brands but gradually, Lowry gained in confidence and barring one or two blips, mainly down to tyres, he was a regular in the top eight in the first half of the season. That form continued and despite overshadowing the team's lead rider Atsu Watanabe, Ian was unlucky not to score a podium although it's expected that if he stays with Philip Neill's team for 2010, he'll most certainly put that right . . .

Simon Andrews

MSS Colchester Kawasaki

Enigmatic is a word oft used to describe Simon Andrews and so it has come to pass that his 2009 campaign will be referred to, once again, in a similar manner. Blindingly fast yet prone to jumping off more than he should, it's not quite a 'win-it-or-bin-it' philosophy, more one that he's simply unlucky. In Nick Morgan's team, the Kawasaki has been transformed from also-ran to race winning potential. Andrews was well on the way to his first Superbike victory at Mallory when he was taken out by the errant Brookes, but just one podium, gifted when Camier was disqualified at Cadwell in all fairness, is scant reward for such a promising season and his talent deserves better.

Results	
Position:	6
Points:	163.5
Poles:	0
Front Rows:	3
Best Grid:	2nd
Races:	23
Wins:	0
Podiums:	1
Best Result:	3rd
Fastest Laps:	0

R1	Brands Hatch Indy:	7th + 11th
R2	Oulton:	C + 8th
R3	Donington:	C + 4th
R4	Thruxton:	4th + 6th
R5	Snetterton:	10th + 11th
R6	Knockhill:	4th + 6th
R7	Mallory:	C + 15th
R8	Brands Hatch GP:	NS + NS
R9	Cadwell:	5th + 3rd
R10	Croft:	C + 5th
R11	Silverstone:	9th + 7th
R12	Oulton:	6th + 9th + C

Julien Da Costa

MSS Colchester Kawasaki

Results	
Position:	7
Points:	163
Poles:	0
Front Rows:	0
Best Grid:	5th
Races:	26
Wins:	0
Podiums:	0
Best Result:	4th
Fastest Laps:	0

R1	Brands Hatch Indy:	11th + 10th
R2	Oulton:	12th + R
R3	Donington:	7th + 11th
R4	Thruxton:	10th + 10th
R5	Snetterton:	9th + 6th
R6	Knockhill:	R + 8th
R7	Mallory:	5th + 10th
R8	Brands Hatch GP:	10th + 11th + R
R9	Cadwell:	6th + 4th
R10	Croft:	9th + 9th
R11	Silverstone:	10th + 6th
R12	Oulton:	7th + R + 6th

The reigning World Endurance Champion has almost sneaked into the top ten unnoticed aboard the second of the MSS Kawasakis and for a debut shot at BSB, the Frenchman has to be commended. Nothing majorly spectacular, but a dogged consistency, spoiled only by the occasional breakdown, has seen him rack up the results and he has been a regular fixture in the top ten. But the one thing Da Costa hasn't done is prove to be as quick as team-mate Andrews, who has set a pretty high benchmark, and one wonders whether or not he'll be back for another shot. Whilst seventh place is good, is it good enough to retain his ride?

Sylvain Guintoli

Worx Crescent Suzuki

Results		
Position:		8
Points:		147
Poles:		1
Front Rows:		2
Best Grid:		Pole
Races:		13
Wins:		1
Podiums:		3
Best Result:		1st
Fastest Laps:		0

R1	Brands Hatch Indy:	1st + 2nd
R2	Oulton:	3rd + 3rd
R3	Donington:	NS + NS
R4	Thruxton:	Inj.
R5	Snetterton:	Inj.
R6	Knockhill:	Inj.
R7	Mallory:	Inj.
R8	Brands Hatch GP:	Inj.
R9	Cadwell:	8th + 7th
R10	Croft:	C + 13th
R11	Silverstone:	7th + 8th
R12	Oulton:	5th + 5th + 5th

Breezing into the championship like a breath of fresh air, no one really knew what to expect of the ex MotoGP racer although excitement was high. Any doubts that he could cut the mustard were quickly dispelled with a history-making pole position and race win at Brands Hatch which he followed up with a hat trick of podiums over the next three races. This Frenchman meant business and could take the game to Camier. But at Donington, his season ended in the most surreal of fashions and he was to sit out the next five meetings before a brave but tentative comeback towards the end of the season. It's a case of what might have been and now he's WSB-bound, it's one which may never be answered.

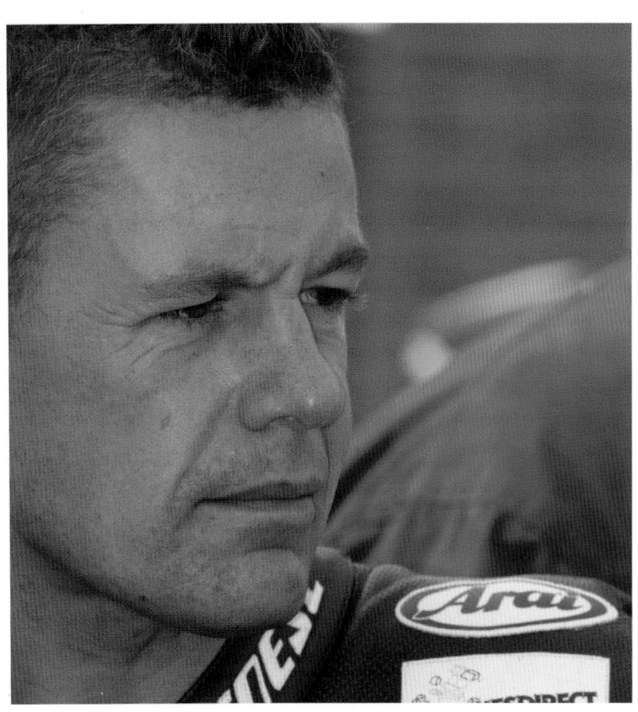

Chris Walker

Motorpoint Henderson Yamaha

The old stager was reunited with his old boss Rob McElnea and with great things expected of the all-new Yamaha this season; it really did look as if the fans' favourite was in with a shot of the title. But it wasn't to be the fairytale reunion as 'The Stalker' struggled in the opening salvos and by the time he hit the podium at Donington, he was already dropping down the points table. As ever, he gave it more than his best but the bike was found lacking on a number of occasions, not least when the handlebar snapped at Croft causing him to crash, and as much as it pains us all to admit it, it's going to be tough for Chris to come back from this season.

Results		
Position:		9
Points:		141
Poles:		0
Front Rows:		1
Best Grid:		3rd
Races:		26
Wins:		0
Podiums:		2
Best Result:		2 x 3rd
Fastest Laps:		0

R1	Brands Hatch Indy:	14th + 8th
R2	Oulton:	11th + 9th
R3	Donington:	5th + 3rd
R4	Thruxton:	R + R
R5	Snetterton:	6th + 17th
R6	Knockhill:	7th + 5th
R7	Mallory:	C + 3rd
R8	Brands Hatch GP:	9th + R + 12th
R9	Cadwell:	11th + 6th
R10	Croft:	C + 11th
R11	Silverstone:	R + 11th
R12	Oulton:	9th + 14th + 7th

John Laverty

Buildbase Kawasaki

Results		
Position:		10
Points:		130.5
Poles:		0
Front Rows:		1
Best Grid:		2nd
Races:		25
Wins:		0
Podiums:		1
Best Result:		4th
Fastest Laps:		0

R1	Brands Hatch Indy:	12th + 13th
R2	Oulton:	C + NS
R3	Donington:	9th + 9th
R4	Thruxton:	8th + 11th
R5	Snetterton:	13th + 5th
R6	Knockhill:	C + C
R7	Mallory:	C + 4th
R8	Brands Hatch GP:	7th + 13th + 5th
R9	Cadwell:	9th + 5th
R10	Croft:	13th + 10th
R11	Silverstone:	6th + R
R12	Oulton:	10th + 6th + R

The reigning Privateers' Cup champion had high hopes of mixing it up with the factory boys having signed for Stuart Hicken's Buildbase Kawasaki team but his season couldn't have got off to a worse start what with problems at Brands, including being hit with a jump start penalty, and then crashing out at Oulton. But in determined fashion, the middle of the three racing brothers from Northern Ireland started his fight back and became a regular runner in the pack which was always inevitably chasing Camier. A career best front row at Cadwell was very nearly backed up with an odd podium and if J-Lav gets another shot, he'll be well placed to step it up a gear.

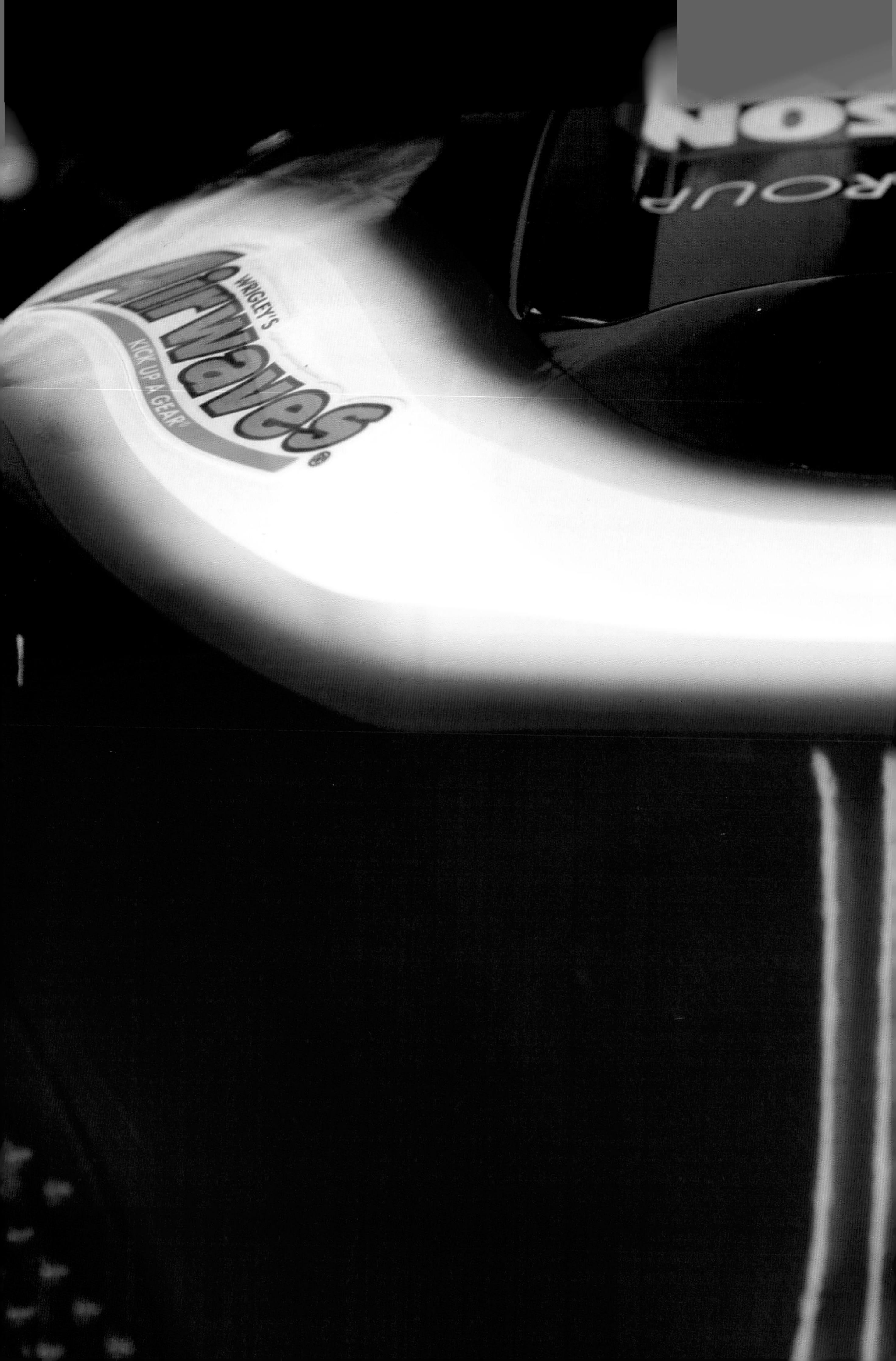
WRIGLEY'S
KICK UP A GEAR

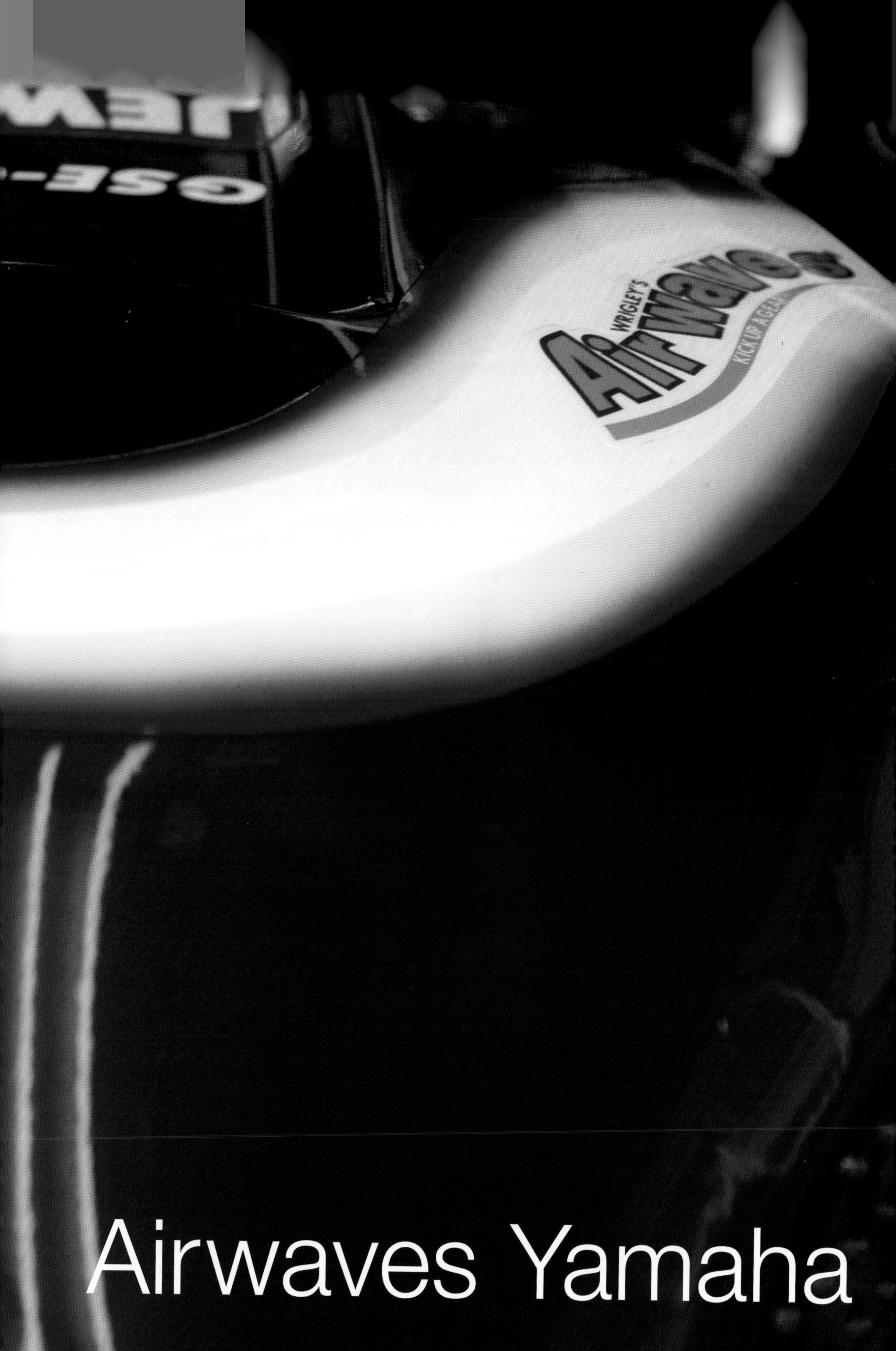

Airwaves Yamaha

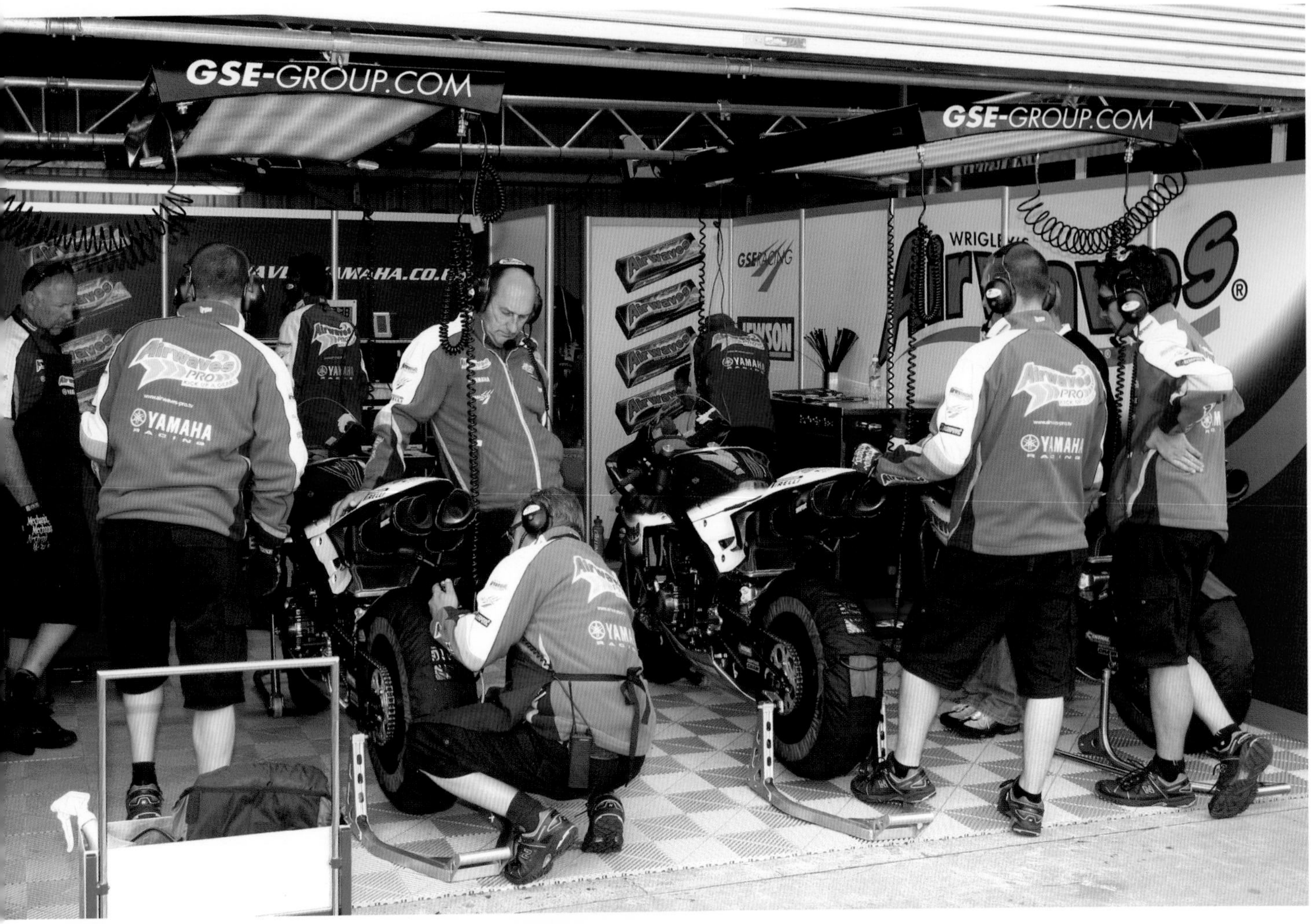

GSE RACING
PIRELLI
YAMALUBE

Airwaves
PRO
YAMAHA
RACING
Racing
PIRELLI

WRIGLEY'S
Airwa
AHA
Airwaves
GSEGROUP
JEWS

Airwaves Yamaha

Machinery: Yamaha YZF-R1
Principal: Colin Wright
Located: Burton on Trent, Derbys
Pedigree: British Superbike Champions 1999, 2000, 2005, 2008 & 2009

After years with Ducati, the current champions made the shock switch to Yamaha power for 2009, with engines identical to those used by the official World Superbike Belgarda Team with Ben Spies and Tom Sykes.

Having won the title with Shane Byrne last season, the squad retained Leon Camier and drafted in James Ellison from Hydrex Honda to make a formidable pairing who were strong from the off, Camier being particularly impressive as Ellison struggled to get dialled in as quickly as he would have liked.

Camier stole the show in no uncertain terms, scorching to a total of 19 wins as he wrapped up GSE Racing's fifth BSB crown with ease and Ellison kept his side of the bargain with a late season flourish to claim runner-up spot also.

23 victories out of the 26 races, and setting the fastest lap in 22 of them, plus 14 additional podiums underlined their supremacy and hopefully, if a title sponsor to replace Airwaves can be found, the team will be a formidable one to retain their crown next season, although just who their riders will be is anyone's guess!

Riders:

Leon Camier		**James Ellison**	
Number:	2	Number:	7
DOB:	04 August, 1986	DOB:	19 September, 1980
Lives:	Wimborne, Dorset	Lives:	Kendal, Cumbria
Races:	70	Races:	74
Wins:	22	Wins:	4
2008 Position:	5th British Superbike Championship	2008 Position:	7th British Superbike Championship

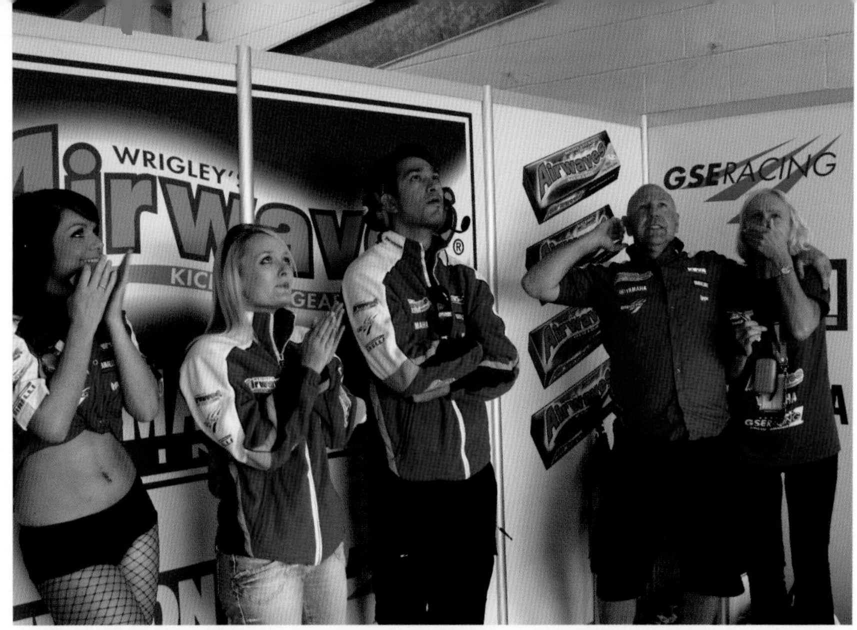

WRIGLEY'S
Airwaves
KICK UP A GEAR
GSERACING

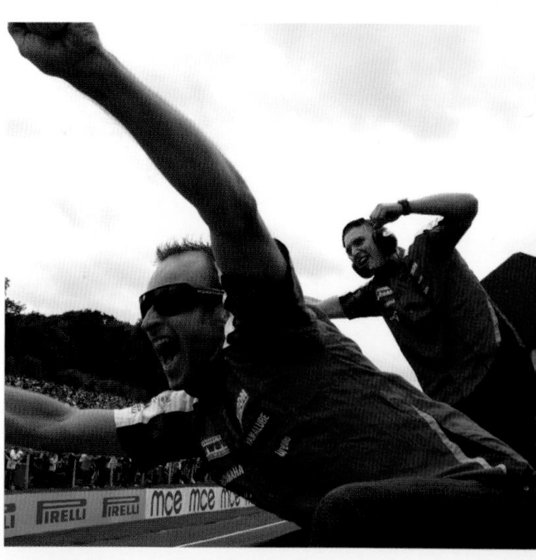

PIRELLI
mce

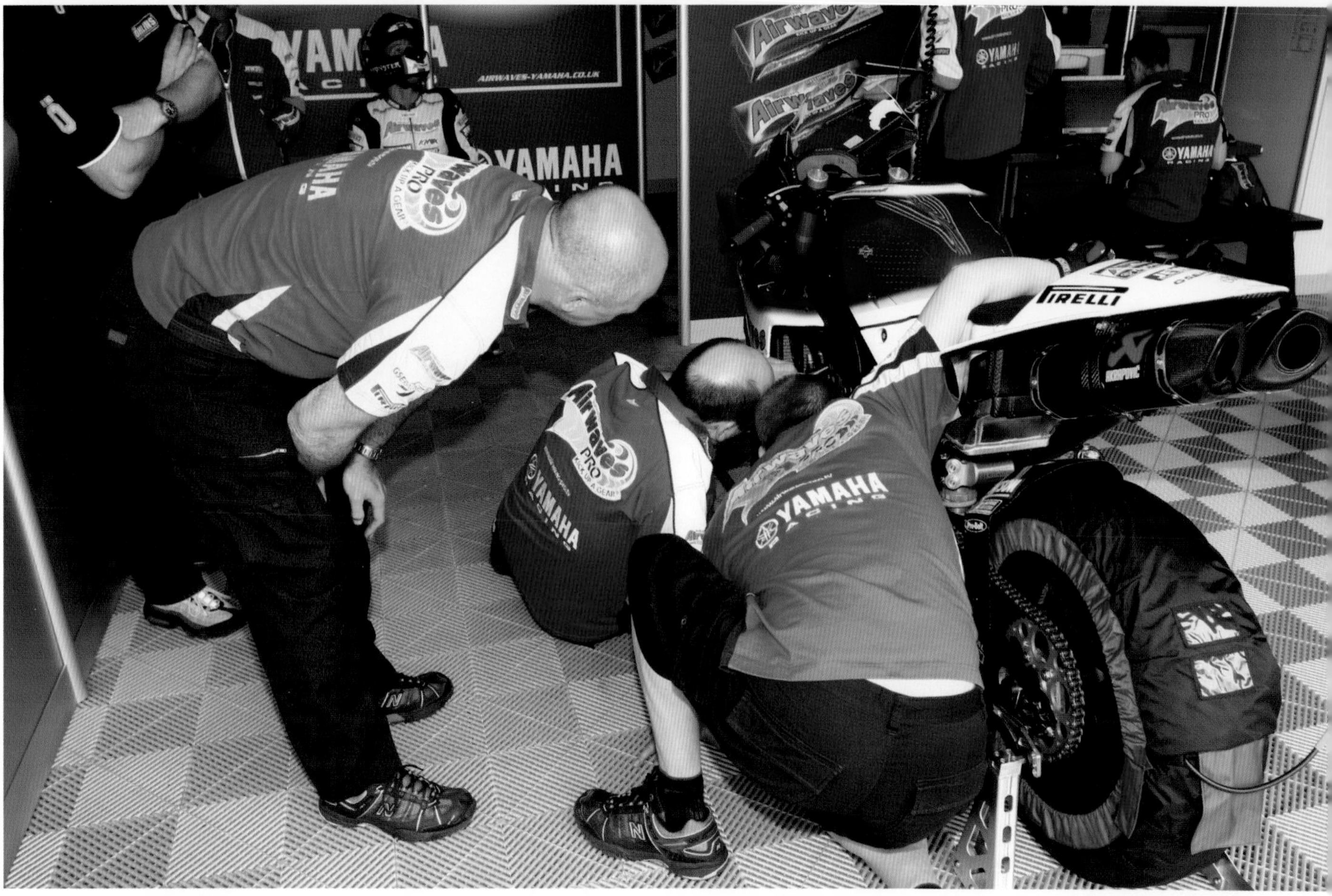

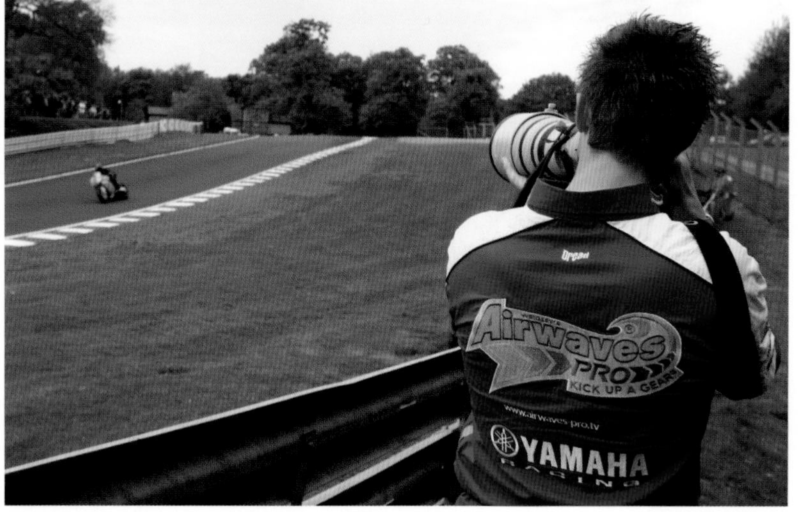

YAMAHA
AIRWAVES-YAMAHA.CO.UK
YAMAHA
PIRELLI

Airwaves
PRO
KICK UP A GEAR
www.airwaves-pro.tv
YAMAHA
RACING

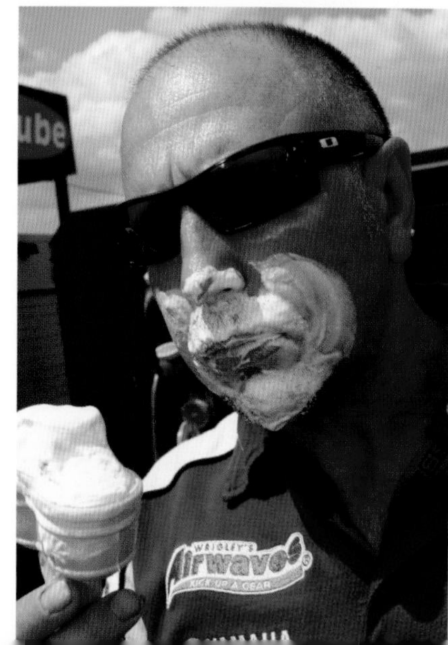

WRIGLEY'S
Airwaves
KICK UP A GEAR

YAMAHA
JEWSON
YAMALUBE

MONSTER
ENERGY
JEWSON
Airwaves
TEKNIC
WRIGLEY'S
Airwaves
KICK UP A GEAR
JEWSON
KNOX
SHOEI
GSE GROUP
YAMAHA

JEWSON

MONSTER
ENERGY
JEWSON
Airwaves
TEKNIC
WRIGLEY'S
Airwaves
SHOEI
YAMAHA
YAMALUBE

WRIGLEY'S
Airwaves®
KICK UP A GEAR®
brembo

YAMAHA
RACING
YAMA

HM Plant Honda Racing

Machinery
HONDA
GENUINE PARTS

HM Plant Honda

Machinery: Honda CBR1000RR Fireblade
Principal: Havier Beltran
Located: Louth, Lincs
Pedigree: British Superbike Champions 2006 & 2007

2009 saw a brand new line up with a pair of Australians in the shape of Glen Richards and Josh Brookes entrusted to win back the title that was last held by Ryuichi Kiyonari in 2006 and 2007 in Honda colours.

However, it was a season to forget for the team as far as BSB was concerned as a plethora of problems beset them virtually from day one, what with Brookes having immigration problems causing him to miss round one and then being involved in a couple of controversial incidents which led to a two-meeting ban.

To add to their strife, Richards broke his leg at Knockhill, effectively ending his rather mediocre campaign and leading to a number of riders being drafted in to deputise for most of the rest of the season, none of whom could manage a podium finish between them.

To his credit, Brookes came away with ten podium finishes with Richards recording just the one in the Brands opener, and for the team that won the 2006 and 2007 BSB titles with Ryuichi Kiyonari, (who made a surprise one off comeback for the team without major success at Croft), it hasn't been a vintage year for the Louth-based team.

Riders:

Josh Brookes

Number:	25
DOB:	28 April, 1983
Lives:	Sydney, Australia
Races:	17
Wins:	0
2008 Position:	3rd World Supersport Championship

Glen Richards

Number:	45
DOB:	30 September, 1973
Lives:	Adelaide, Australia
Races:	128
Wins:	0
2008 Position:	British Supersport Champion

Steve Plater	Brands Hatch Indy
Steve Brogan	Mallory Park, Brands Hatch GP
Karl Muggeridge	Brands Hatch GP, Cadwell Park
John McGuinness	Cadwell Park
Ryuichi Kiyonari	Croft

HONDA
HM plant
HITACHI
HONDA
Milspec
HONDA

HM plant

AKRAPOVIĆ
Snap-on
Honda Racing

HONDA
Castrol
HONDA
HITACHI

Honda Racing
Honda
HITACHI

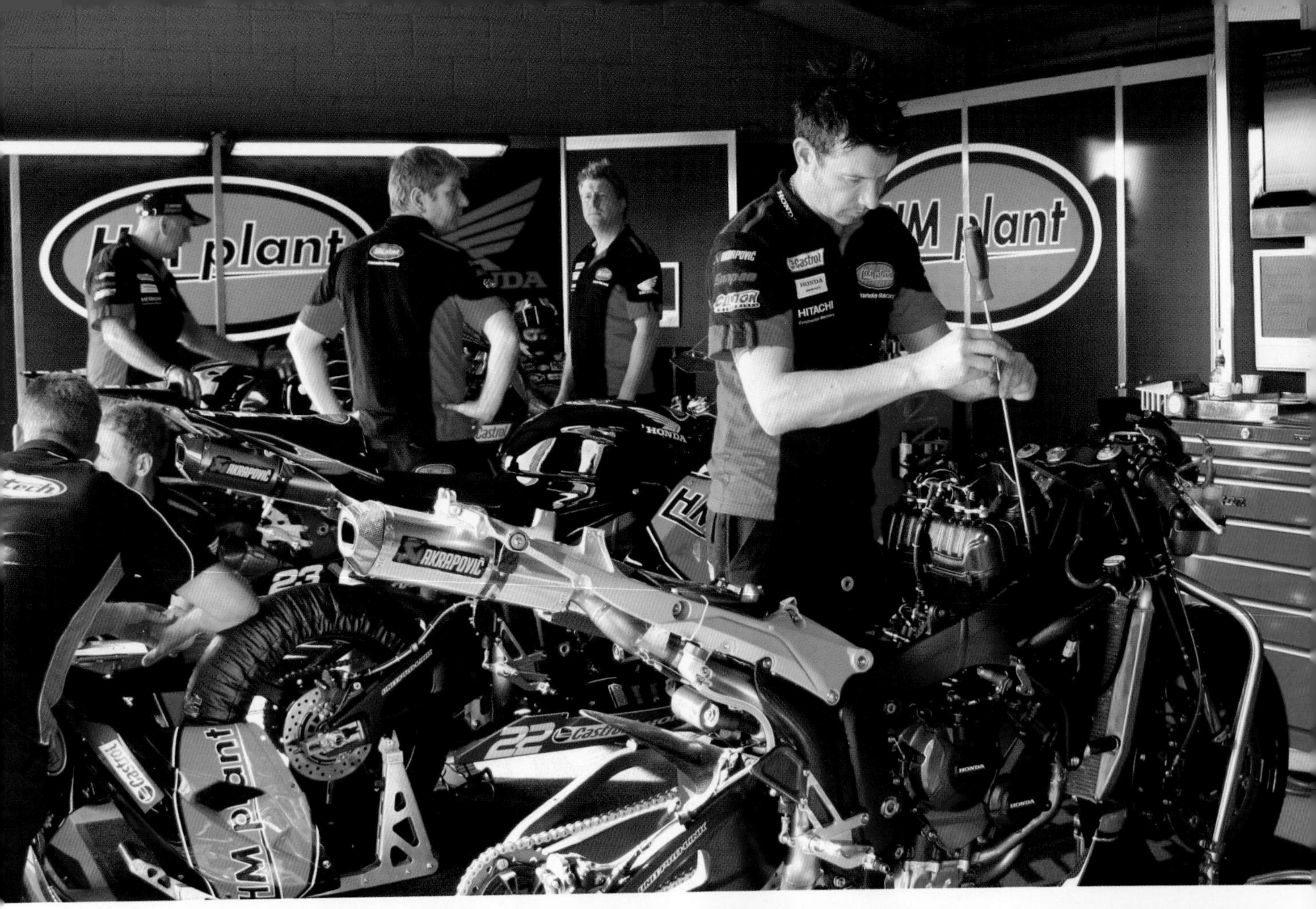

HITACHI
HM plant
GAERNE
Milspec
HONDA

Honda
HITACHI
HONDA
GENUINE PARTS
Arai
GAERNE
Milspec
HM plant
HONDA

Arai
HM plant
Castrol
HONDA
HITACHI
ASTRO
AKRAPOVIC
Snap-on
CLAPA
Honda Racing
HITACHI Construction Machinery
EXIDE
PIRELLI
HONDA

WP
HONDA

Arai HELMET

Castrol
HITACHI

HITACHI

Hydrex Honda

SMR
HARRIS
CJ
HYDREX
Honda
RED TORPEDO
BOOTH & PARTNERS

Putoline
Arai

HYDREX
Honda
HYDREX
RED TORPEDO
REVIT

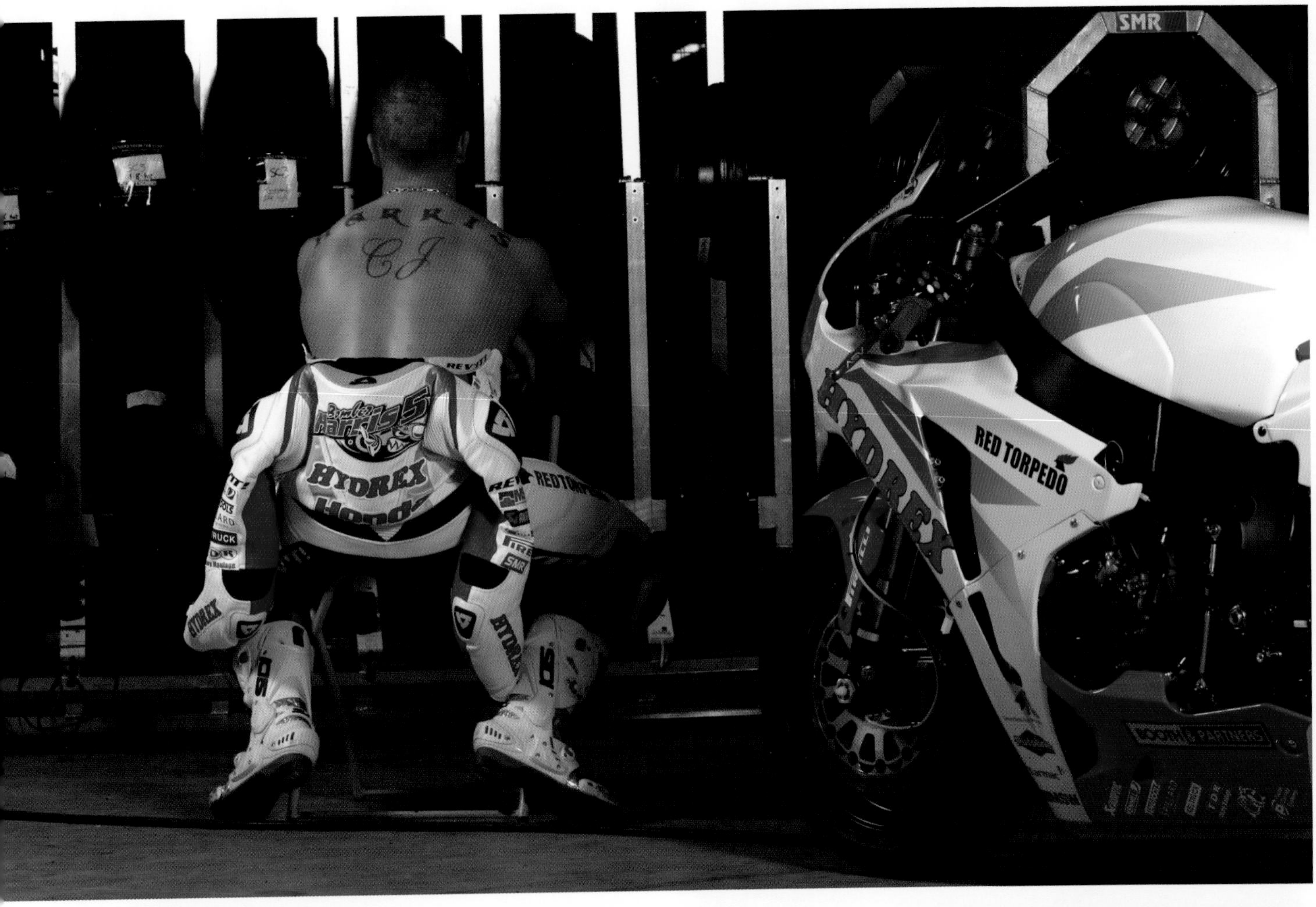

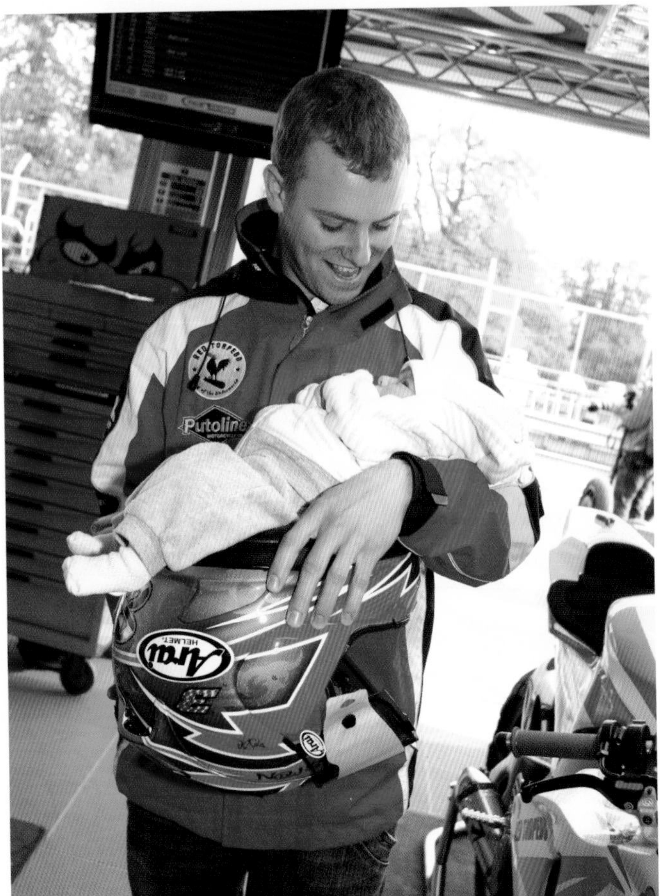

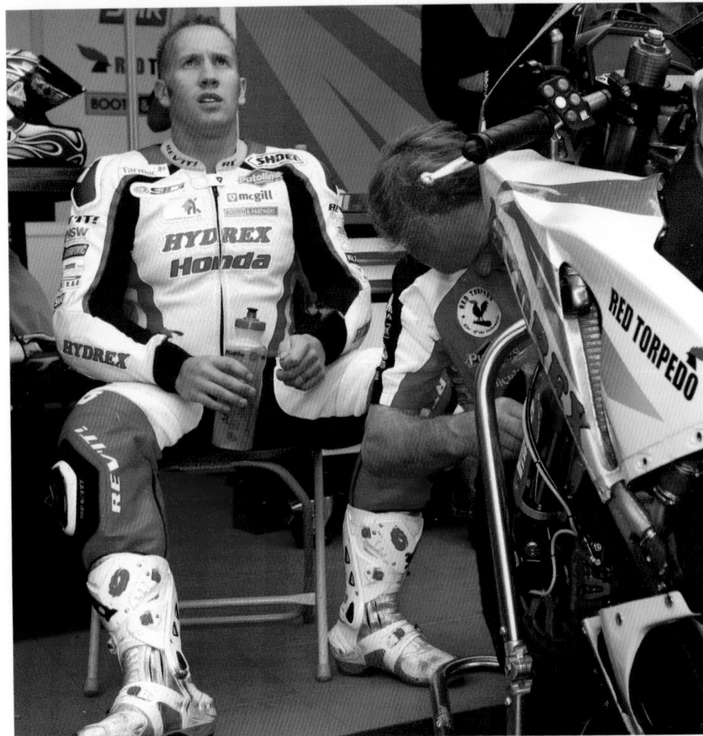

Hydrex Honda

Machinery: Honda CBR1000RR Fireblade
Principal: Shaun Muir
Located: Guisborough, Cleveland
Pedigree: Podium finishers in BSB, NW200 & TT, Ulster GP winners

After an impressive 2008 season, notably with James Ellison and which included a WSB wild card fourth placing at Donington, the Northerners were many people's favourites to emerge as dark horses this season.

Karl Harris was aiming to put a disastrous 2008 campaign behind him and was reunited with the team in which he claimed his debut podium two seasons back. He also made some big lifestyle changes over winter, including employing a personal coach.

Scottish ace Stuart Easton won the Macau GP for Shaun Muir's dedicated team last November and his reward has been a full season with the Hydrex team. Following on from his first half of the season performances, he landed his and the team's first win amidst sensational scenes at Croft.

As Easton finished as top Honda in the series, Harris was given his P45 after Cadwell and in came Tommy Hill. Hill did a sterling job for the team with a brace of podiums in the final round at Oulton to conclude a memorable year for Shaun Muir and his team.

Riders:

Karl Harris	
Number:	5
DOB:	21 October, 1979
Lives:	Sheffield, Yorks
Races:	135
Wins:	0
2008 Position:	11th British Superbike Championship

Stuart Easton	
Number:	3
DOB:	21 July, 1983
Lives:	Hawick, Scotland
Races:	54
Wins:	2
2008 Position:	13th British Superbike Championship

Tommy Hill
Croft, Silverstone, Oulton Park

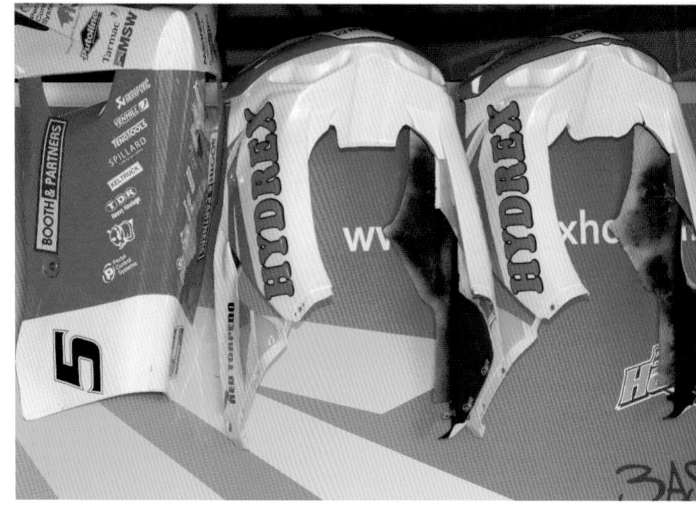

LONDON
Tarmac
SPERIAN

HYDREX
Honda
BKS
SHOEI
PIRELLI
HYDREX
33
BOOTH & PARTNERS

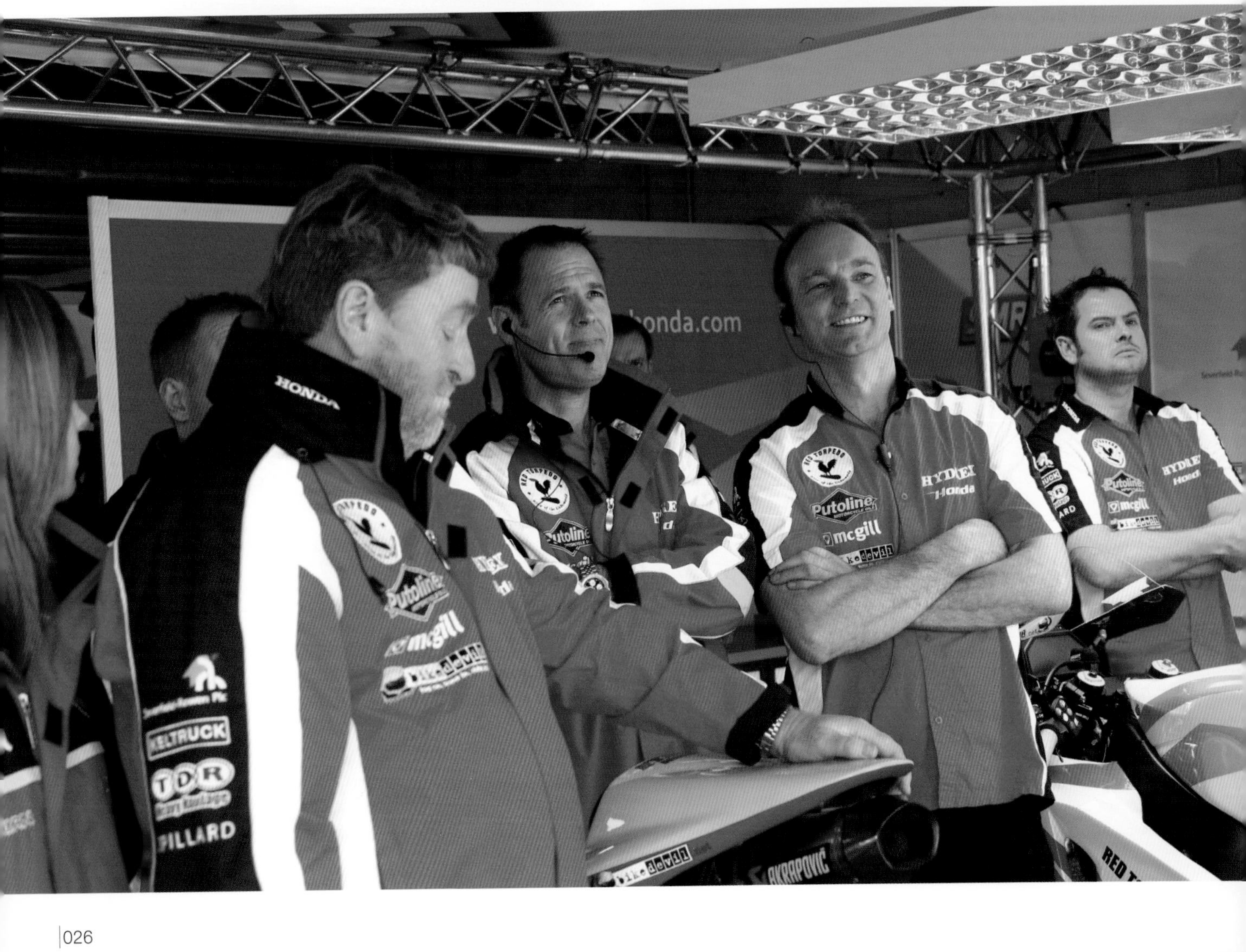

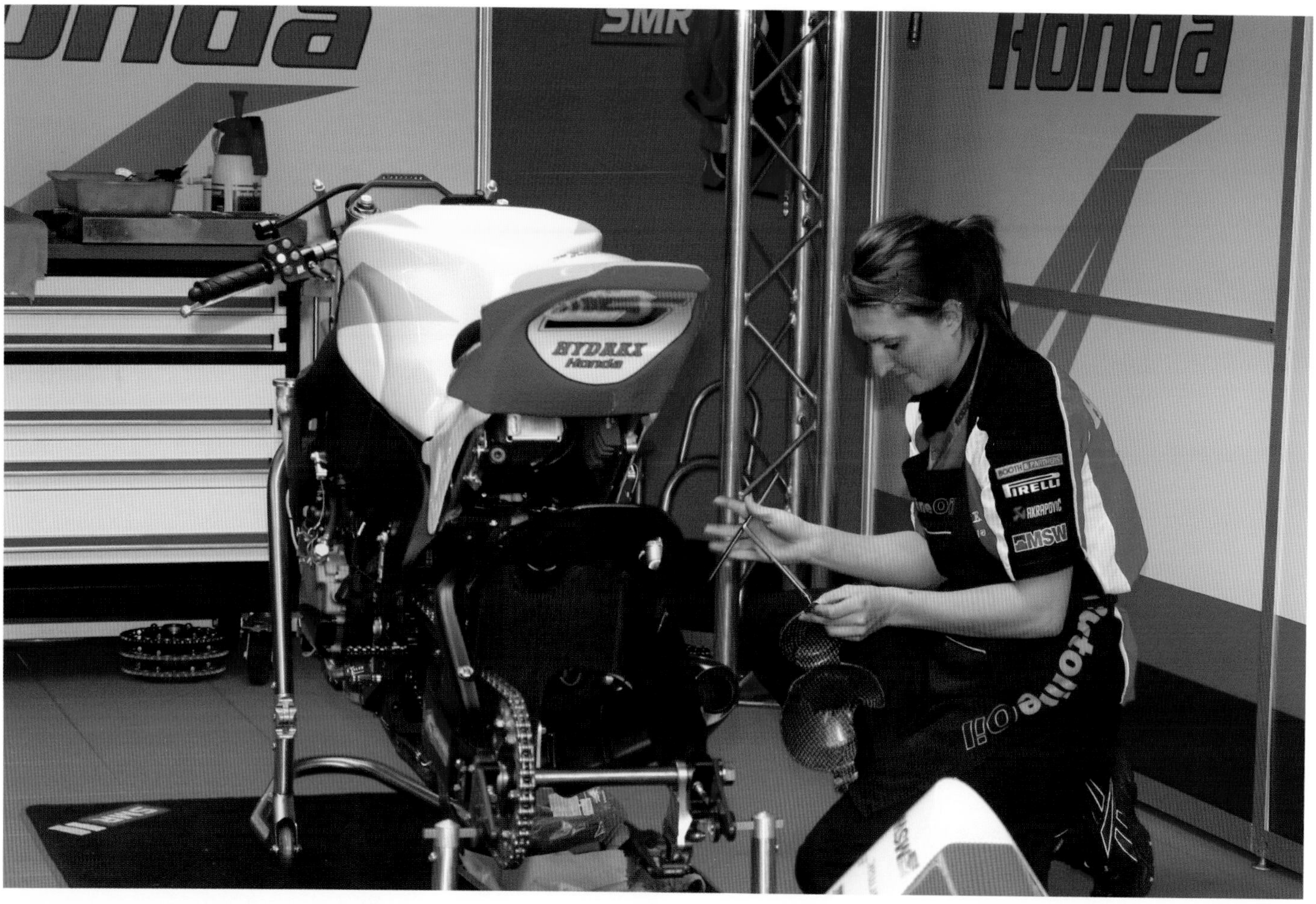

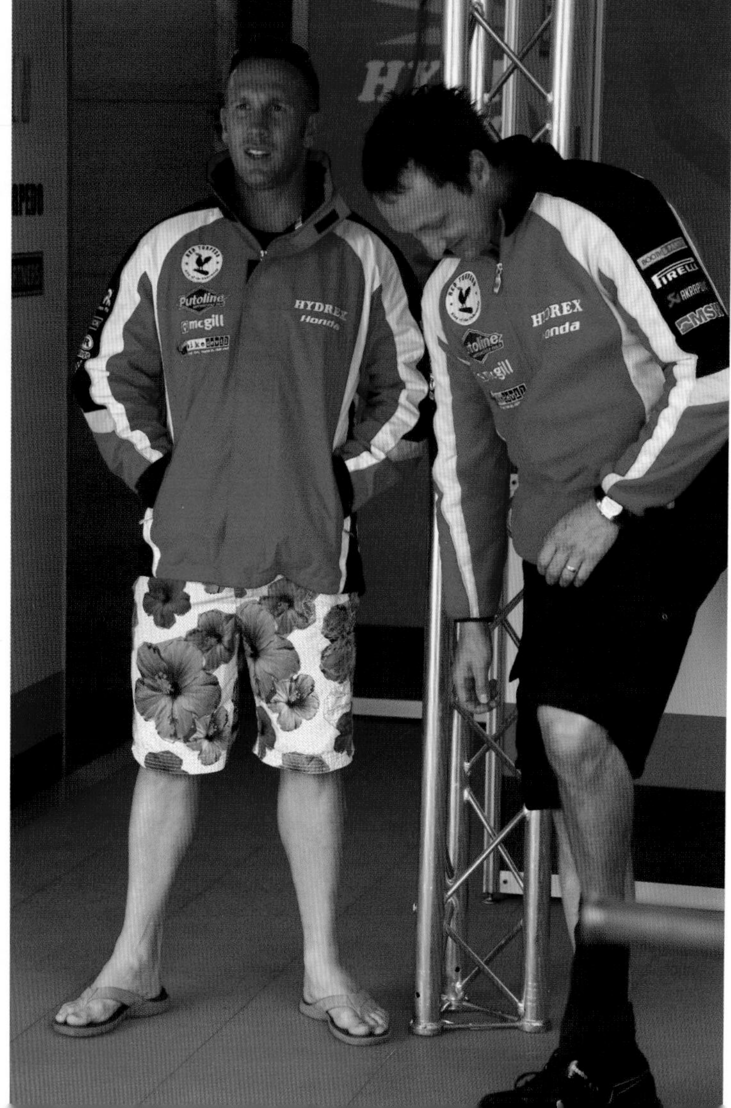
HYDREX
Honda
Putoline
mcgill
PIRELLI
MSW

BKS
Tarmac
SPERIAN
Putoline
mcgill
Adaptaflex
Severfield-Rowen Plc
BOOTH & PARTNERS
Vent-Axia
MSW

Honda
HYDREX
Honda
Tarmac
Putoline
mcgill
Arai
PBM
HYDREX
Honda
SIDI
MSW
HYDREX
Honda

Motorpoint Henderson Yamaha

Motorpoint Henderson Yamaha

Machinery: Yamaha YZF-R1
Principal: Rob McElnea
Located: Scunthorpe, North Lincs
Pedigree: British Superbike Champions 1996, 1997 & 1998

Reverting to a two-rider team after last year's single bike effort with Karl Harris, ex GP racer Rob McElnea retained his long association with Yamaha and looked as if he had his best shot at the title in recent years.

A decade ago, Chris Walker finished second for the team in BSB and the veteran returned to the team with whom he had much of his success. But again it wasn't to be for the four-times runner-up, who only managed the two podiums this season amidst a number of niggling little problems which cost him countless points.

A surprise addition was the ex Virgin Cup rider Graeme Gowland who spent some of last season in World Supersport and, although the genial Geordie has limited Superbike experience, he really excelled in his rookie season and after the Mallory Park race one shenanigans, found himself on the podium.

Rumour has it that Rob Mac's squad may be missing from the BSB paddock next season but it's hard to imagine the place without them so hopefully, they can get the necessary deals in place for 2010.

Riders:

Chris Walker	
Number:	9
DOB:	25 March, 1972
Lives:	Newark, Nottingham
Races:	156
Wins:	20
2008 Position:	31st World Superbike Championship

Graeme Gowland	
Number:	8
DOB:	23 January, 1986
Lives:	Northumberland
Races:	23
Wins:	0
2008 Position:	35th World Supersport Championship

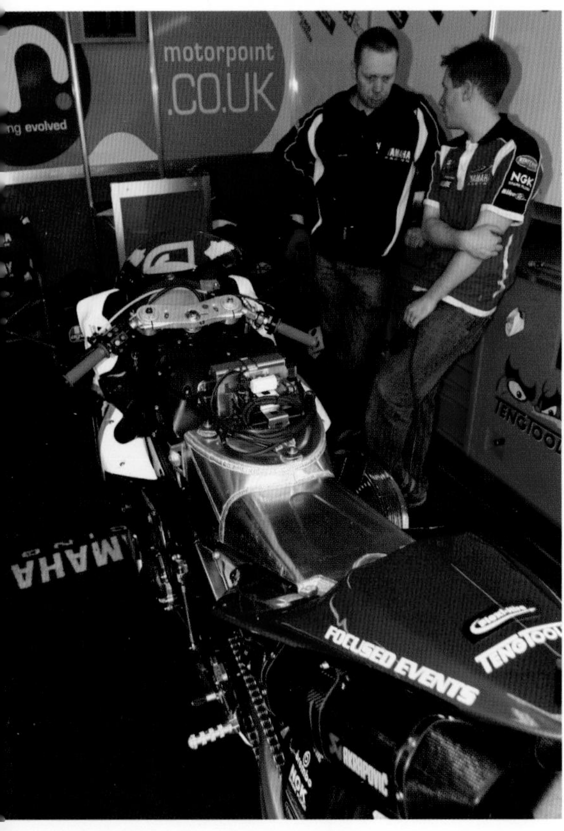

ROBMACRACING
YAMAHA
RACING
motorpoint
FOCUSED EVENTS
BIKETEK
KENT CAMS
brembo
NGK
KENTHAL

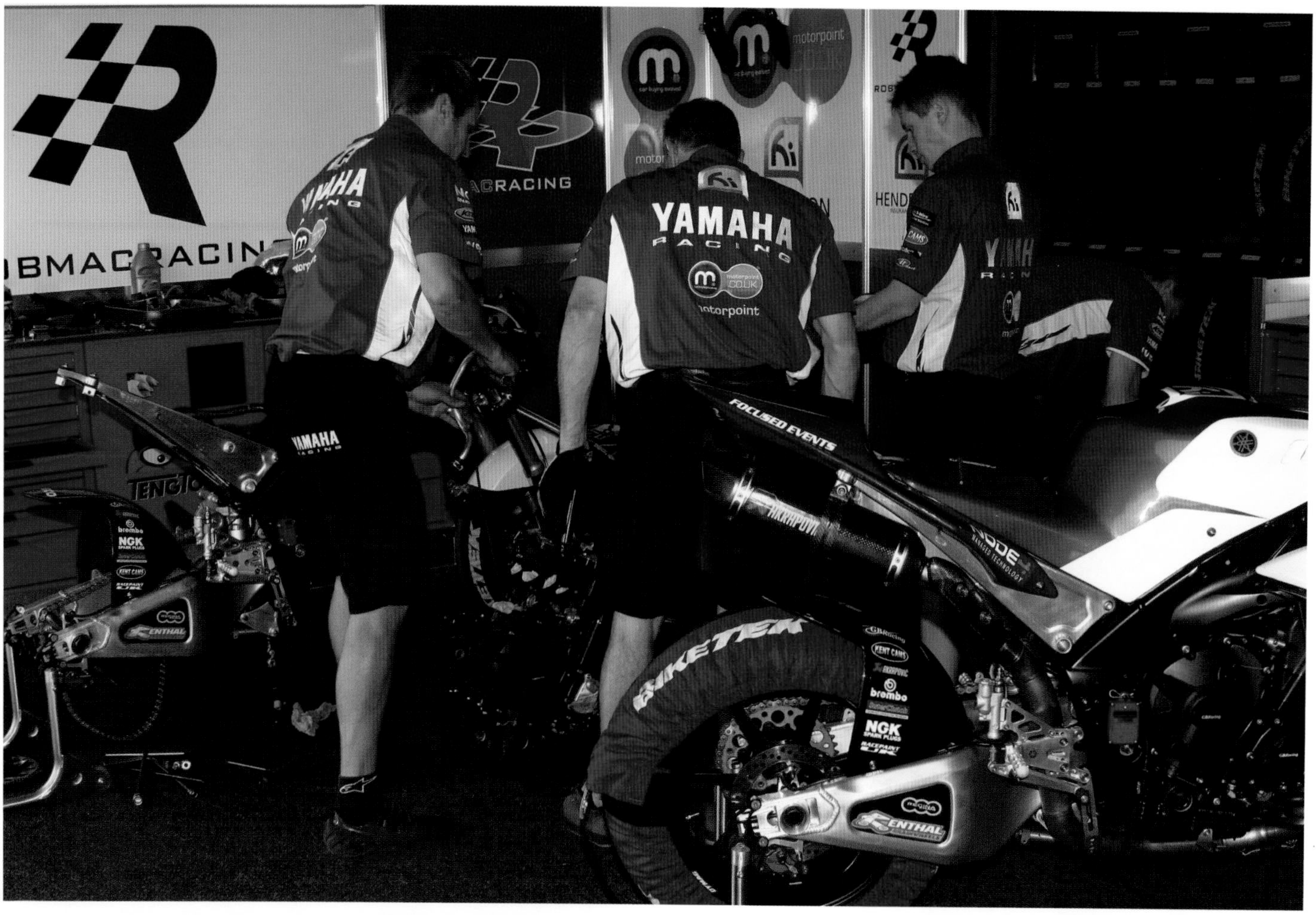

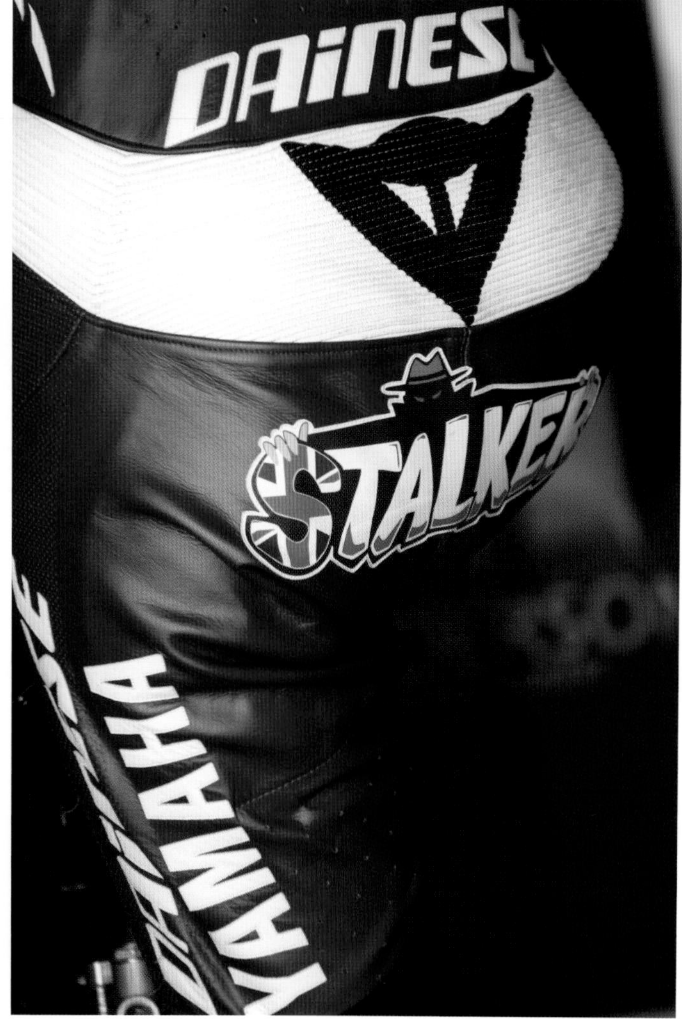

DAINESE
STALKER
YAMAHA

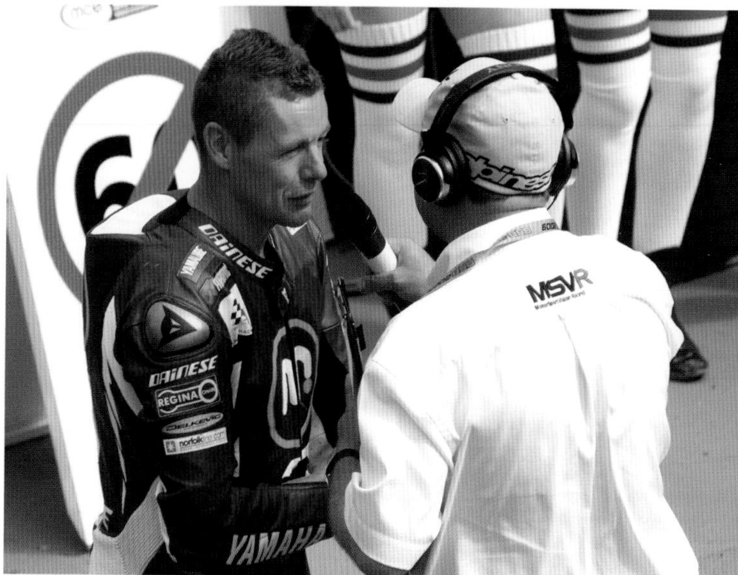

DAINESE
REGINA
YAMAHA
MSVR

car buying evolved
NGK
SPARK PLUGS
YAMALUBE
IVECO
YAMAHA

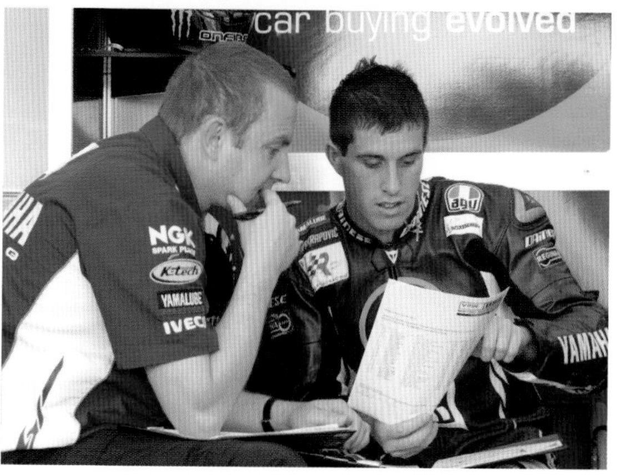

DAINESE
YAMAHA
YAMAHA
YAMAHA
HENDERSON
YAMAHA RACING

YAMALUBE
AKRAPOVIC
DAINESE
Flexi-Hire
KENT CAMS

YAMAHA RACING

HENDERSON
INSURANCE BROKERS
CO.UK
SONIC
HEL
AKRAPOVIC
YAMAHA
HENDERSON
INSURANCE BROKERS
PIRELLI
AKRAPOVIC

HENDERSON
INSURANCE
motorpoint
YAMAHA
RACING

NGK
HENDERSON
motorpoint
YAMAHA
RACING

MSS Colchester Kawasaki

Simon
Andrews

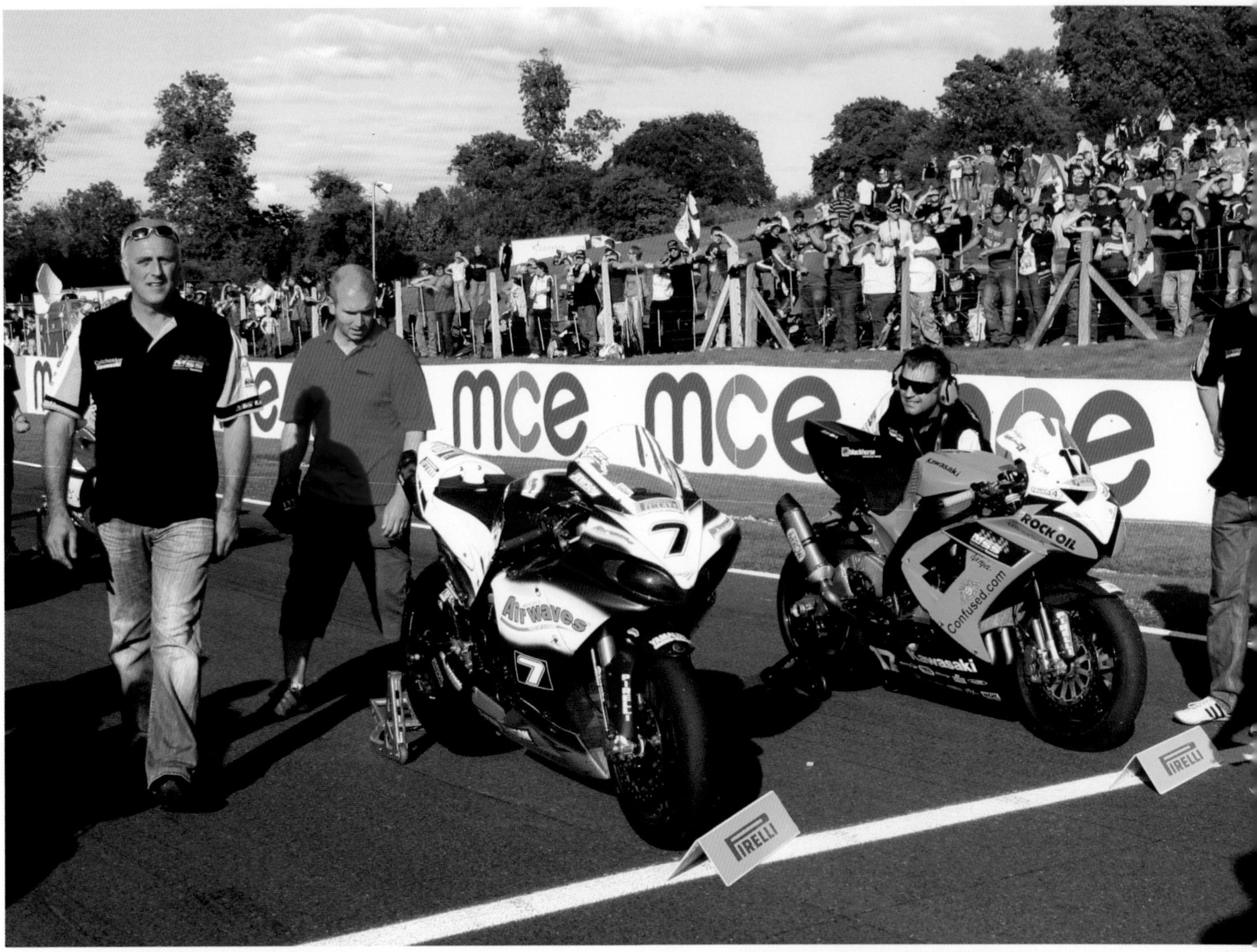

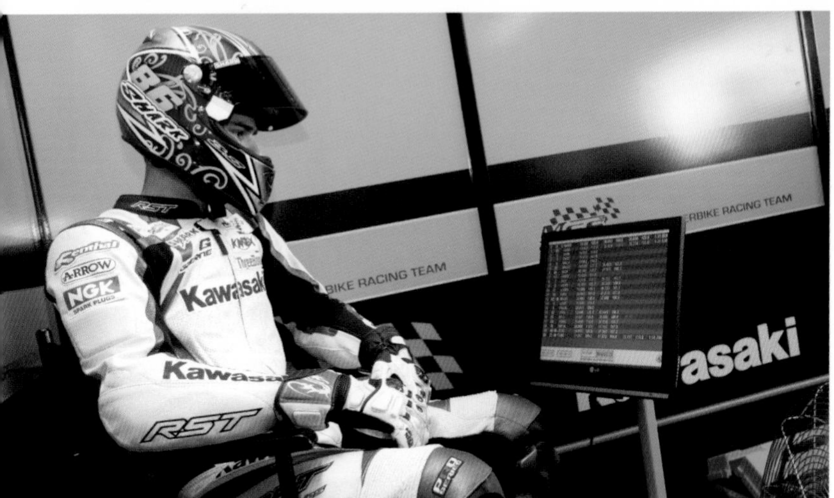

mce
mce
mce
Airwaves
7
ROCK OIL
Confused.com
Kawasaki
17
PIRELLI
PIRELLI

86
RST
ARROW
NGK
Kawasaki
Kawasaki
RST
BIKE RACING TEAM
ERBIKE RACING TEAM
asaki

GOODRIDGE
ARROW
ROCK OIL
MSS
Kawasaki
17
ICOM
ICOM
touch 4
touch 4
ROCK OIL

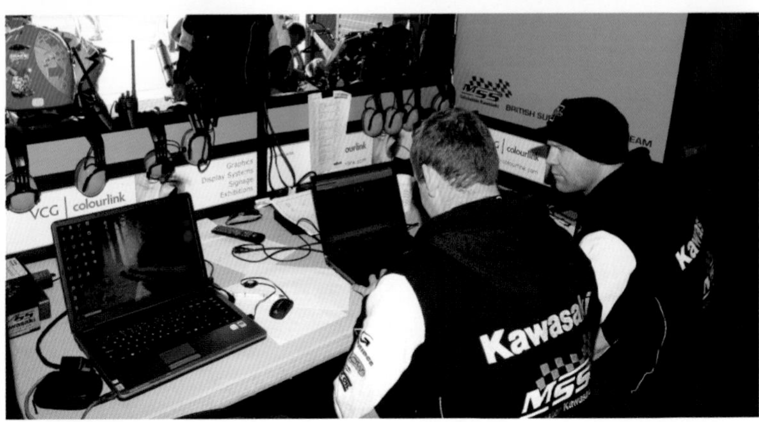

VCG | colourlink
Kawasaki
MSS

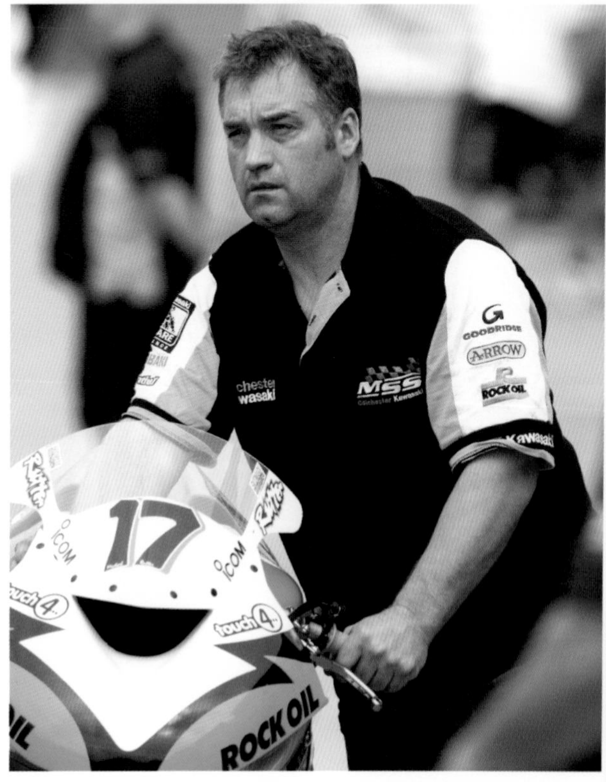

MSS Colchester Kawasaki

Machinery: Kawasaki ZX-10R
Manager: Nick Morgan
Located: Colchester, Essex
Pedigree: British Supersport Race Winners

Nick Morgan's team were granted official factory Kawasaki status for 2009 and with it signed riders with proven track records.

The nomadic Simon Andrews had proved his mettle over recent seasons by being a regular thorn in the sides of the factory riders and reigning World Endurance Champion Julien Da Costa had a winning pedigree after a brief flirtation with National Superstock a few years ago for the team.

However, whereas it's widely recognised that the ZX-10R had work to do if it was to be constantly at the cutting edge, both Andrews and Da Costa proved that myth wrong. They consistently ran at the front and confirmed their competitiveness with a fine debut podium for both Andrews and the team at Cadwell.

Andrews, who recovered from a wrist operation that saw him miss Brands, has been seriously knocking on the door and but for a wayward Honda at Mallory would have surely broken his BSB podium top-step duck but his time will come.

Riders:

Simon Andrews

Number:	17
DOB:	14 August, 1983
Lives:	Evesham, Worcs
Races:	73
Wins:	0
2008 Position:	8th British Superbike Championship

Julien Da Costa

Number:	86
DOB:	03 September, 1981
Lives:	Beziers, France
Races:	34
Wins:	0
2008 Position:	1st World Endurance Championship

Michael Rutter
Brands Hatch GP

Colchester Kawasaki

Kawasaki

Ninja
86
Kawasaki

touch4
Kawasaki
MSS
Colchester Kawasaki
Kawasaki
MSS
Colchester Kawasaki
Kawasaki
MSS
Colchester Kawasaki

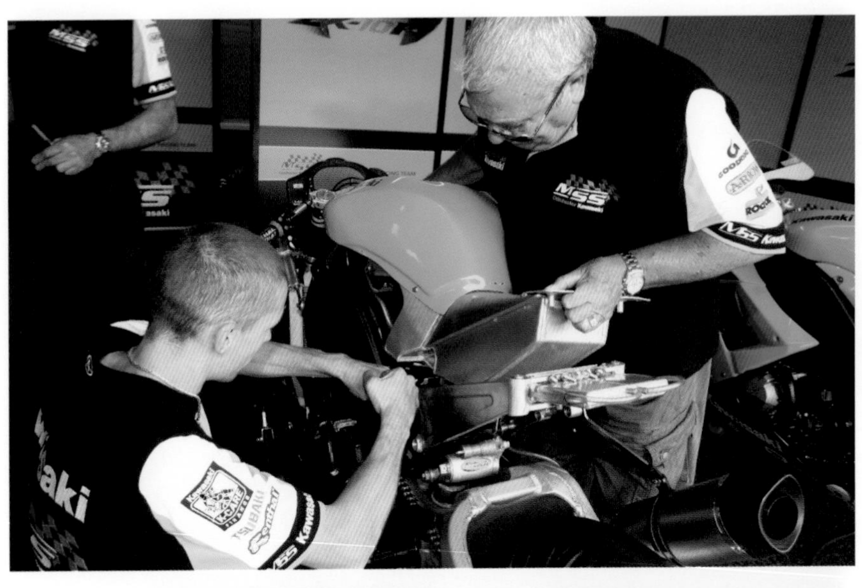

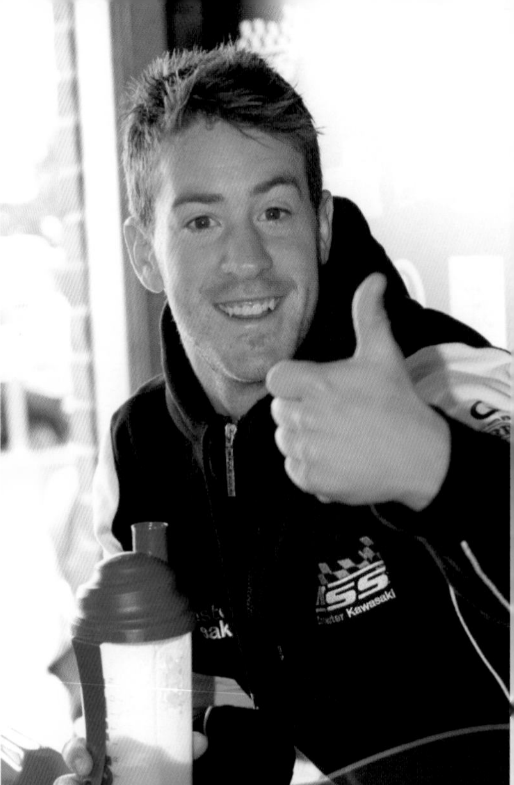

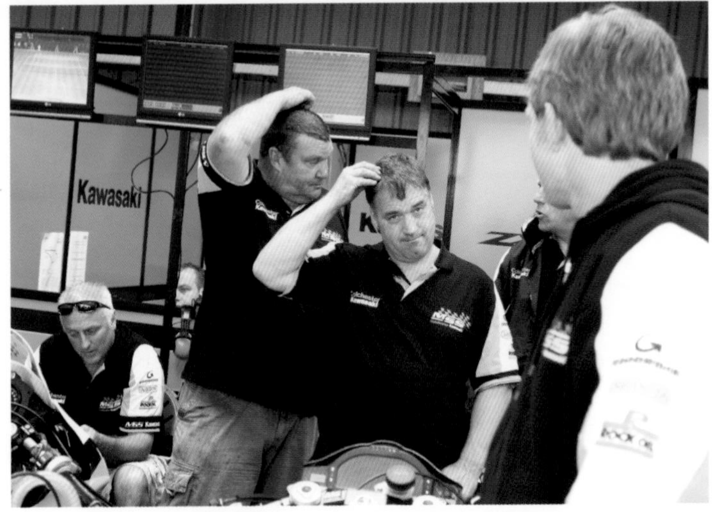

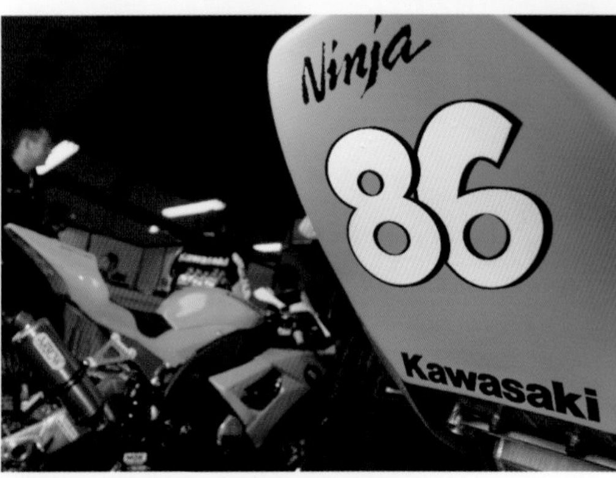

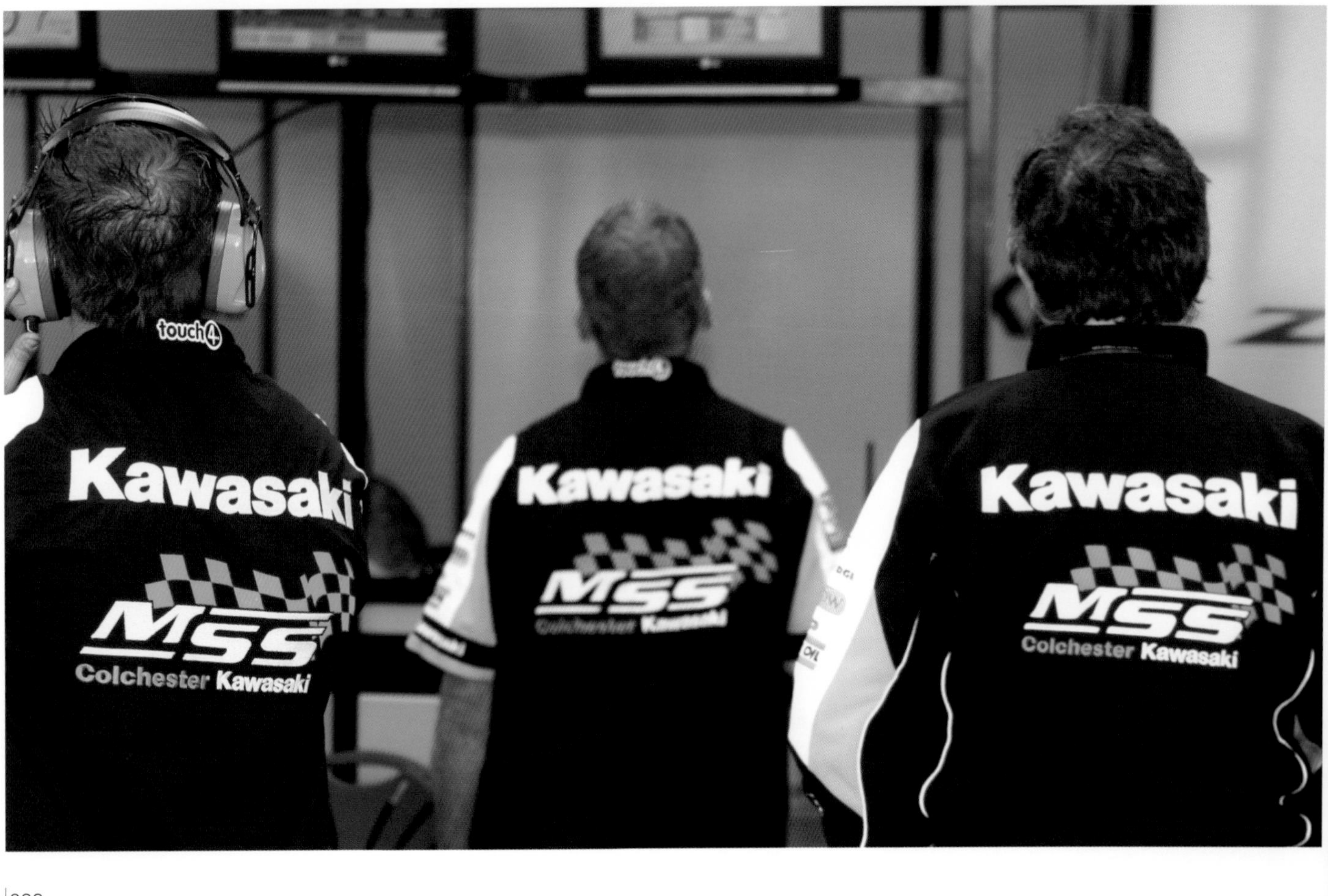

icom
touch 4

Kawasaki
MSS Kawasaki

Kawasaki
ROCK OIL

Kawasaki
17
Kawasaki
17

Relentless Suzuki by TAS

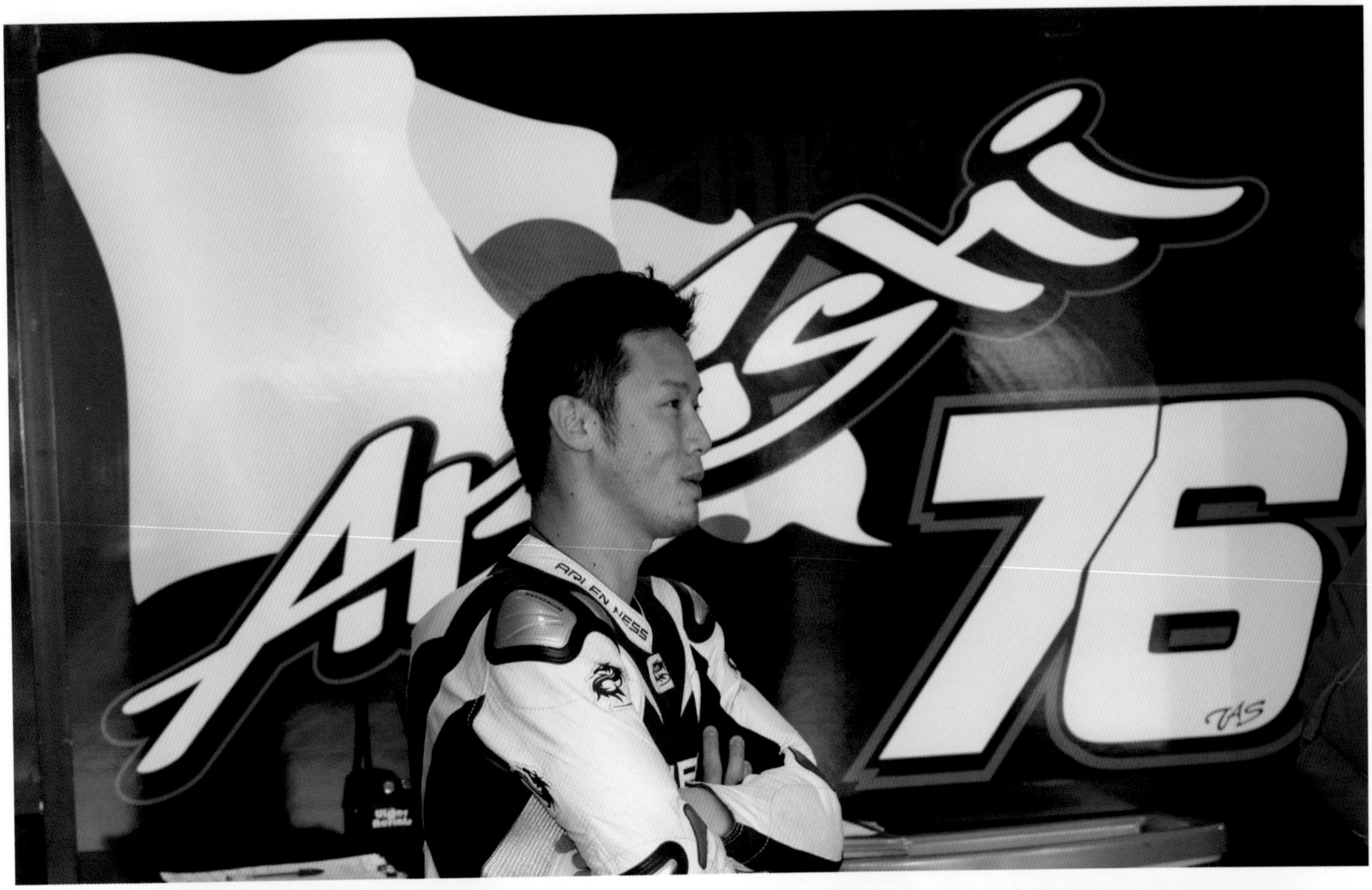

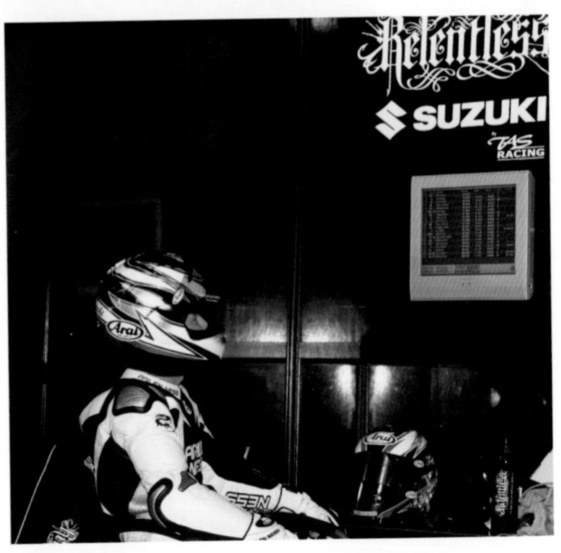

Arai
76
ARLEN NESS
TAS
Relentless
SUZUKI
TAS RACING
Arai
ARLEN NESS
SBK
NGK
Bendix
MOTUL
ARLENNESS
SUZUKI
MOTUL
Beacon

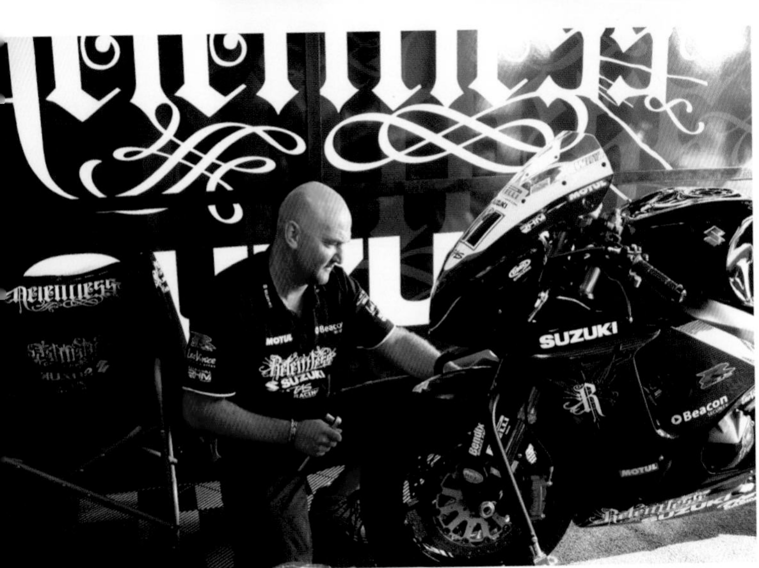

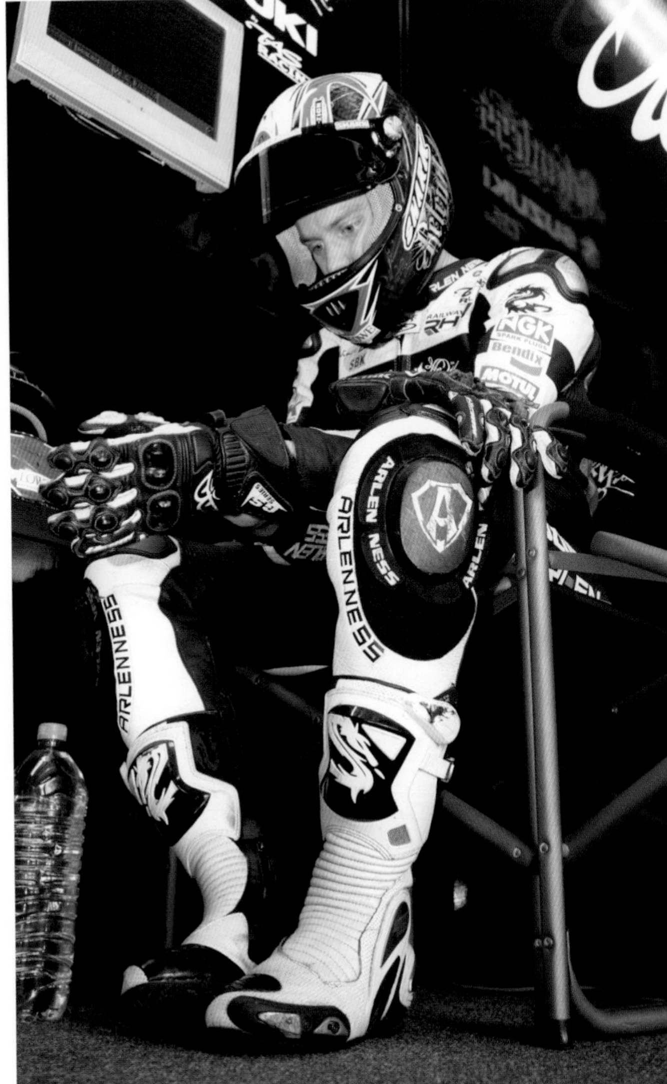

Relentless Suzuki by TAS

Machinery: Suzuki GSX-R1000 K9
Owner: Philip Neill
Located: Moneymore, Northern Ireland
Pedigree: British Supersport Champions 2007

It was all change this term for Northern Ireland's top team with TAS Suzuki doubling up to a two-rider team as they signed up ex Rizla Suzuki man, and former Japanese Champion, Atsu Watanabe and promoted home-grown Supersport prodigy Ian Lowry to the premier class.

Doyens of the road racing scene, they were aiming to be a major force on the short circuits once again, and with Watanabe having a year's apprenticeship behind him coupled with Lowry's raw talent, they were hoping for further success after the team's debut BSB season in 2008.

Lowry, who contracted swine flu in mid season, was particularly impressive and finished in an amazing fifth place in his rookie season but Watanabe was still inexplicably off the pace and is doubtful to return to these shores.

Coupled with a disastrous closed roads campaign of the NW200, TT and Ulster GP by their high standards, they had to rely on Alastair Seeley's domination in National Superstock 1000 to land the team's major silverware this season.

Riders:

Atsushi Watanabe	
Number:	76
DOB:	22 September, 1976
Lives:	Hamamatsu, Japan
Races:	47
Wins:	0
2008 Position:	14th British Superbike Championship

Ian Lowry	
Number:	11
DOB:	22 September, 1986
Lives:	Newry, Northern Ireland
Races:	26
Wins:	0
2008 Position:	3rd British Supersport Championship

Alastair Seeley
Silverstone, Oulton Park

Lowry
SUZUKI
MOTUL
NO HALF MEASURES
NO HALF MEASURES
SBK
SBK

Beacon
MOTUL
PIRELLI
NGK
Bendix
NO HALF MEASURES
SUZUKI
Beacon
SECURITY
SBK
NGK
MOTUL
34
SUZUKI
RACING
PIRELLI

Buildbase Kawasaki

BUILDBASE
Kawasaki

Buildbase Kawasaki

Machinery: Kawasaki ZX-10R
Owner: Stuart Hicken
Located: Peggs Green, Leics
Pedigree: BSB Race Winners

No one has more experience of racing Kawasakis than the team formerly known as Hawk who had enjoyed copious amounts of previous success with the 750cc ZX-7R fours.

Team boss Stuart Hicken runs a tight ship and for 2009, signed two of the most underrated and consistent riders in BSB, namely John Laverty and Tristan Palmer to run in Buildbase colours.

Between them, they have won the Privateers Cup for the past two seasons and even on lower spec bikes, were regular points scorers. However, each had a tough start to the season, Laverty crashing out at Oulton and Palmer missing Thruxton after a big practice smash.

As the season progressed, Laverty in particular kicked on and came very near to giving Buildbase their first podium of the season at Mallory. He was back on the pace next time out at Brands to end up in a creditable top ten placing in the series although the affable Palmer ended up outside the top twenty after missing the final round.

Riders:

Tristan Palmer	
Number:	6
DOB:	17 August, 1982
Lives:	New Arley, Warks
Races:	93
Wins:	0
2008 Position:	10th British Superbike Championship

John Laverty	
Number:	4
DOB:	06 July, 1982
Lives:	Toomebridge, Northern Ireland
Races:	63
Wins:	0
2008 Position:	British Superbike Cup Champion

James Hillier
Oulton Park

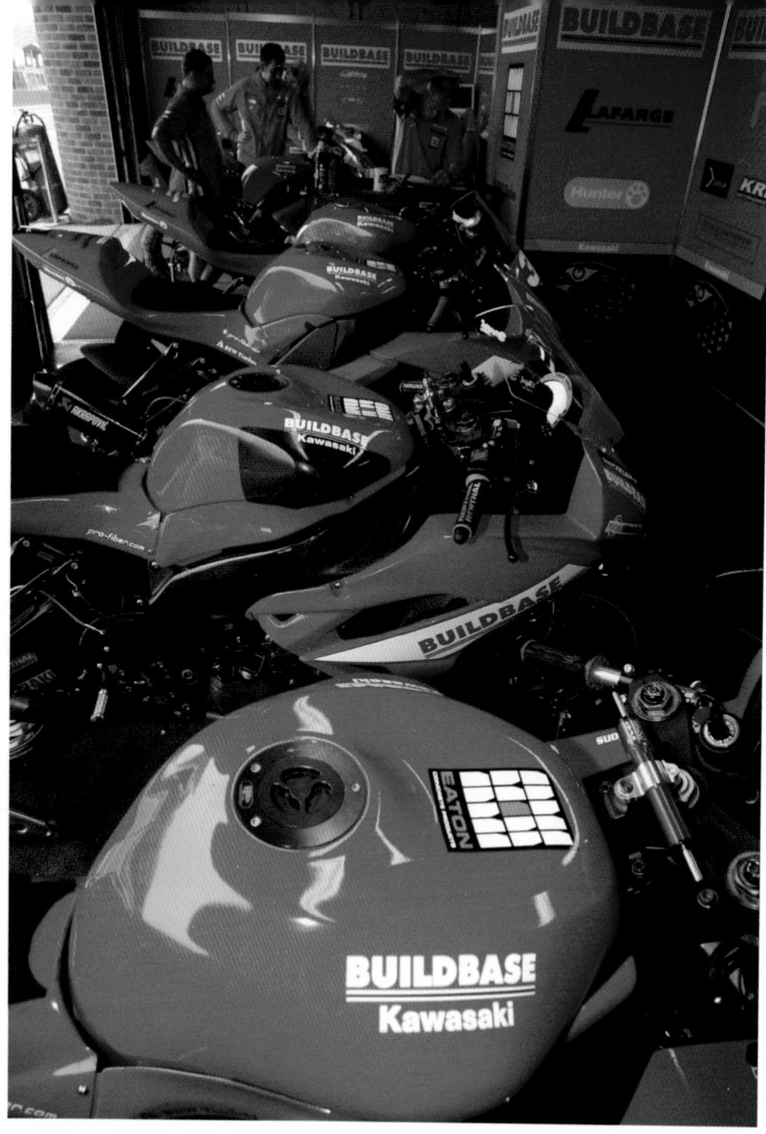

BUILDBASE
LAFARGE
Hunter
BUILDBASE
Kawasaki
EATON
BUILDBASE
Kawasaki

BUILDBASE
SHOEI

BUILDBASE
BUILDBASE
BUILDBASE
BUILDBASE
ARROW
OXFORD
FUCHS
LAFARGE
Hunter
Kawasaki
TRiS

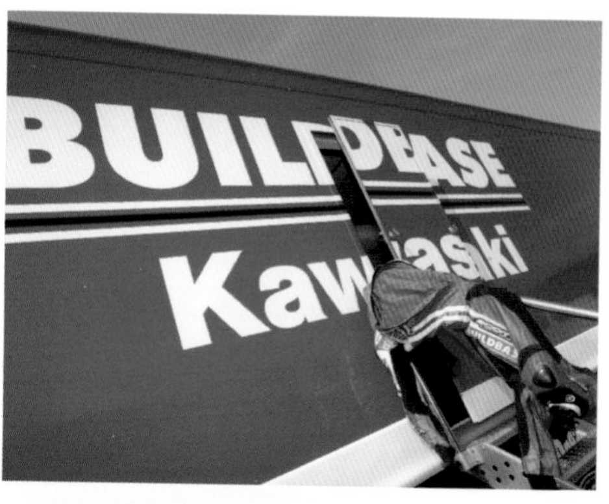

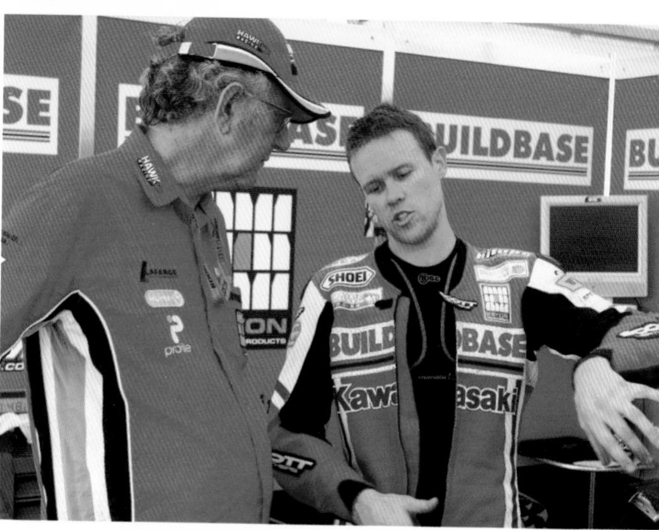

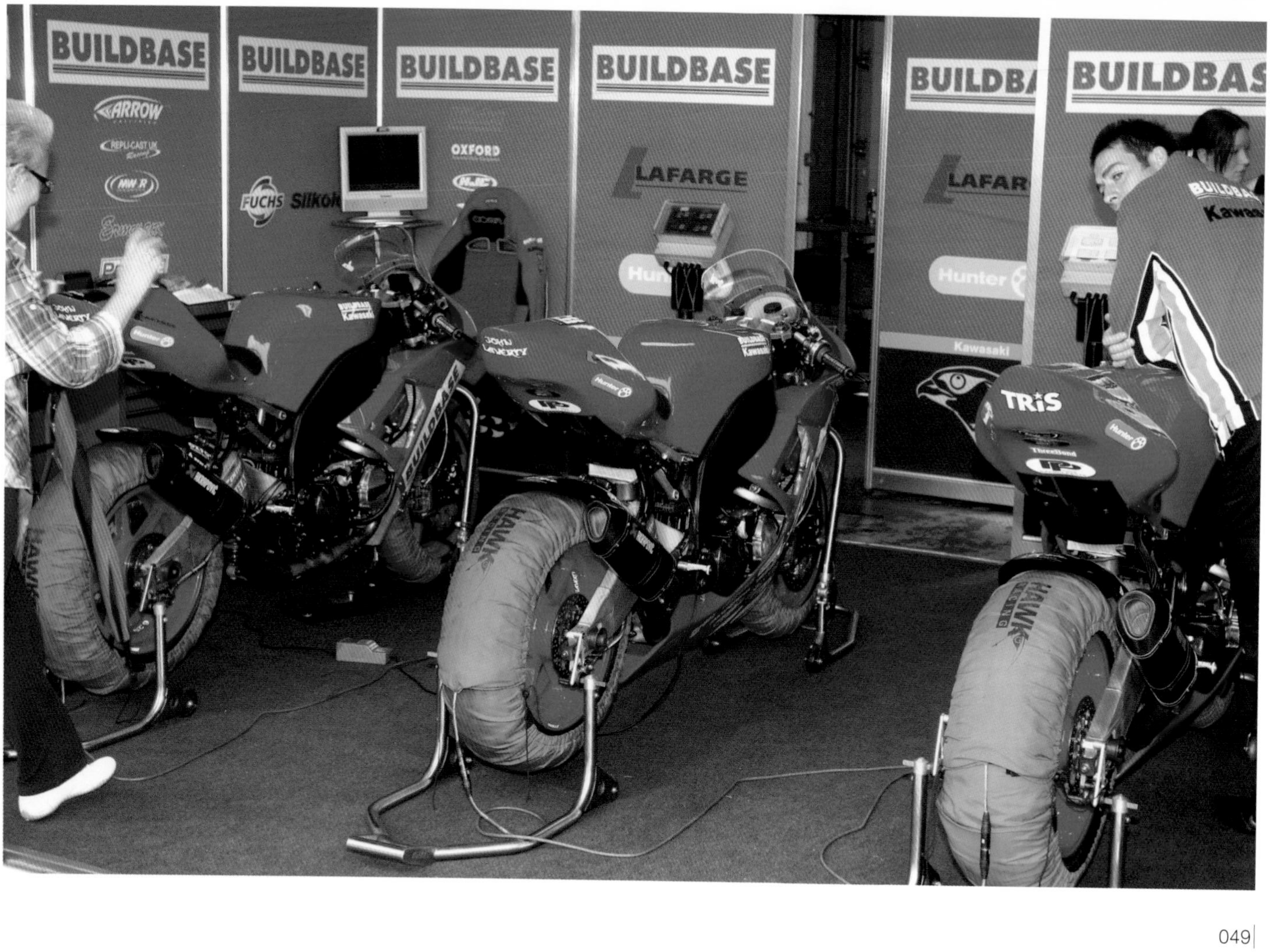

BUILDBASE
SHOEI
ANDREWS

PIRELLI
TRiS
Hunter
ThreeBond

OXFORD
HJC
BUILDBASE
Kawasaki
TRiS

TRiS
Hunter
Hunter
ThreeBond

BUILDBASE
Kawasaki
SHOEI
BUILDBASE
Kawasaki
SHOEI

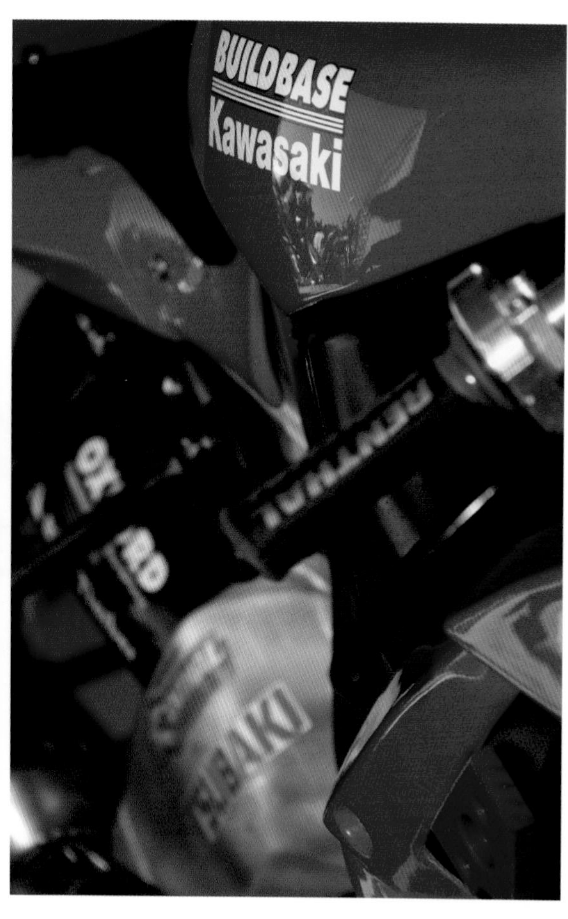

BUILDBASE
Kawasaki
TSUBAKI

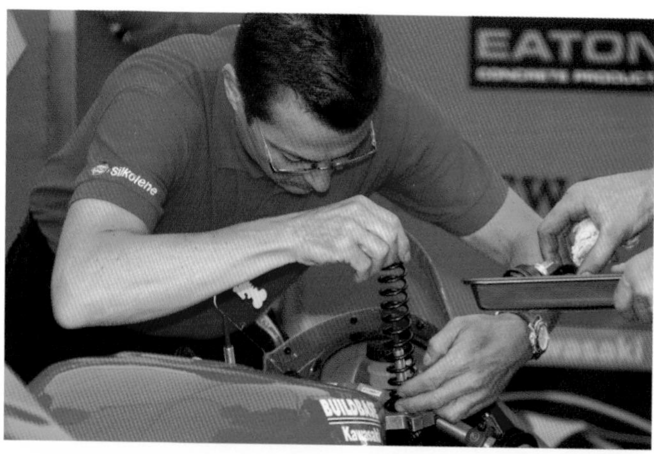

EATON
Silkolene
BUILDBASE

BUILDBASE
BUILDBASE
ARROW
Kawasaki
WWW.PROBIKE.C
BUILDBASE

BUILDBASE
BUILDBASE
BUILDBASE
BUILDBASE
BUIL
EATON
FUCHS
ARROW
REPLAY
SHOEI
BUILDBASE
Silkolene
BUILDBASE
TSUBAKI
PROBIKE
EXTRA
WebCrea
SHOEI
SHOEI
SHOEI

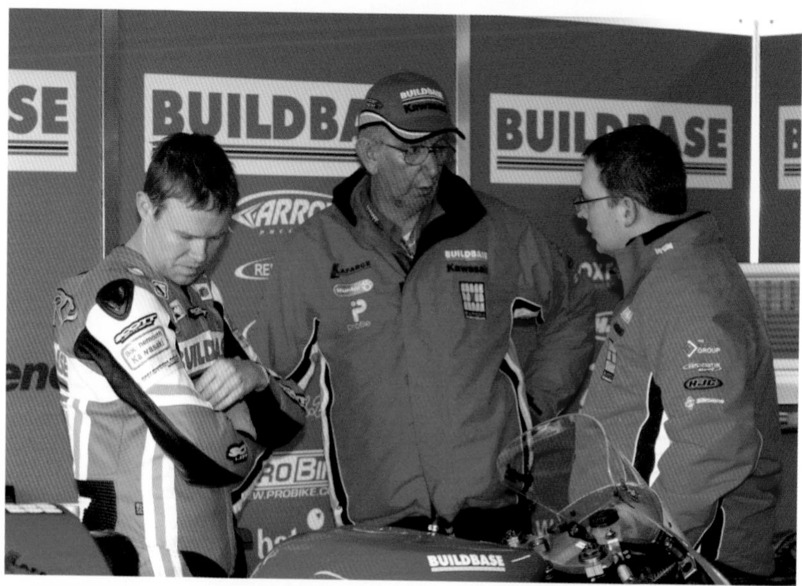

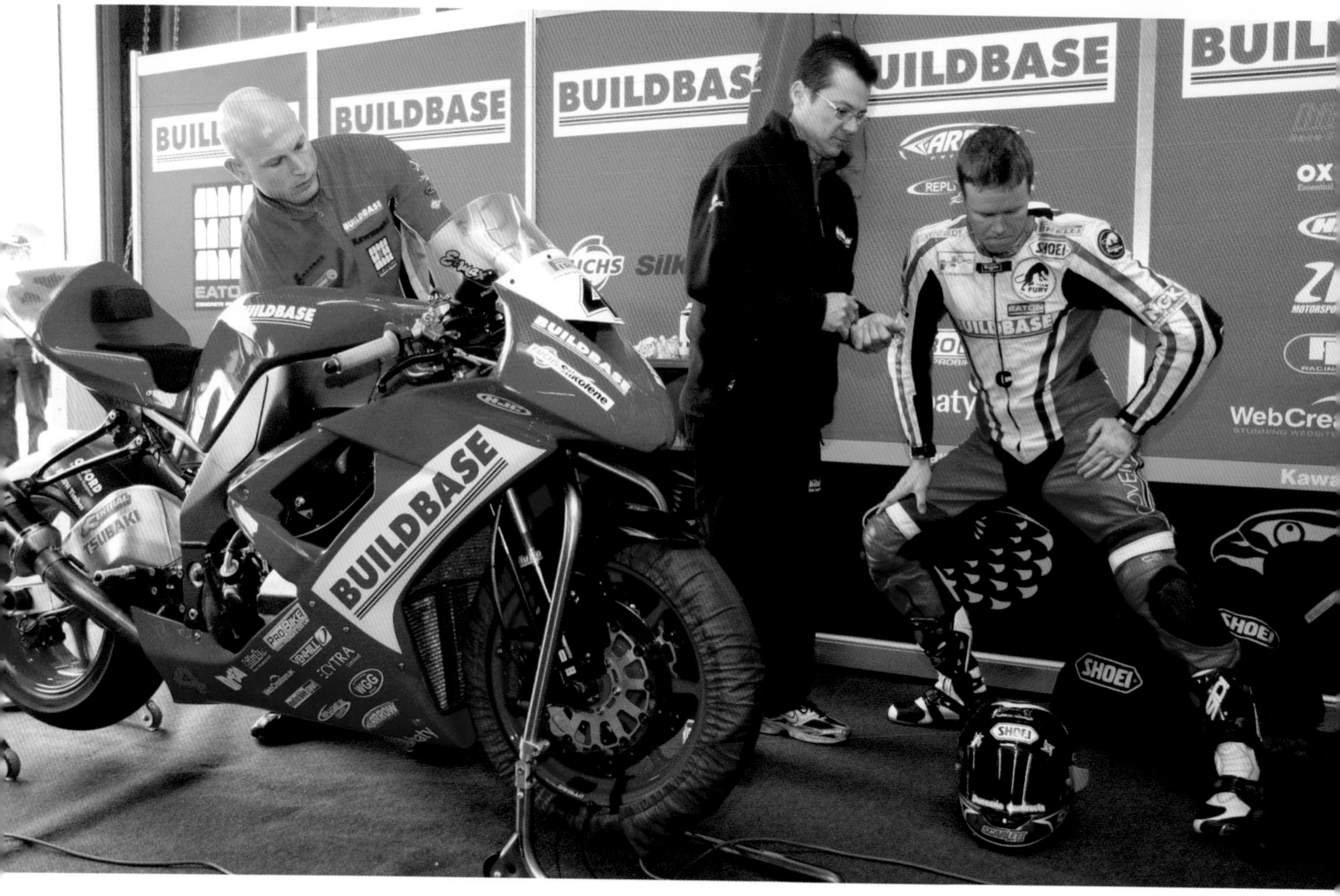

Worx Crescent Suzuki

Worx Crescent Suzuki

Machinery: Suzuki GSX-R1000 K9
Principal: Jack Valentine
Located: Verwood, Dorset
Pedigree: British Superbike Champions 2004

After the success of 2008 with Tom Sykes, Paul Denning's team was whittled down to just one rider for this season but the nucleus of the team remained the same for the arrival of cosmopolitan Frenchman Sylvain Guintoli.

The ex MotoGP rider sensationally won on his debut at Brands and was taking the fight to the rest when his season was cruelly disrupted with that infamous formation lap crash at Donington involving Josh Brookes which left Guintoli with a serious leg injury.

Having spent the majority of his career in the MotoGP paddock with 118 GP starts and a best result of fourth at Motegi in 2007, 'Guinters' has British roots having lived here for many years and has an English wife so BSB didn't hold any culture shocks and he unexpectedly returned at Cadwell Park but couldn't recapture his early season form.

Sadly, his tenure in BSB was to be brief and he's been drafted into the Alstare team in World Superbikes next season meaning British fans will never get to witness his undoubted great potential.

Riders:

Sylvain Guintoli

Number:	50
DOB:	24 June, 1982
Lives:	Montelimar, France
Races:	13
Wins:	1
2008 Position:	13th MotoGP World Championship

Michael Rutter
Thruxton, Snetterton, Knockhill

Tommy Hill
Mallory, Brands Hatch GP

CRESCENT
EXPRESS Insurance
MOTOREX
DataPacific

GUINTERS
P1
+·6

WORX

SHOEI
Adaptaflex
NGK
SPARK PLUGS
EXPRESS Insurance
Vent-Axia

EXPRESS
Insurance
CRESCENT
WORX
GSX
CRESCENT

WORX
SUZUKI
you've got the power

WORX
SUZUKI
WORX

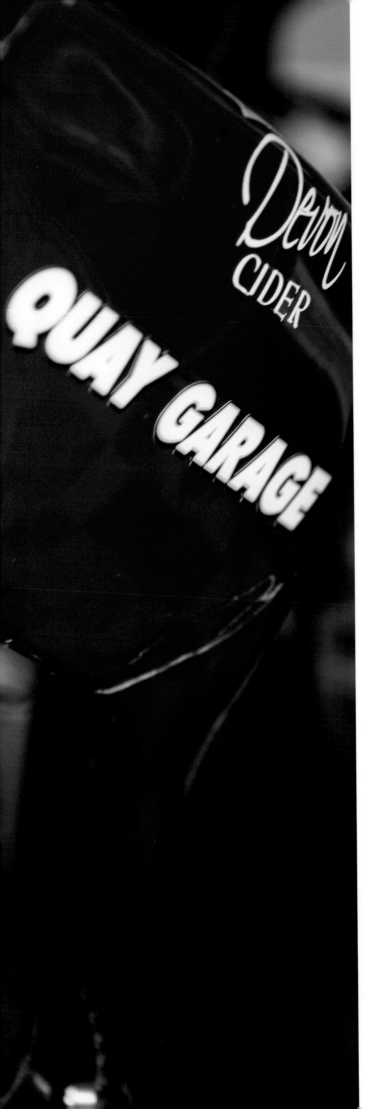

Quay Garage Honda

Machinery: Honda CBR1000RR Fireblade
Owner: Ian Woolacott
Located: Braunton, Devon
Pedigree: British Superbike Cup Champions 2005 & 2009

The team started out last year with tall Devonian, James Buckingham, who has been a stalwart of the Superbike Cup class for many seasons, and indeed landed the crown in 2005.

Still suffering from serious leg injuries sustained in 2006, 'Big Bucks' decided to hang his leathers up after three rounds and as a result, the team drafted in ex BSB works star Gary Mason, who was racing in the USA at the time.

Following on a superb season last year, Mason, quite simply, has once again been a revelation and his front row qualifying performance at Thruxton backed up his dozen top ten placings in the increasingly competitive races as he landed the Mirror.co.uk Cup crown with two meetings to spare for team boss Ian Woolacott.

Riders:

Gary Mason

Number:	101
DOB:	04 May, 1979
Lives:	Lichfield, Staffs.
Races:	134
Wins:	0
2008 Position:	3rd British Superbike Cup

James Buckingham
Oulton Park

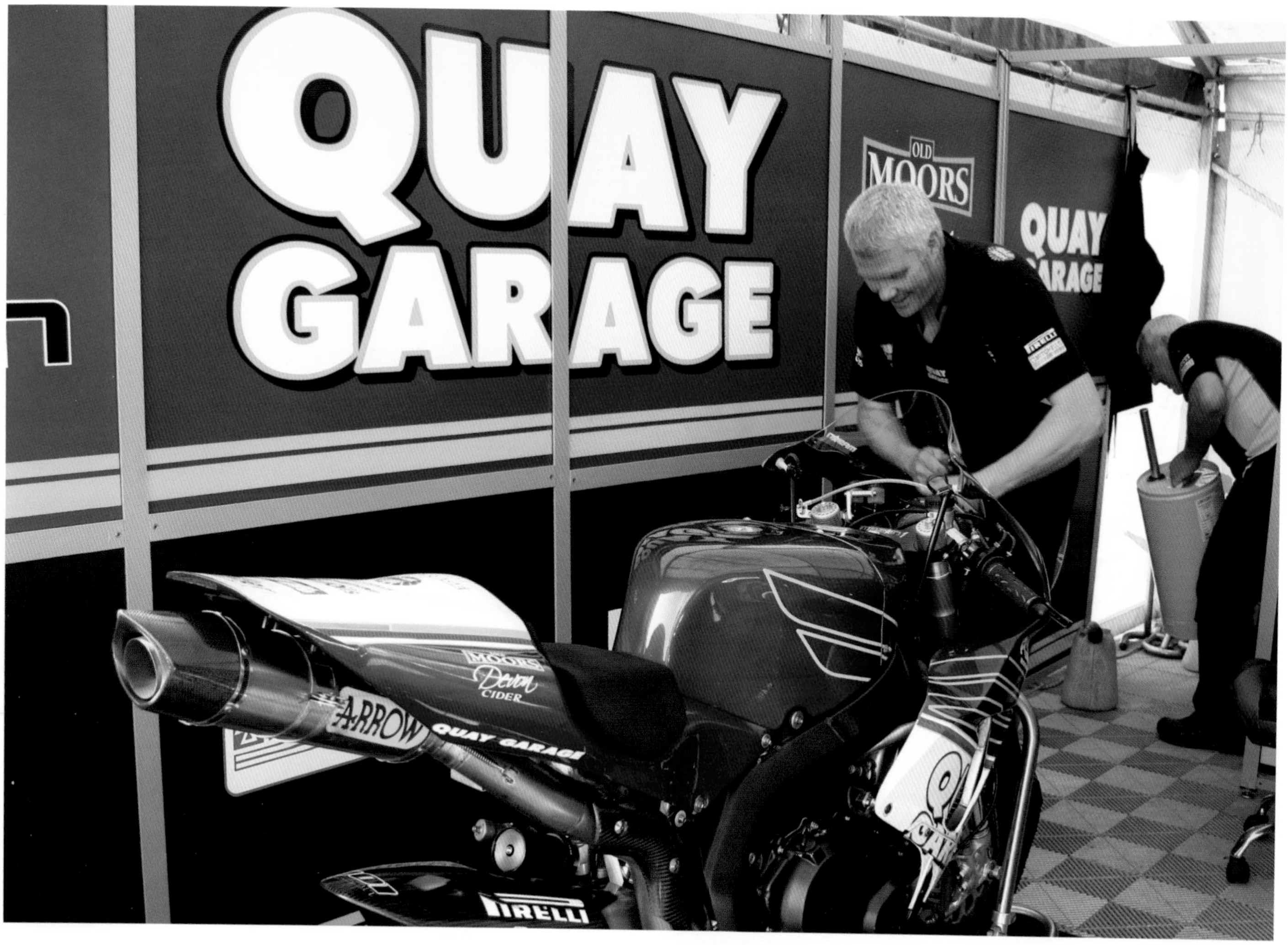

Q8 Oils
Q8 Oils
execflyer
PIRELLI
101

www.quaygarage.co.uk

QUAY
GARAGE
#101
MASON

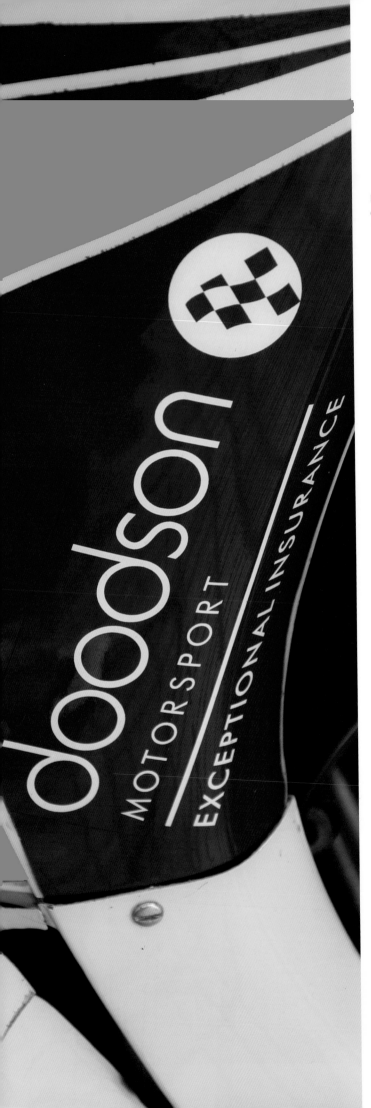

Hardinge Doodson Motorsport Honda

Machinery: Honda CBR1000RR Fireblade
Owner: Tom Tunstall
Located: Denby Dale, West Yorkshire
Pedigree: World Championship Experience

Having served his apprenticeship in the Superteen and British 250cc series, genial Yorkshireman Tom Tunstall went off to race in Europe, returning at the start of 2007 to contest the British Superbike Cup where he eventually finished third.

Denied a victory but accumulating more than a dozen podiums in that 2007 campaign, Tunstall did everything but claim a win in the Cup class last season and so it has come to pass, as once again he just missed out on climbing the top step of the podium.

Tom scored a triple podium at Brands to add to those at Donington and Thruxton as well as claiming more silverware at Snetterton and Knockhill before rounding the season off with more success at Silverstone and Oulton to reward his hard working yet compact team.

Rider:

Tom Tunstall

Number:	21
DOB:	21 June, 1978
Lives:	Huddersfield, West Yorkshire
Races:	74
Wins:	0
2008 Position:	4th British Superbike Cup

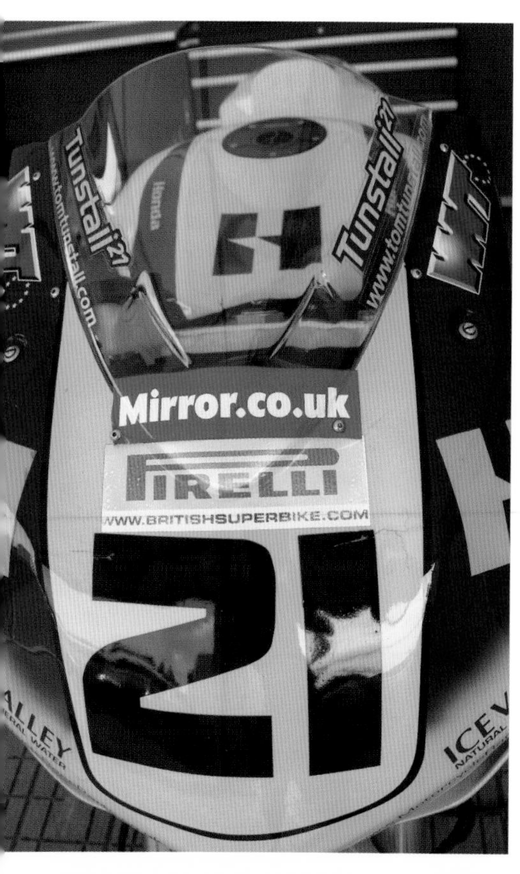

Tunstall21
www.tomtunstall.com
Mirror.co.uk
PIRELLI
WWW.BRITISHSUPERBIKE.COM
21

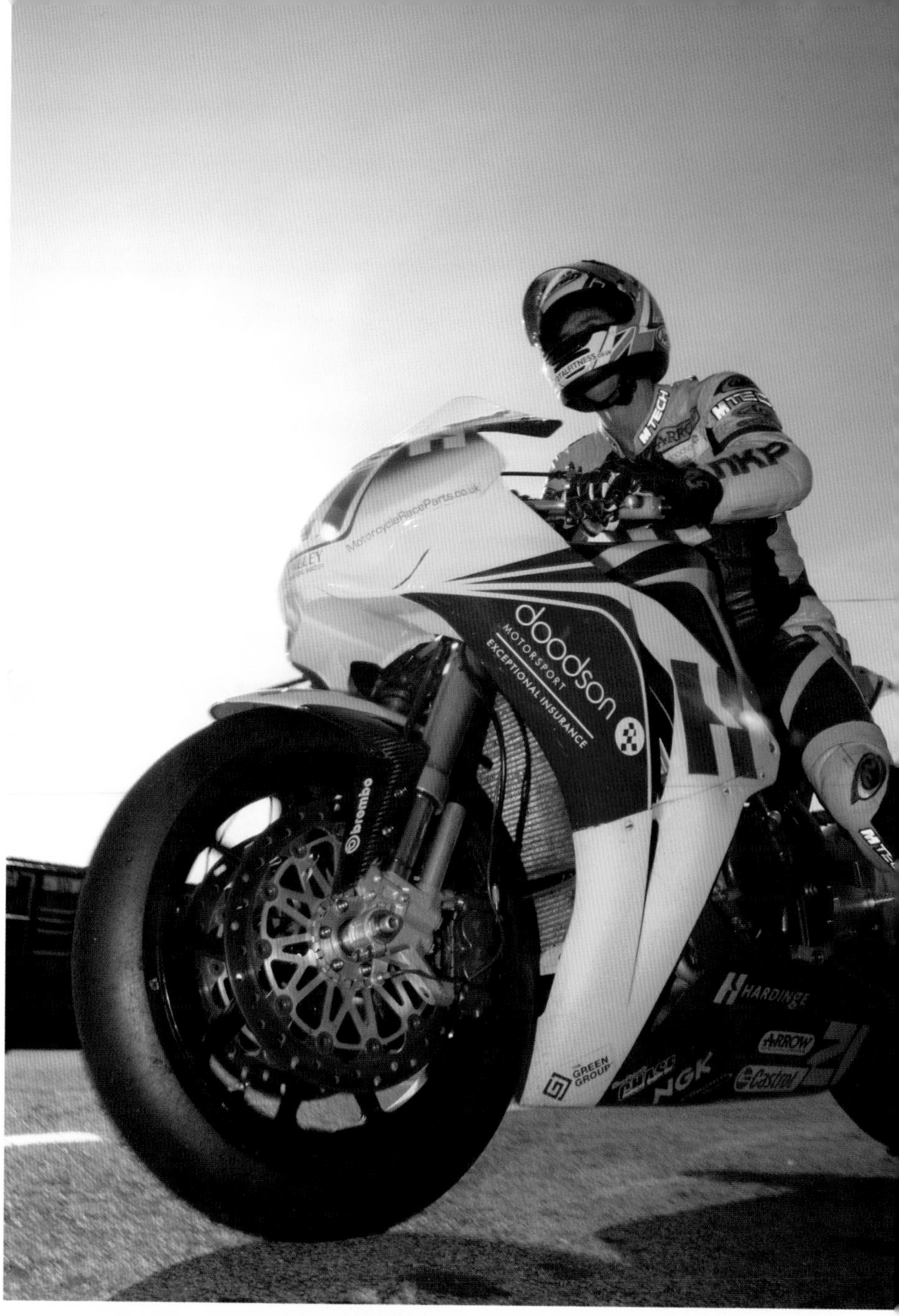

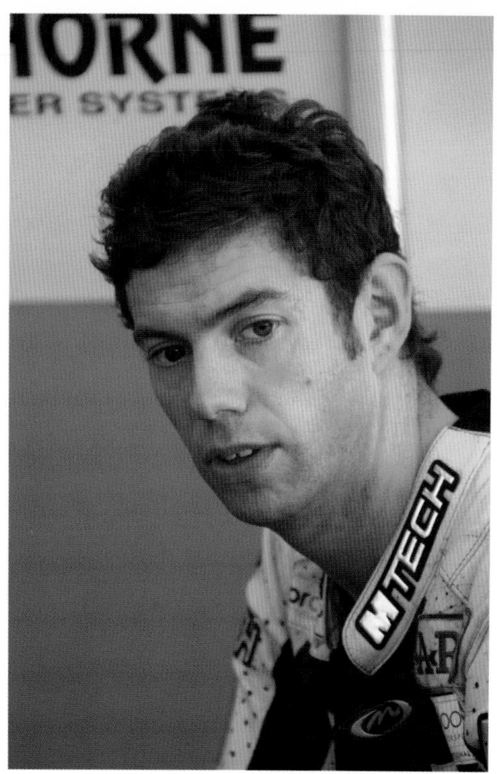

MotorcycleRaceParts.co.uk
doodson
MOTORSPORT
EXCEPTIONAL INSURANCE
brembo
HARDINGE
ARROW
NGK
Castrol
M TECH

HORNE
M TECH

HARDINGE
ICE VALLEY
NATURAL MINERAL WATER
NGK
Renthal
TSUBAKI
M.A. HORNE
TYRE HEATER SYSTEMS
RacePar
.co.uk
Tunstall
21
ARROW
doodson

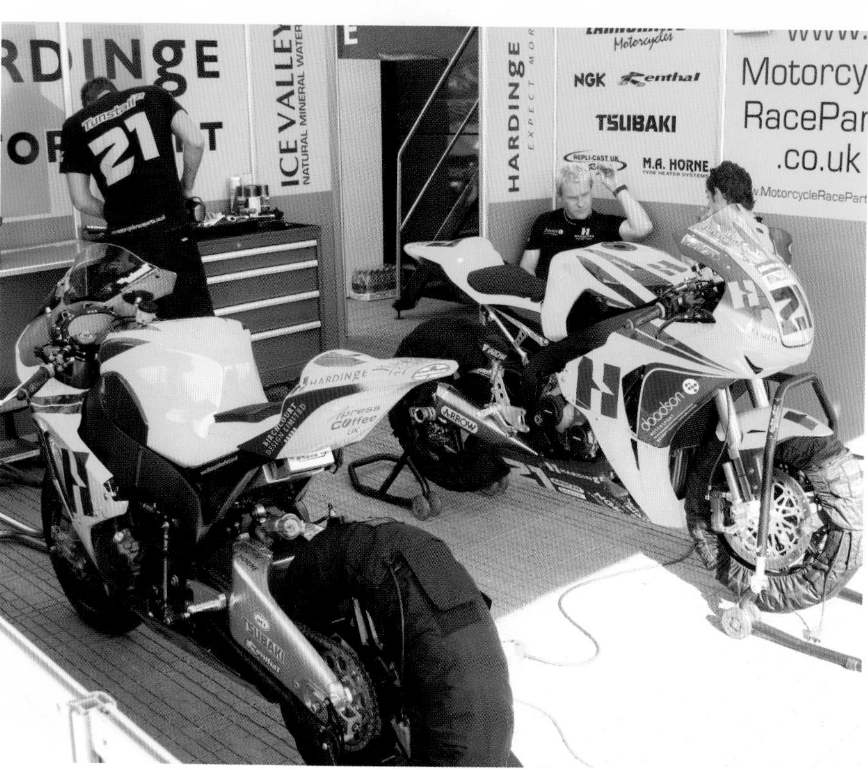

Team Maxxis Adept Yamaha

Machinery: Yamaha YZF-R1
Owner: John Jameson
Located: Liverpool
Pedigree: British Superbike Cup Champions 2006

Having won the British Superbike Cup in 2006 with Chris Martin, the team underwent several rider changes in 2007 before settling with the venerable Australian David Johnson who rode for them throughout last season.

'The Aussie DJ' is a class act who has suffered from his fair share of bad luck, but despite that, was a regular points scorer on the lower leaderboard placings in 2008 and was looking good this season until a 150mph crash at Brands in August saw him break his foot.

As a result, the team drafted in Superstock 1000 regular Howie Mainwaring as a replacement for the rest of the season and he responded with a number of consistent, if unspectacular, rides scoring points in all bar one of the meetings he contested.

Riders:

Howie Mainwaring

Number:	68
DOB:	09 April, 1986
Lives:	Frodsham, Cheshire
Races:	50
Wins:	0
2008 Position:	15th National Superstock 1000cc Championship

David Johnson
Brands Hatch Indy to Brands Hatch GP (not Knockhill)

MAXXIS
SHARK
maxxis.co.uk
BICKERS
PIRELLI

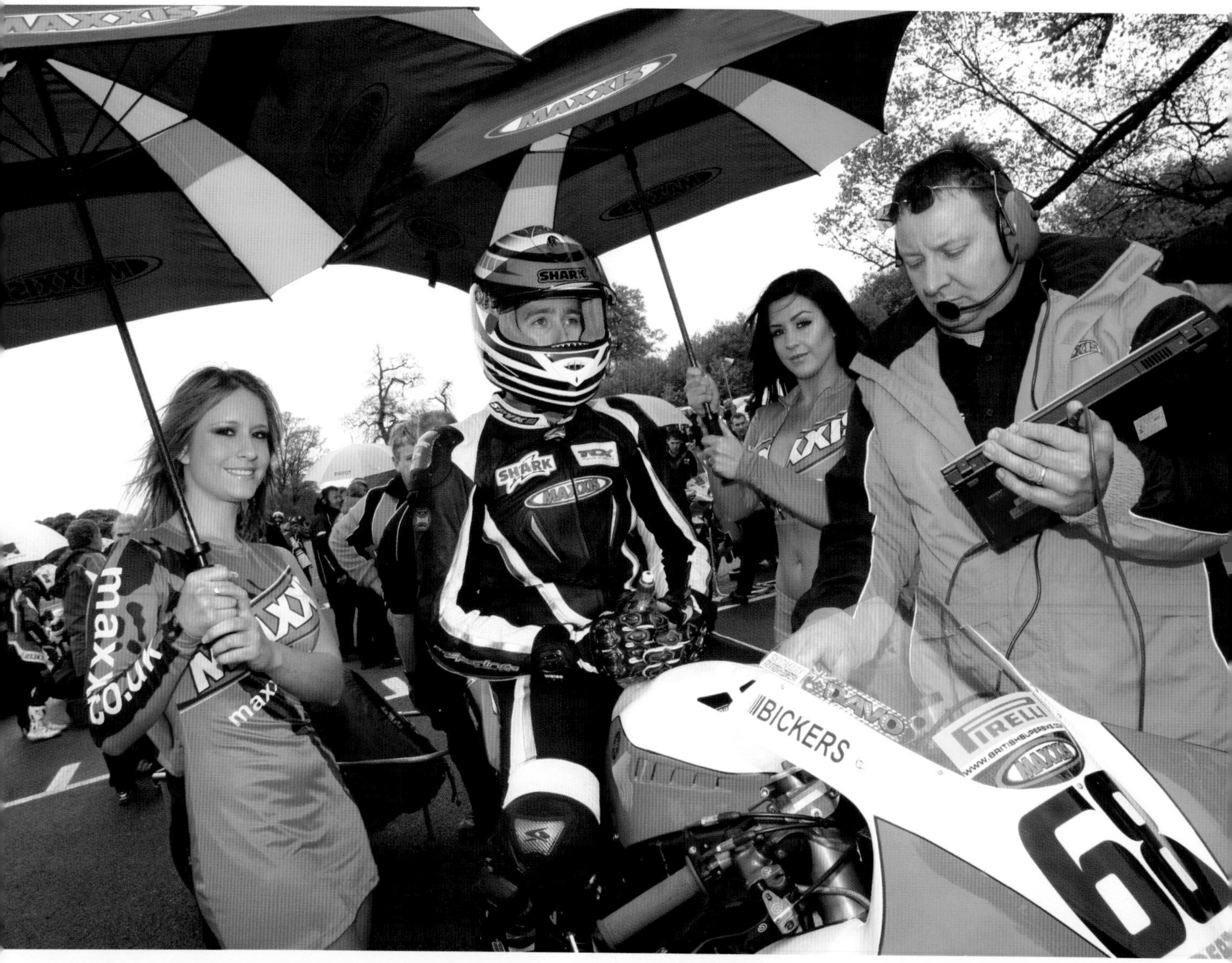

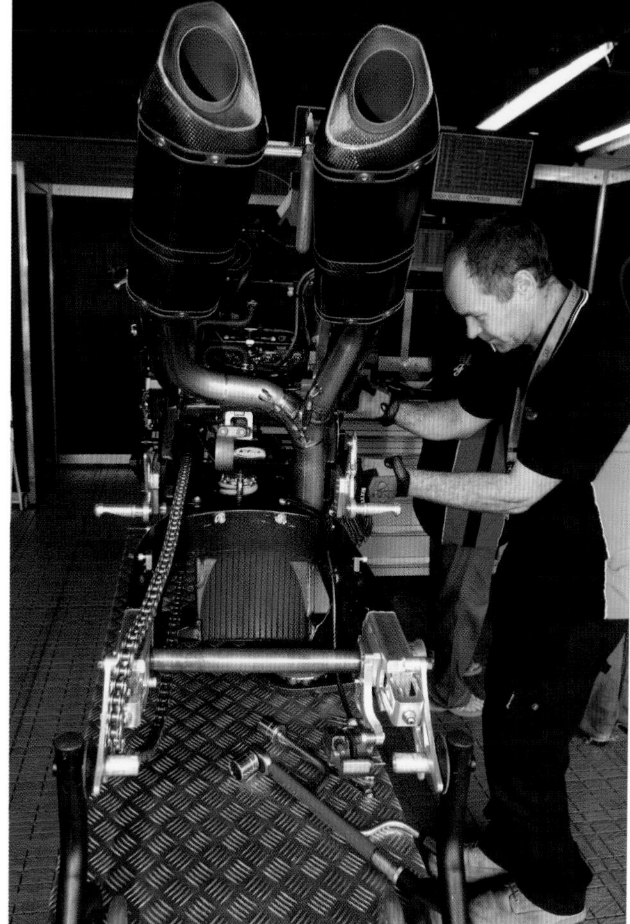

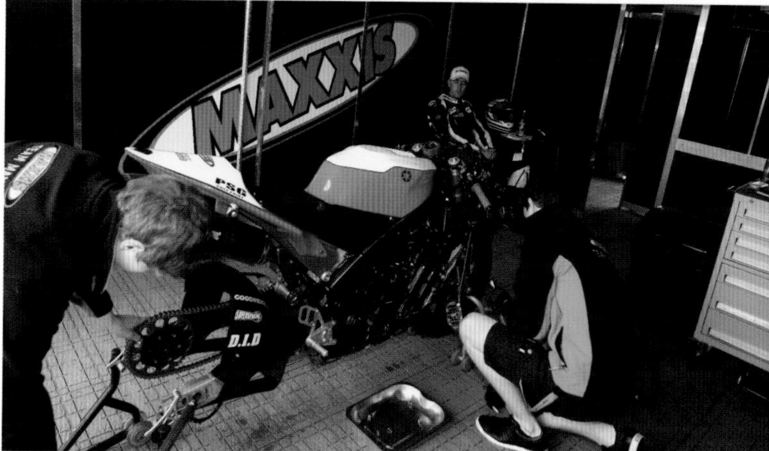

MAXXIS
D.I.D

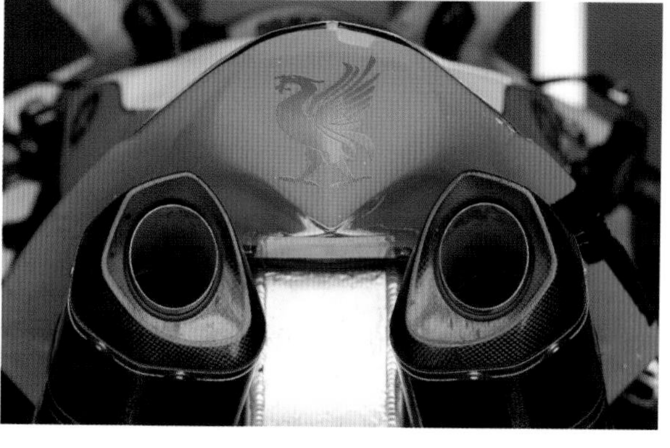

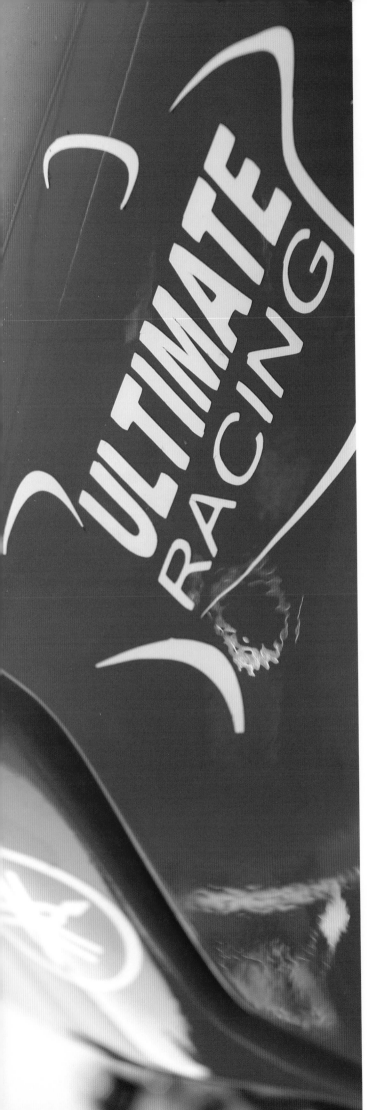

Ultimate Racing Yamaha

Machinery: Yamaha YZF-R1
Owners: Ian Drake, David & Peter Hickman
Located: Silverstone, Northants
Pedigree: Superbike Cup Runners-Up

Former Superstock front-runner Peter Hickman, along with his Ultimate Racing team, made the move up to the Mirror.co.uk Cup class this season and having done a few rounds towards the end of last year, is proving he's well capable of challenging.

Indeed, despite his junior years, 'Hicky' has plenty of Superbike experience and was part of the Hawk Racing set up a couple of seasons back meaning he knows what's required to race against the world's best.

As media-savvy as they come, Hickman, who part owns the team along with dad Dave and sponsor Ian Drake, performed with such consistency that he claimed a superb runner-up placing behind Gary Mason in the series to round off a very successful season.

Rider:

Peter Hickman	
Number:	60
DOB:	08 April, 1987
Lives:	Alford, Lincolnshire
Races:	68
Wins:	0
2008 Position:	3rd National Superstock 1000cc Championship

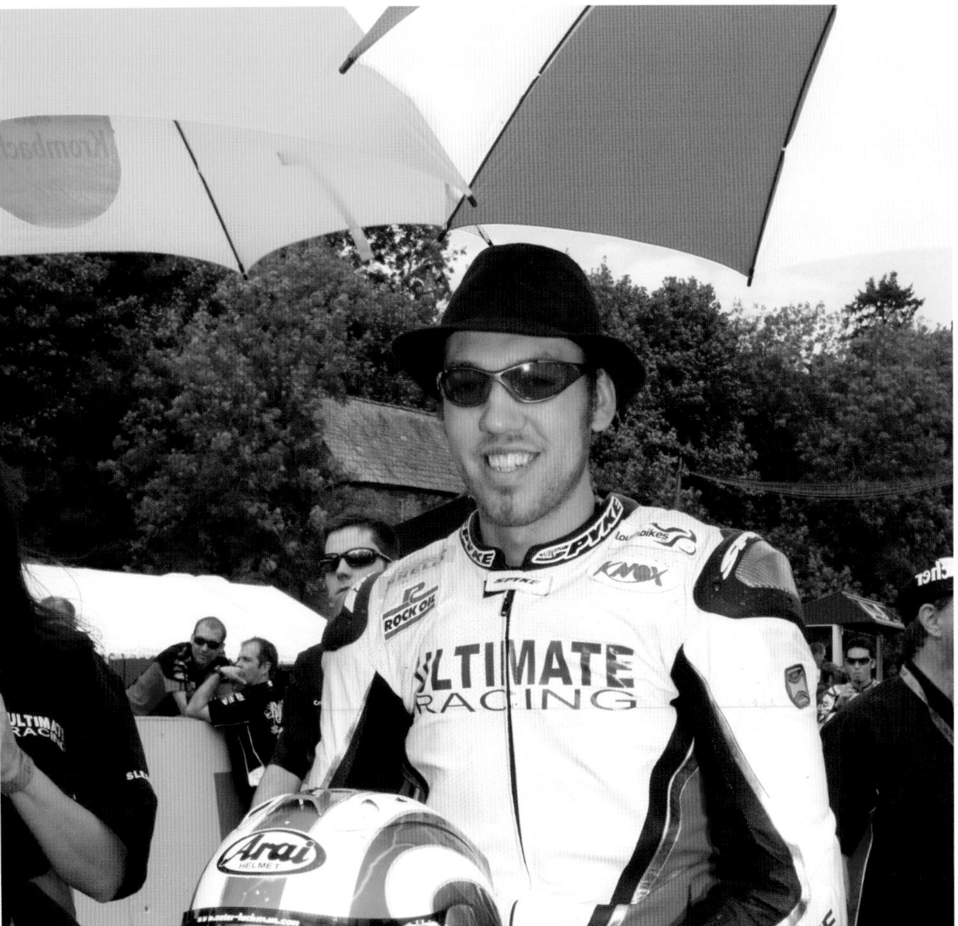

PIRELLI
WWW.BRITISHSUPERBIKE.COM
60
Mirror.co.uk
SLEAFORD
Pro-Bolt

Hicky

ULTIMATE
RACING
SLP
Racing
LOGISTICS
LTD

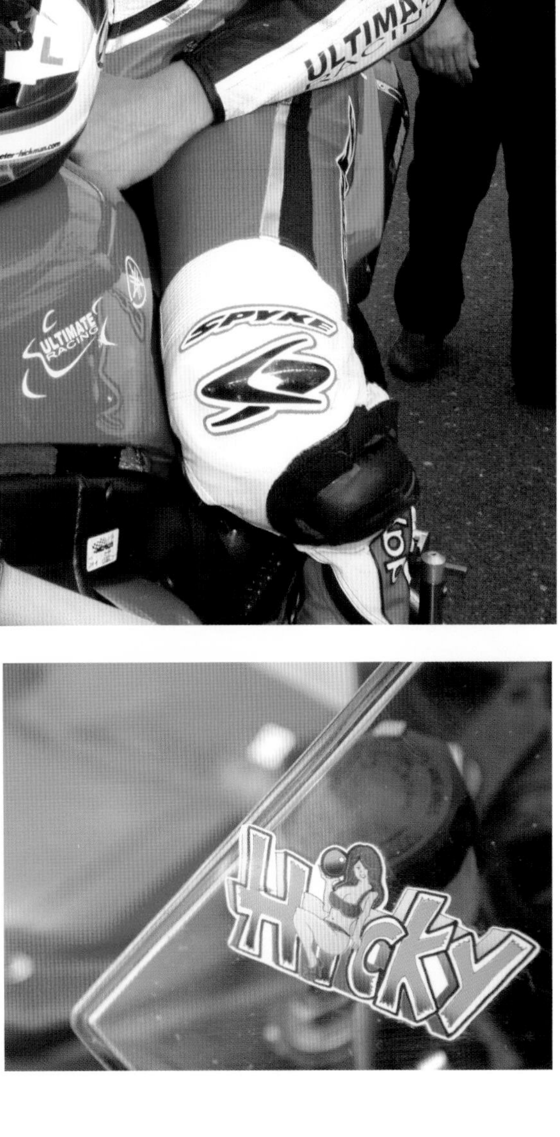

Riders Racing Honda

Machinery: Honda CBR1000RR Fireblade
Owner: Phil Jessopp
Located: Bridgwater, Somerset
Pedigree: Superbike Cup Race Winners

After acquiring a pair of Stobart Hondas towards the end of 2007, the team had a brief outing in readiness for 2008 whereby Martin Jessopp ended up being a major contender for the privateer's crown in the early part of the season.

An accident at Donington hampered his bid but he bounced back to show remarkable consistency to claim runner-up spot on the immaculately turned out bikes, the only blot being he didn't manage to win a race.

Earlier in the season, Martin scored seven podiums in the opening eight races before a morning warm up spill sidelined him at Snetterton with a broken shoulder but he came back at Mallory and followed that up with a hat trick of runner-up places at Brands but didn't make the podium again, although he did finish third in the final standings.

Rider:

Martin Jessopp

Number:	60
DOB:	04 November, 1985
Lives:	Yeovil, Somerset
Races:	46
Wins:	0
2008 Position:	2nd British Superbike Cup

Riders
Racing
martinjessopp.com
Riders
of Brit

Jessopp
40

Jessopp
Riders
Racing
40

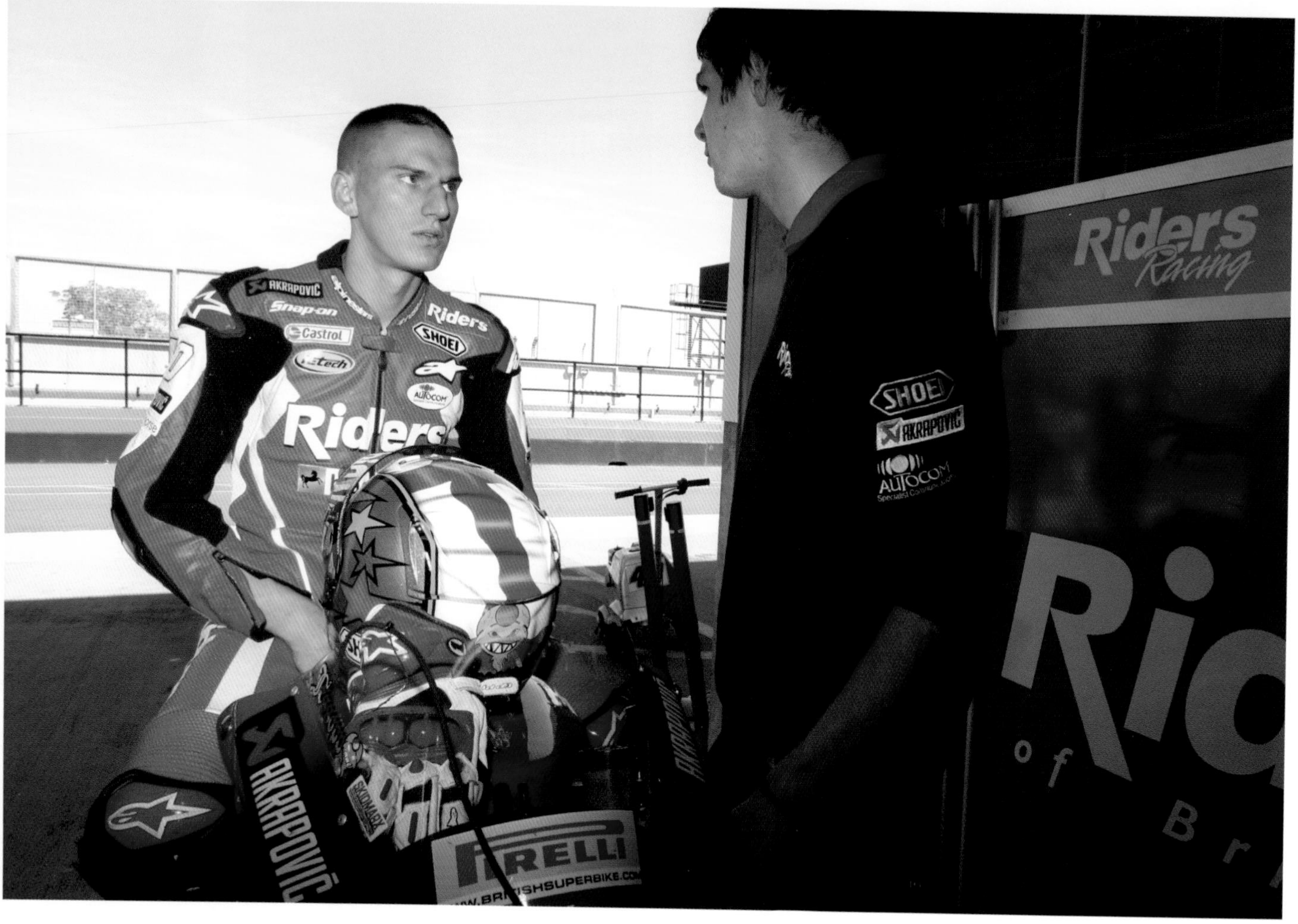

Team NB

Machinery: Suzuki GSX-R1000K6
Owner: Marcus, Elizabeth, Thomas & Charlotte Bridewell
Located: Devizes, Wiltshire
Pedigree: Superbike Cup Race Winners

After cutting his teeth in the UK, Tommy made the transition to the European paddocks at the start of 2008 and has had reasonable success in the Suzuki Cup, Italian Superbike Championship and FIM Superstock 1000 before returning to the UK.

Very much a family affair, the machine was the one campaigned by his late brother Ollie in 2007 before his accident at Mallory and quite simply, Tommy astounded everyone by winning on his return to this season's Mirror.co.uk Cup at Snetterton.

Tom and his family are unique. Firm favourites with race fans and fellow competitors alike, and it would be a crying shame if no top team takes a chance on him, especially after those stunning performances netted seven wins in total.

Rider:

Tommy Bridewell

Number:	46
DOB:	04 August, 1988
Lives:	Devizes, Wilts
Races:	33
Wins:	0
2008 Position:	Italian Superbike Championship & Suzuki GSX-R750 Cup

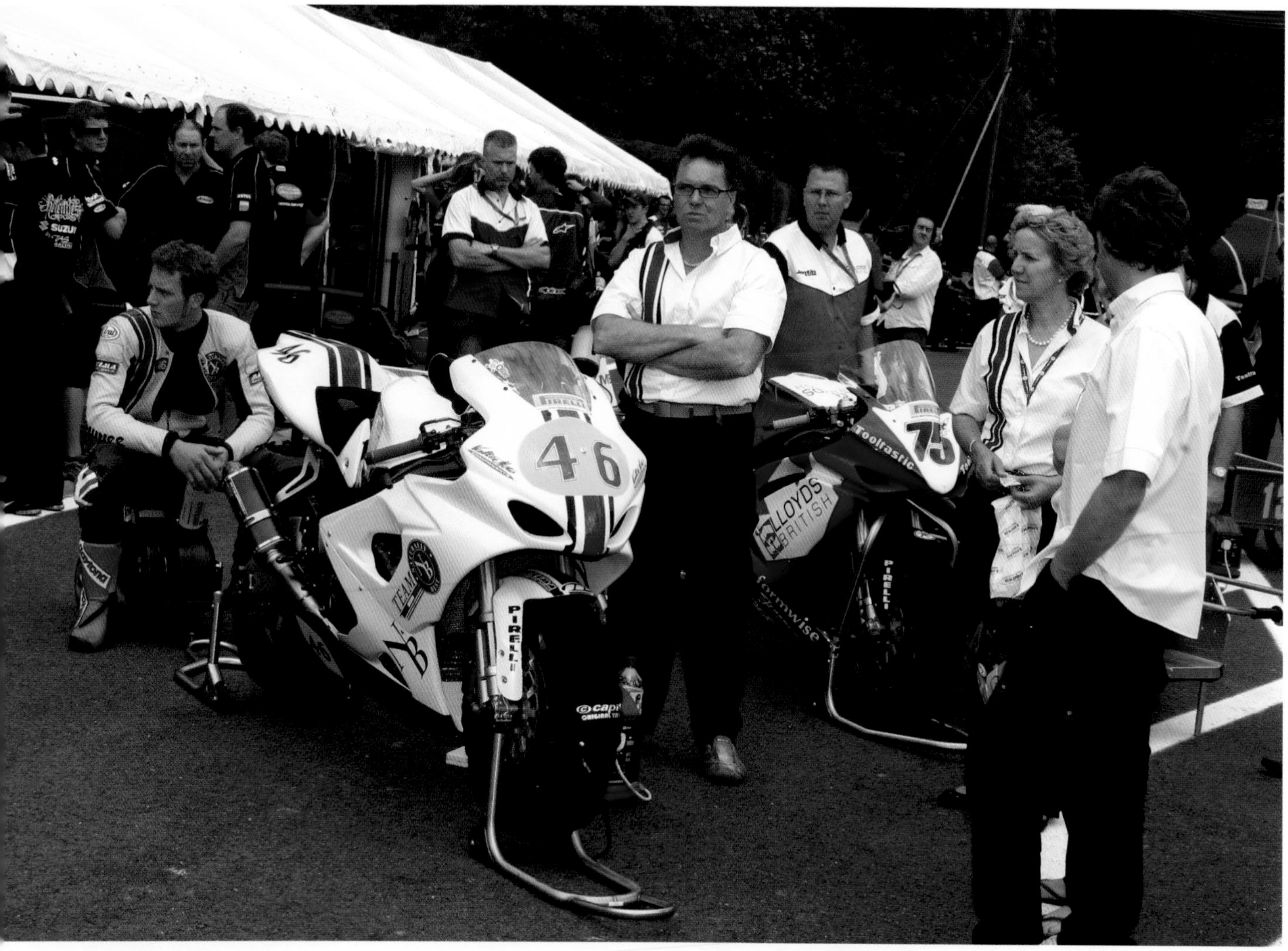

NATURALLY
NB
46

46
COMPONENTS

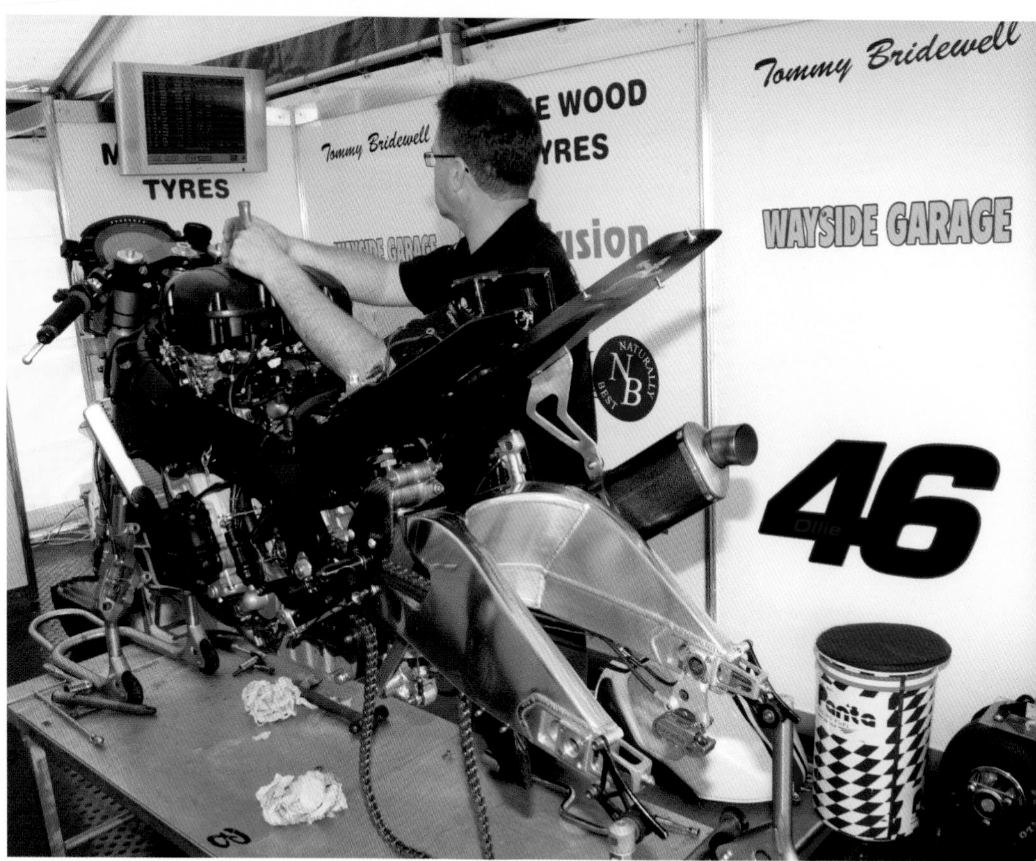
Tommy Bridewell
Tommy Bridewell
TYRES
WAYSIDE GARAGE
NATURALLY BEST
NB
46

MSVR behind the scenes

BSB

BSB

BSB

VISK

JUMP START
BSB

DIABLO
SUPERCORSA

IT TOOK EMOTION TO CREATE THE ULTIMATE BSB TYRE

The Diablo Supercorsa BSB is the *special edition* road legal tyre, brought to you by Pirelli. Developed through use within the British and World Superbike Championships and now available for use on the road. The Diablo Supercorsa BSB benefits from input from some of the world's best Supersport riders and has achieved an incredible 5 lap records during the 2008 British Supersport Championship. The Diablo Supercorsa BSB is produced with the latest technology and offers the rider the unrivalled riding experience of a track derived tyre, for the road. The 0° steel belt construction gives consistent feed back, a high level of stability and the ultimate riding sensation. The advanced tread pattern design gives maximum side grip performance, providing greater rider confidence right through the corner.

Arai
HELMET
Putoline Oil
RED TORPEDO
redtorpedo.com
BOOTH & PARTNERS
mcgill
HYDREX
3
mcgill
Putoline Oil
Tarmac
SPERIAN
RED TORPEDO
redtorpedo.com
BOOTH & PARTNERS

ROUND
01

Brands Hatch Indy

13th April

Hunter
ThreeBond
SHOEI
4

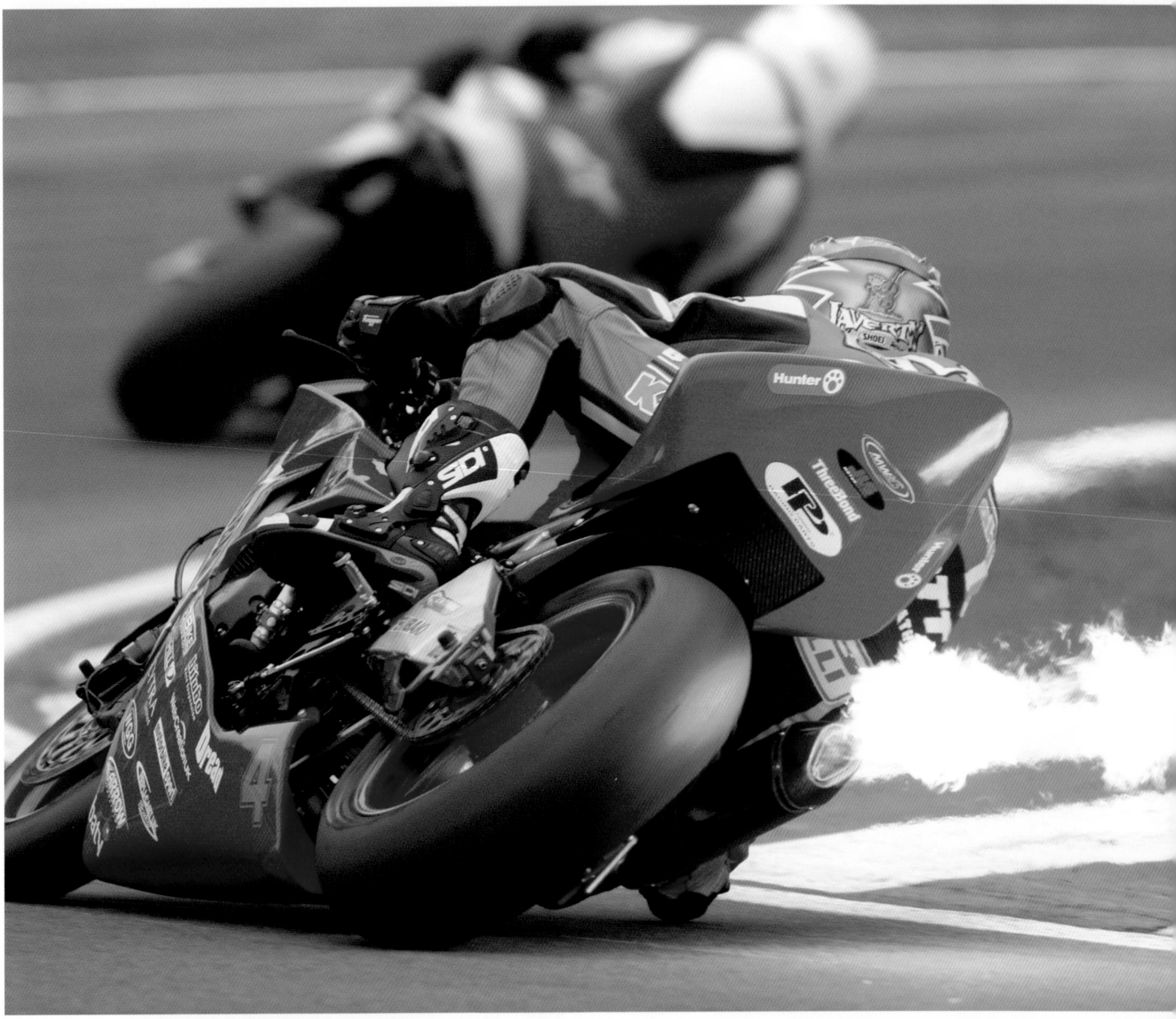

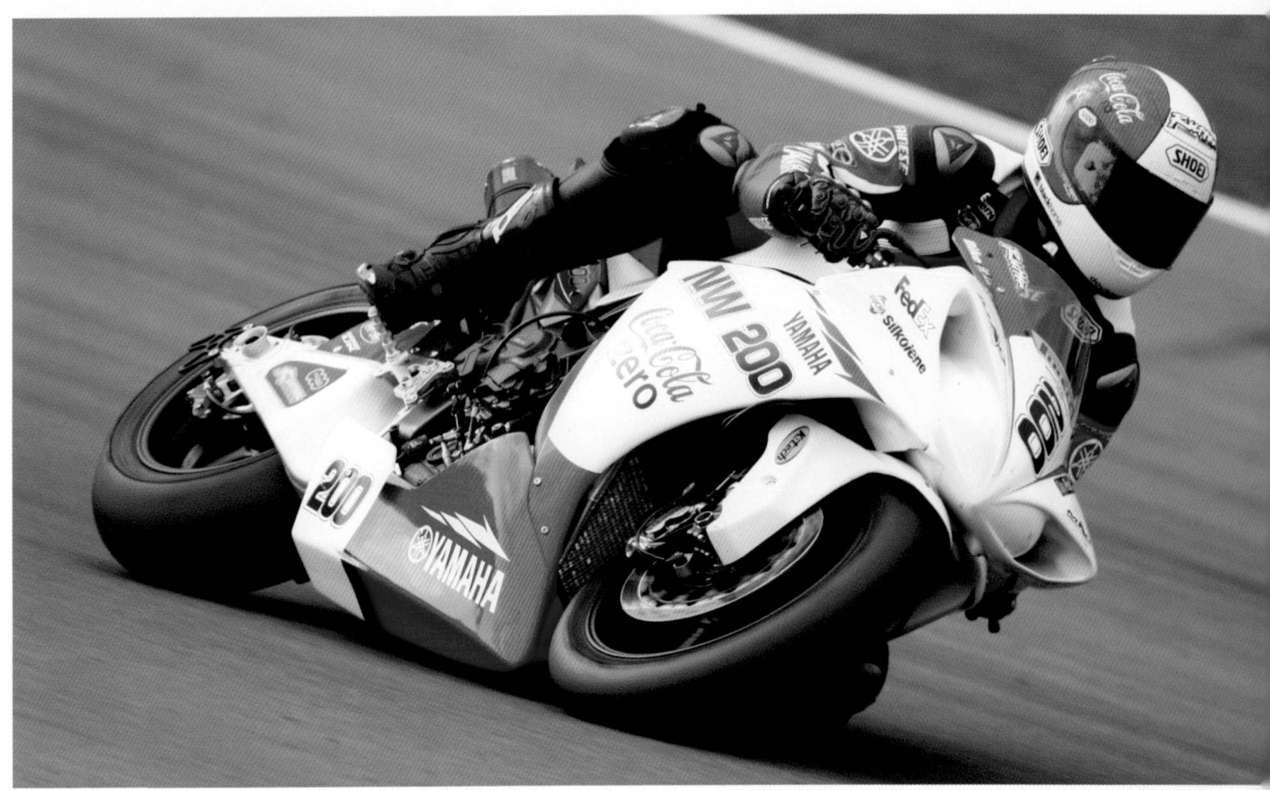

NW 200
YAMAHA
Coca-Cola
Zero
FedEx
Silkolene
SHOEI
200
YAMAHA

Left: John Laverty's season got off to a fiery start

Below: Camier limbers up before mounting his untried R1

Right & bottom: Guintoli makes sure the established names know he is here to win!

Arai
HELMET
RST
HONDA
CLAPA
HITACHI
Construction Machinery
ASTRO
CLAPA
RST
HITACHI
Construction Machinery
GLEN
EXIDE
BATTERIES
HM plant
PIRELLI
WWW.BRITISHSUPERBIKE.COM
HONDA
45
HITACHI
Construction Machinery
EXIDE
BATTERIES
HM plant
TECH STYLE
HONDA
RST
Castrol
HONDA

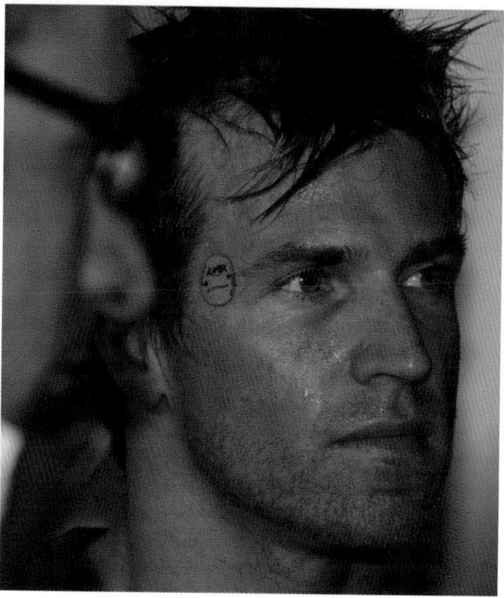

Far left: Glen Richards' concentration is evident in his eyes as he made his HM Plant Honda debut

Above: James Ellison sweats it out on what is basically a stock, road-going R1

86
Kawasaki

BrandsHatch
ViSK
ViSK.COM INSURANCE
0:00
TRiS
86
P12
P14
L23
P17
L23
JOHN LAVERTY

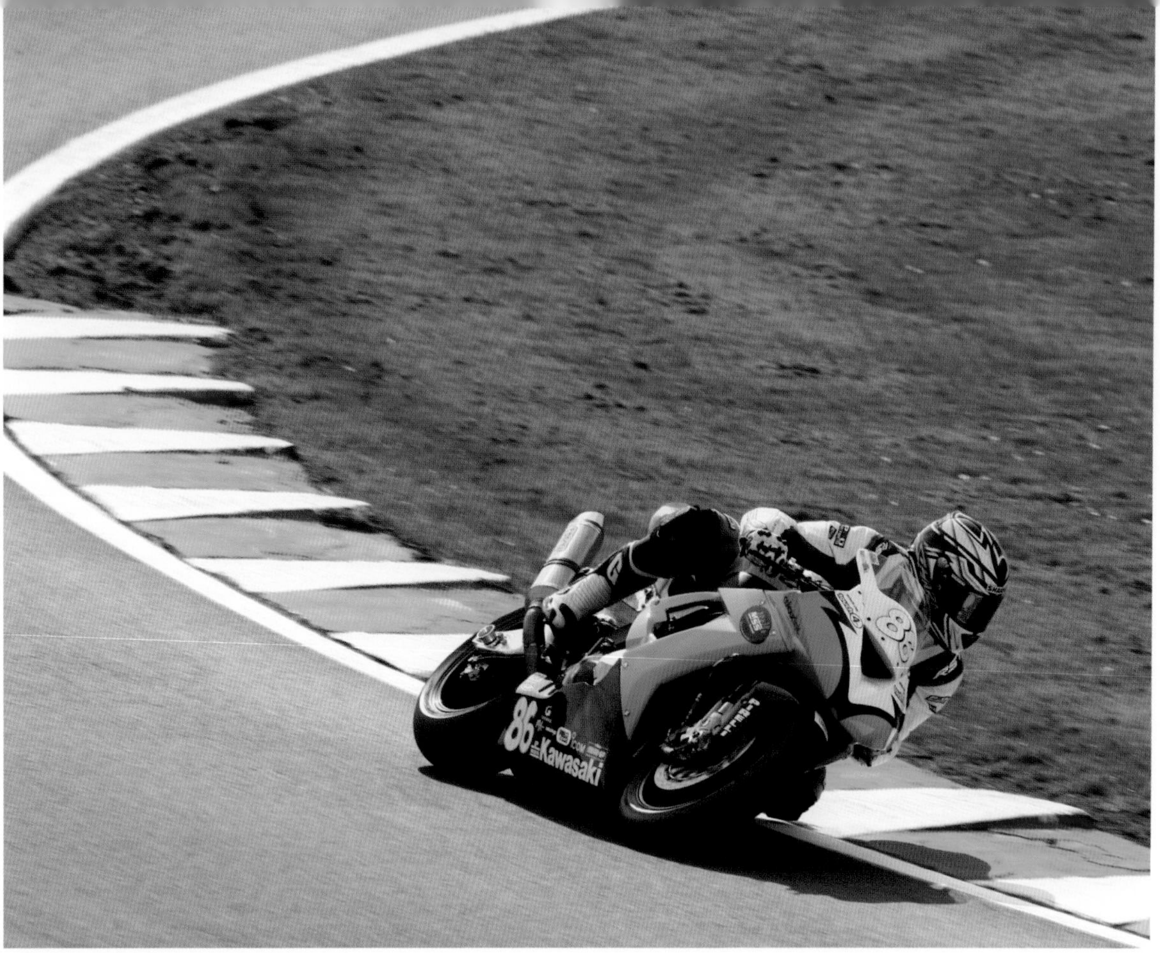

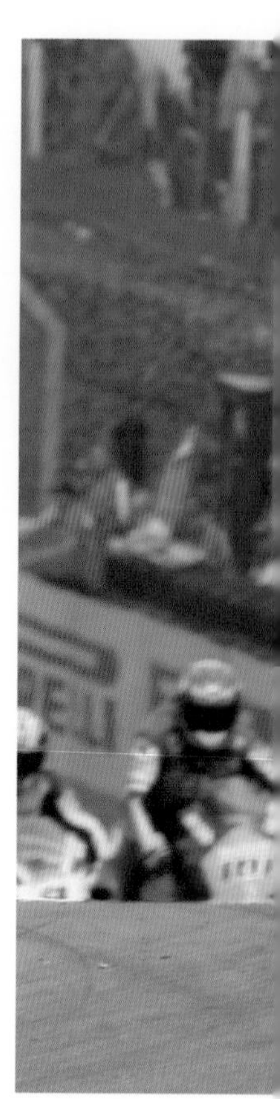

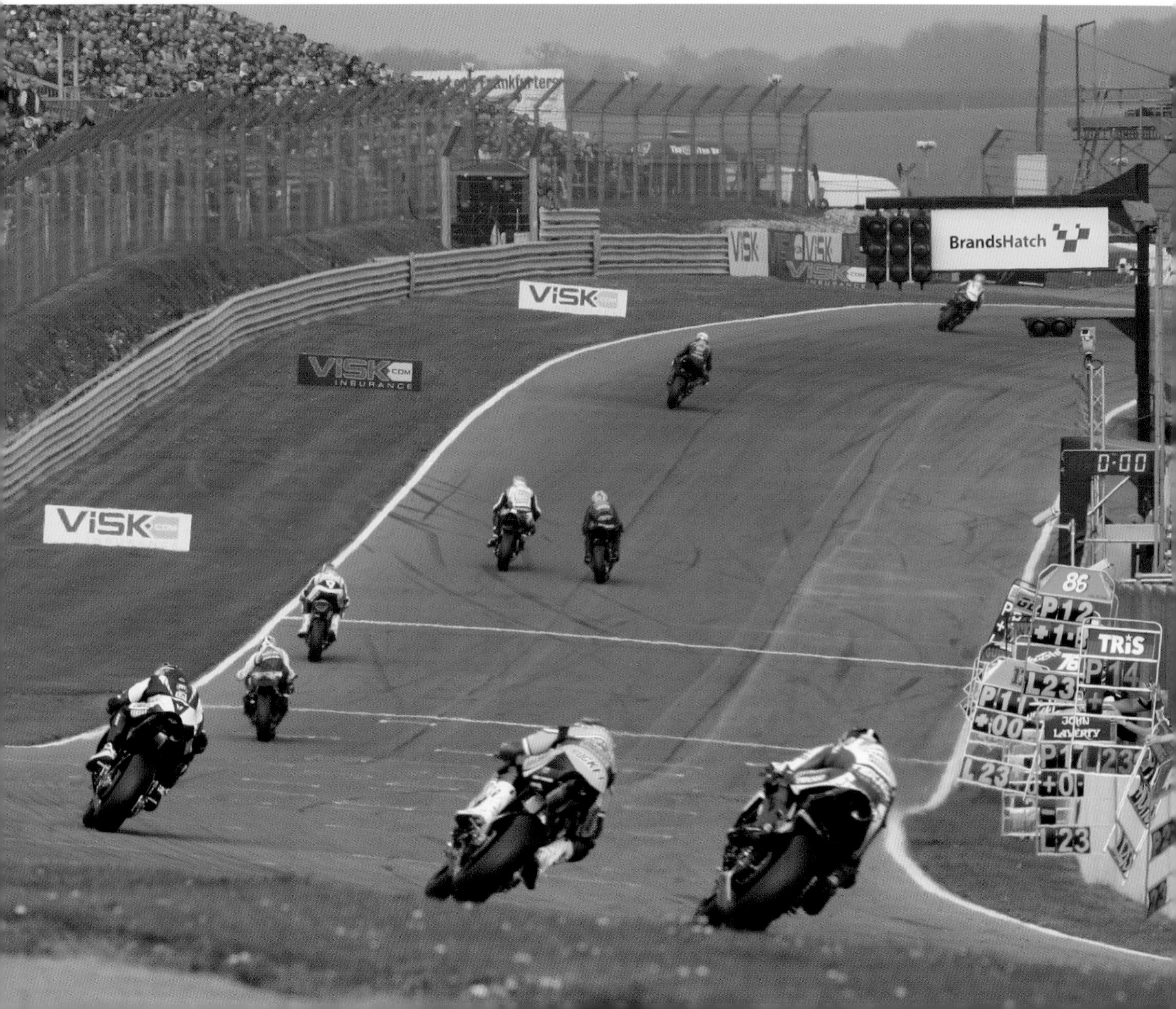

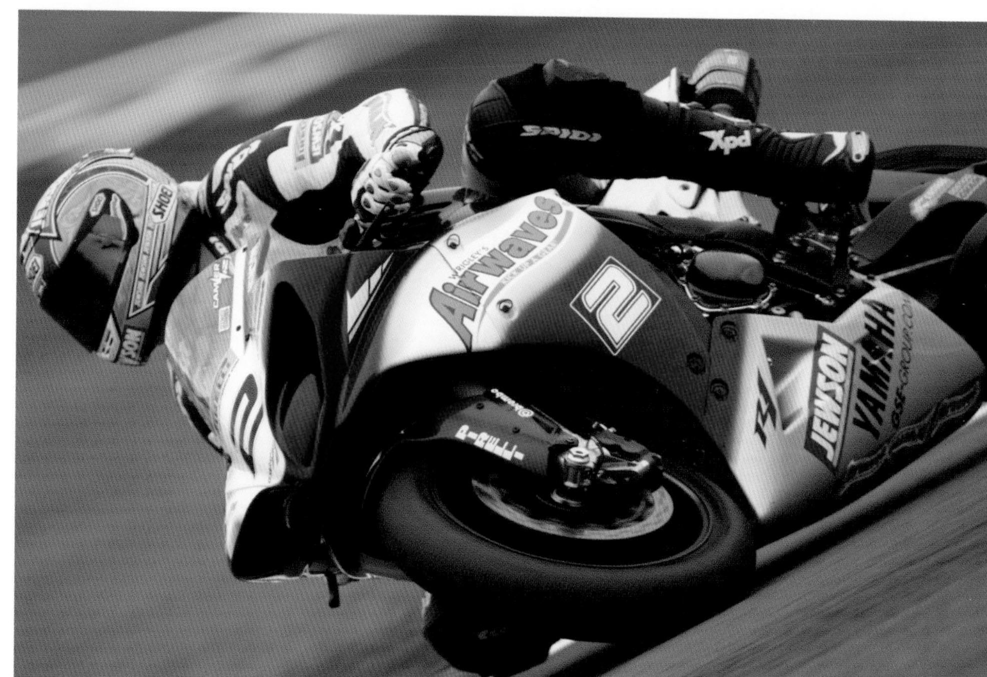

Above: Both Hydrex and HM Plant Hondas were showing well until Plater tipped off at Druids

Left: A packed Brands Hatch crowd witness the unfolding battles

Round 01

Brands Hatch Indy

13th April

FIRST BLOOD TO GUINTOLI…

MotoGP exile Sylvain Guintoli had plenty of testing miles aboard the Worx Crescent Suzuki under his belt and the Frenchman was raring to go, but that was not the case for some of his rivals, with the Airwaves Yamaha duo of Leon Camier and James Ellison not having turned a wheel until first practice.

The odds, it seemed, would be stacked against them, but led by Colin Wright, the Airwaves duo's backroom team soon had them up to speed and as they had to settle for second row starts, Guintoli took the initiative, winning the Swan Combi 50 Roll for Pole at his first attempt.

However, the Frenchman was beaten off the line by Stuart Easton, the young Scot who had earned the Hydrex Honda seat by winning the Macau Grand Prix. Steve Plater, deputising on the HM Plant Honda for Josh Brookes who was having UK entry visa problems, and Glen Richards were both not far adrift.

Richards took the lead after eight laps but by half distance, the Aussie had been taken by his team-mate Plater with Guintoli moving through to second. As Plater tipped off at Druids, it was Camier who had to take avoiding action leaving Guintoli to take a maiden race-winning victory.

"I can't remember the last time that I won," said Guintoli. "I have to sort out my starts, that one was really bad, but I fought and had a lot of fun."

Richards took second, ahead of Easton, Camier and Ellison, while Gary Mason, riding the Quay Garage Honda, was seeing off some of the factory riders as he took sixth place overall and with it the Mirror.co.uk Cup victory.

In race two, Easton was again fast away, pursued this time by his team-mate Karl Harris who was eager to atone for a first race tumble. Behind them, it was Plater, Richards, Guintoli and Camier, with the latter soon on the charge and picking off places.

Camier was up to second at half distance and visibly closing on Easton, making the telling move at Clearways to take the victory, with Guintoli, not to be outdone, nipping through into second place, ahead of Plater who denied Easton a podium finish on the final lap. In the Mirror.co.uk Cup, Mason duly completed the double.

BSB Championship Positions

1	GUINTOLI	45
2	CAMIER	38
3	RICHARDS	31
4	EASTON	29
5	ELLISON	20
6	MASON	17

Cup Championship Positions

1	MASON	50
2	JESSOPP	40
3	HICKMAN	32
4	GILBERTSON	23
5	FAGAN	13
6	MCCORMACK	11

THE THINK! MOTORCYCLE ACADEMY HOSTS BSB STARS

The THINK! Motorcycle Academy has enjoyed another successful season as sponsor of BSB, hosting interviews with a multitude of stars from both past and present. THINK! was at the trackside at every round, consistently entertaining fans throughout the season with some fantastic off-track action.

The interview with racing hero Giacomo Agostini at Brands Hatch where thousands flocked for the chance to meet their idol was a particular highlight. Phil "Prince of Speed" Read appeared alongside Ago and a number of other legends to mark an outstanding weekend for BSB.

The rest of the season proved to be just as memorable as THINK! played host to the 'Roll-for-Poll' press conference at each race and held regular interviews with triple BSB champions John Reynolds and Niall Mackenzie, as well as the best of the current BSB crop - including Leon Camier, James Ellison, Sylvain Guintoli and Simon Andrews. Other guests included Superstock champion and rival pair Steve Plater and Billy McConnell, THINK! regular Jamie Whitham, World Superbike favourite Leon Haslam and young British GP hope Bradley Smith.

Most importantly, THINK! also experienced another successful year promoting safer riding, with innovative and interactive ways of helping riders and drivers learn how to take more care on the roads. With regular interviews, VIP prize giveaways, competitions, a riding simulator and all the latest superbikes on display, THINK! helps to educate visitors about how they can become better, safer riders, including remembering to save racing for the track.

Visit the THINK! Motorcycle Academy online at www.dft.gov.uk/tma

2009 British Superbike Championship riders

Ago & Cooper on the T.M.A. addressing the fans

THINK! Front Row Press Conference

The THINK! Motorcycle Academy

The THINK! Campaign would like to thank its loyal partners for their ongoing support.

ROUND

02 Oulton Park

4th May

WORX
MOTOREX
Oil of Switzerland
AKRAPOVIC

Above & top right: Graeme Gowland & Ian Lowry give it the max

Both Hydrex Hondas were showing well **(left)** while Camier heads the field over Deer's Leap

agv

SUZUKI
SUZUKI
SUZUKI
MOTUL

SHOEI
JEWSON
PIRELLI
7
Airwaves
PIRELLI
PIRELLI

Left: James Ellison takes it right to the edge, almost clipping the kerb and on the white line

Right: Josh Brookes, with his visa issues now resolved, shows his determination

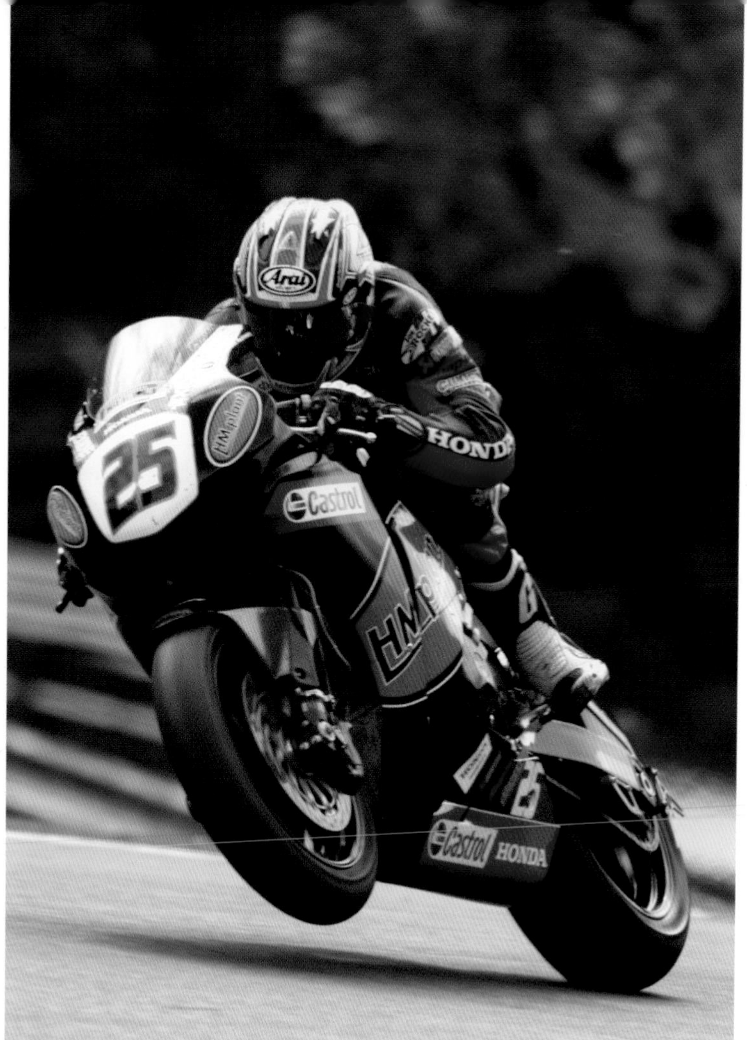

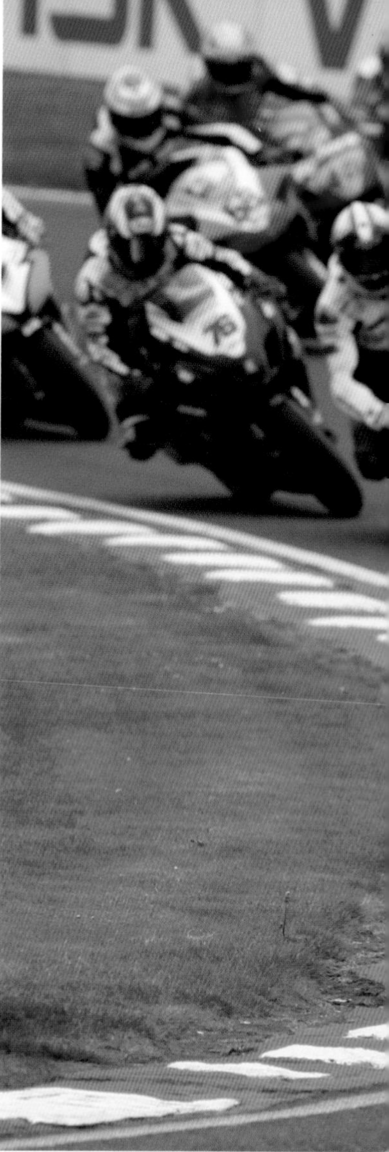

Top right: Lightweight Stuart Easton leading into turn one was to become a regular feature of the 2009 BSB season

Below: Glen Richards is fully committed into the blind crest at Hilltop

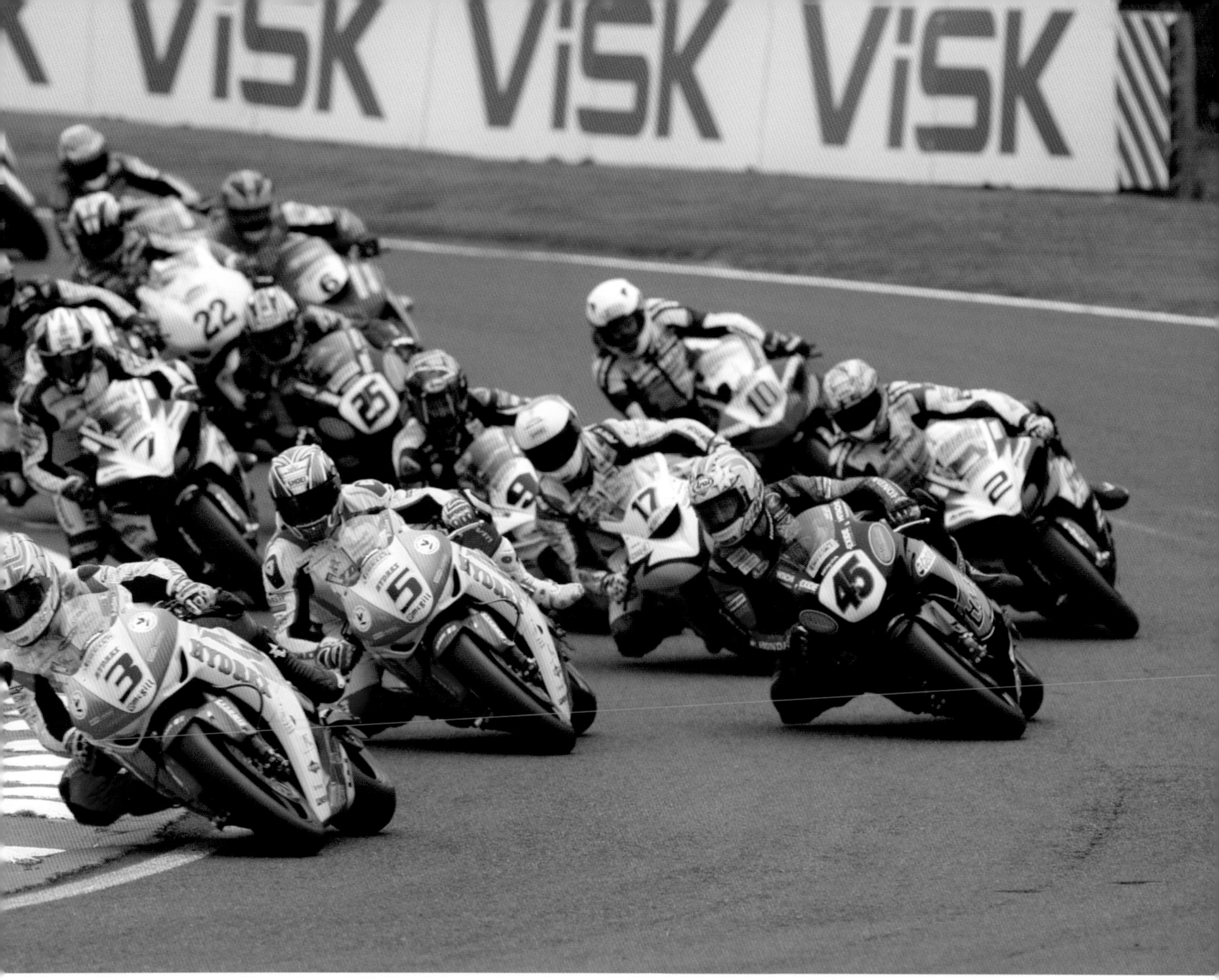
ViSK ViSK ViSK
HYDREX

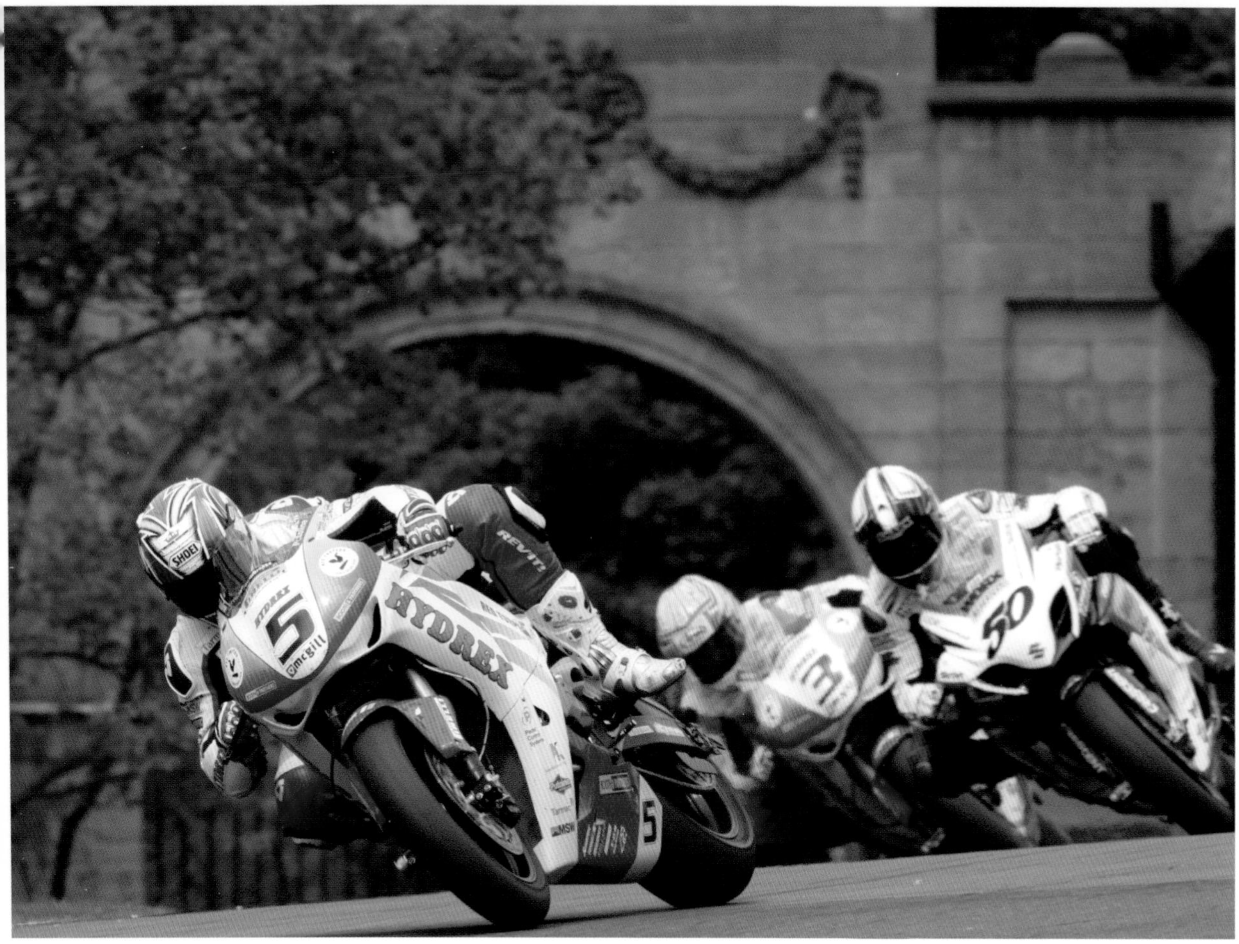
HYDREX

Round 02

Oulton Park

4th May

CAMIER AT THE DOUBLE...

Sylvain Guintoli had the points advantage as they powered into the second round but Leon Camier was keen to grab the initiative and he did that in the closing minutes of the grid decider, putting in a superb pole setting lap to finally break the challenge of Stuart Easton, Karl Harris and the stylish Frenchman, who was quickly learning the rigours of the circuit.

Damp, but drying, was the track dilemma ahead of the opening race, which was declared officially dry, with Easton and Harris forging clear on the opening lap, but soon the red flags were out as John Laverty fell at Hill Top. The Hydrex Honda riders were back out front on the resumption but Camier, who had a few anxious moments as his bike overheated on the grid, and Guintoli were soon harassing them.

Camier swept into the lead at Cascades on the sixth lap leaving Harris in vain pursuit while Guintoli took Easton in the final third of the race to maintain his record of podium finishes. Gary Mason enjoyed another Cup victory, taking ninth just in front of Josh Brookes who, with his visa issues resolved was able to make his HM Plant Honda debut,

Harris always goes well at the Cheshire circuit and still searching for that elusive first victory in the top flight, the former Supersport title winner was out front early on in a second race that saw Simon Andrews making a strong start on the MSS Colchester Kawasaki while Guintoli was sluggish off the line and was left to play catch-up.

Camier was having none of those worries. Fourth on the opening lap, second next time around and leading on the third, he was in charge and powering to a runaway victory, finishing seven seconds clear of the pack. It was the Airwaves Yamaha rider's third consecutive victory and an ominous sign of things to come!

Harris took second from the determined Guintoli with James Ellison heading off the challenges of Glen Richards while Ian Lowry, getting to grips with the Relentless Suzuki, ran sixth just ahead of Gary Mason who was continuing his supremacy in the Cup stakes.

BSB Championship Positions

1	CAMIER	88
2	GUINTOLI	77
3	RICHARDS	52
4	HARRIS	50
5	ELLISON	44
6	EASTON	42

Cup Championship Positions

1	MASON	100
2	JESSOPP	80
3	HICKMAN	64
4	GILBERTSON	34
5	TUNSTALL	26
6	FAGAN	24

ROUND

03 Donington Park

25th May

SUZUKI
Beacon
MOTUL
SHARK
HEL

Right: Andrews leads Da Costa on the MSS Kawasakis

Bottom right: Walker puts in his best performance of the season at his local circuit

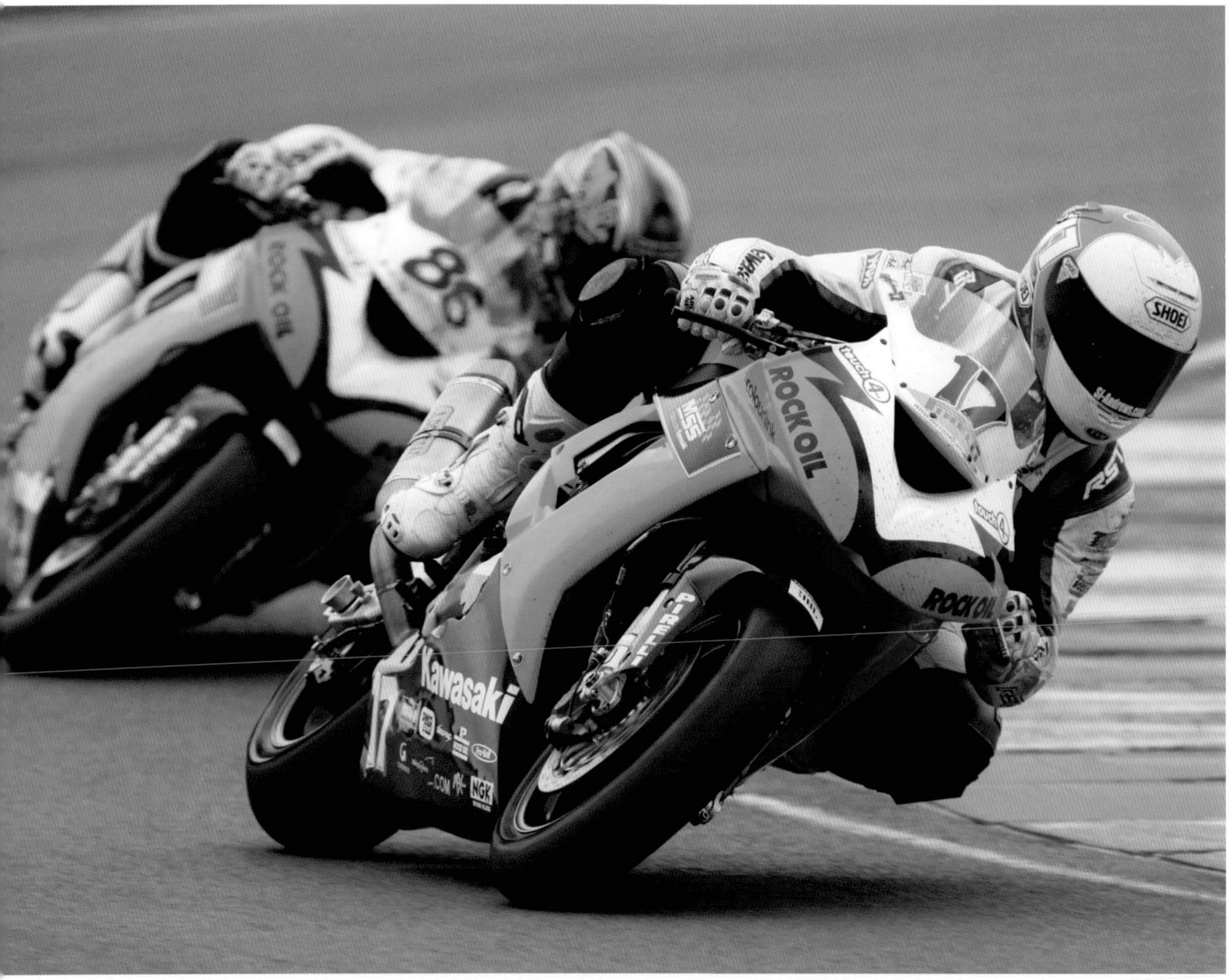
ROCK OIL
Kawasaki
SHOEI
NGK

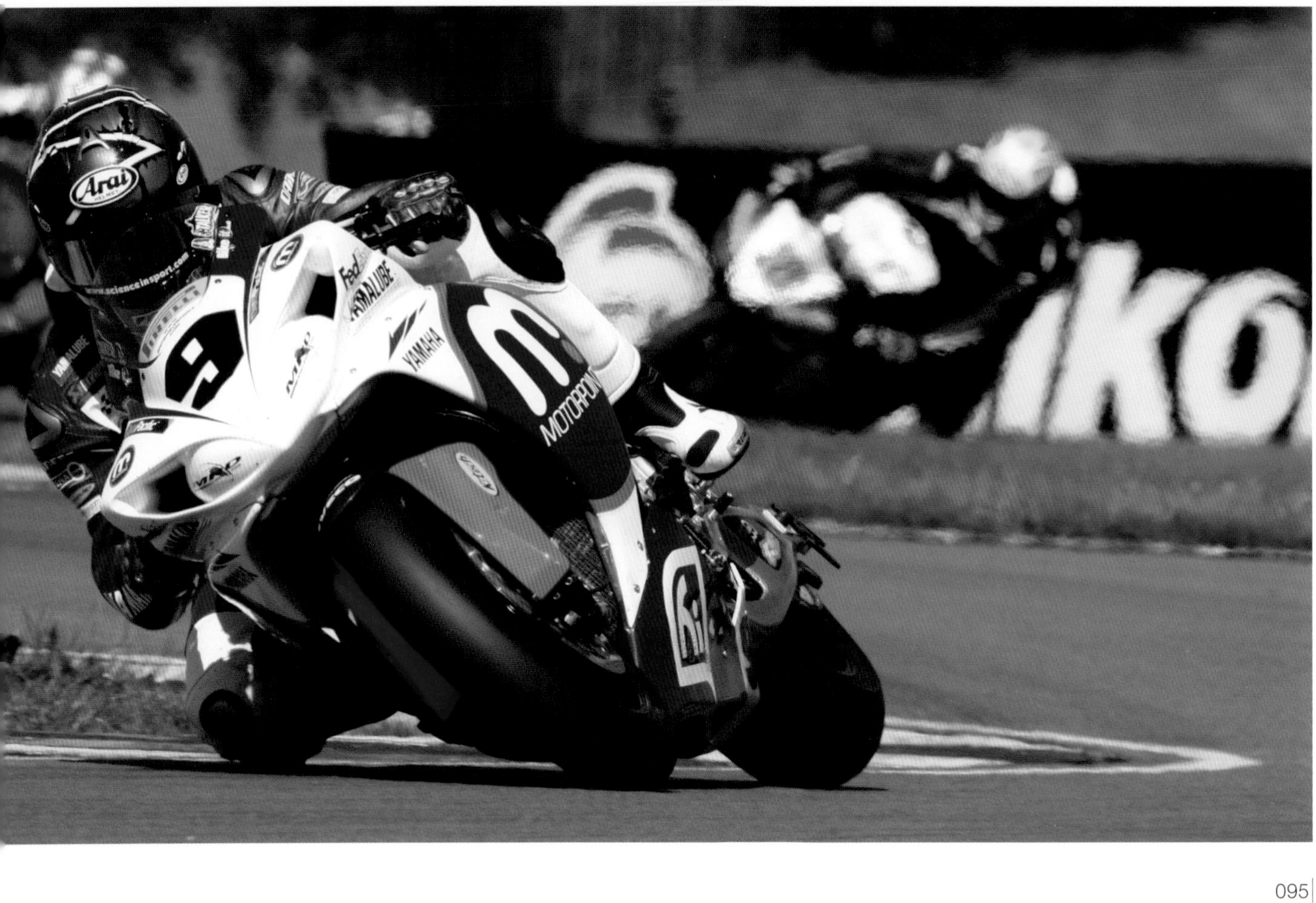
Arai
YAMAHA

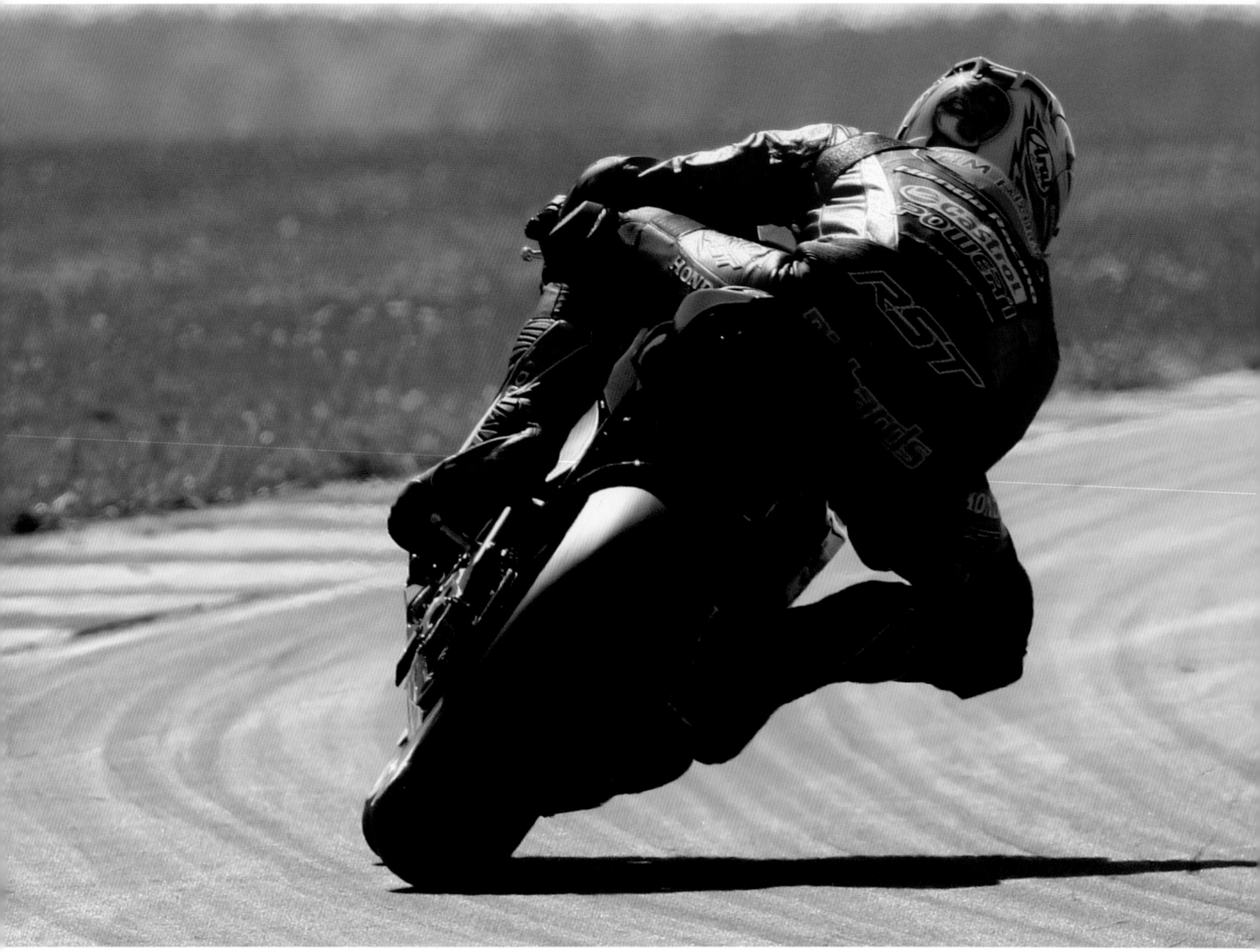
RST

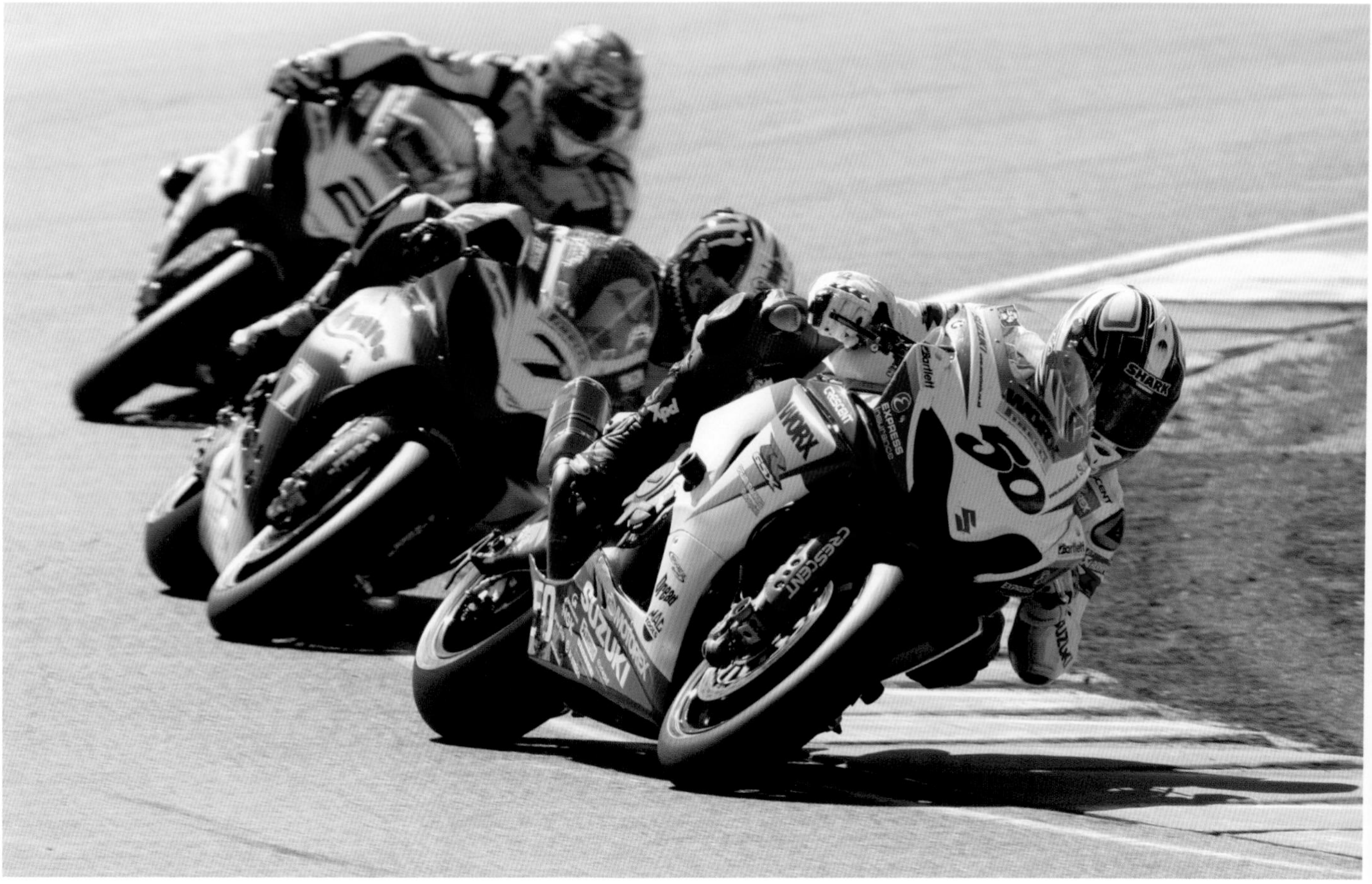
SHARK
SUZUKI
CRESCENT

Above: Andrews tips off while dicing with Easton, Walker and Richards

Far left: Guintoli heads the Yamahas of Camier & Ellison

76
SUZUKI
PIRELLI
MOTUL
Arai
SUZUKI
Beacon

45
17

Top left: Atsushi Watanabe's disappointing form continued

Below: Ellison and Camier took a win each

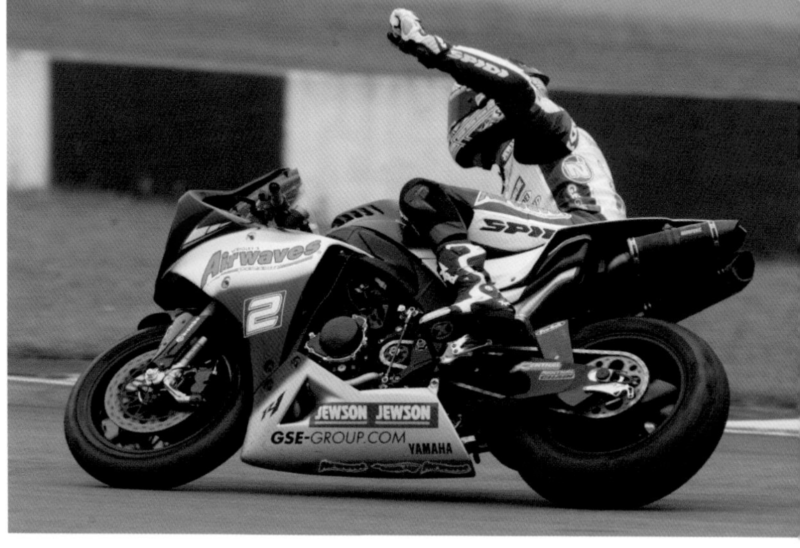

Round 03

Donington Park

25th May

DRAMA AT DONINGTON...

It started routinely, with a hectic scrap for pole, won by the series-leading Leon Camier ahead of Sylvain Guintoli, James Ellison and the impressive Simon Andrews, but then came the first of the controversial moments of the campaign.

HM Plant Honda's Josh Brookes, a third row starter, ran hot into the Melbourne Hairpin on the sighting lap ahead of the opening race and clattered into the unfortunate Guintoli who sustained serious leg injuries.

Opinions varied between brake fade and brain fade but Brookes picked up a suspended one race ban for his part in the incident, and with his own bike damaged in the incident, he was a non-starter at the Leicestershire circuit.

Ellison made the early running after the delayed start with the local hero and former four times runner-up in the series Chris Walker running second on the Motorpoint Henderson Yamaha, ahead of Stuart Easton and Leon Camier. Camier was soon on the move and took the lead from his team-mate Ellison on the fifth lap before easing to victory by a little over three seconds.

Easton took third ahead of Glen Richards, still taking time getting to grips with the Honda Superbike after his title-winning years in Supersport and Superstock. Walker had to settle for fifth from Karl Harris, while Gary Mason, who else, took the Cup glory ahead of Tom Tunstall and Martin Jessopp.

More of the same was expected in race two but it wasn't to be as Richards made the running, chased down by Walker who grabbed the lead on the fifth lap, but was not able to make it stick as Ellison, carving through from fifth, moved out front on the eighth lap. It gave his side of the garage some cheer only for Camier, who had been third, to stop briefly with an electrical problem which left him dead last before speeding through the pack to finish twelfth.

Ellison took the victory, heading off the advances of Stuart Easton while Walker enjoyed his first podium finish since returning to domestic action from the world scene. Simon Andrews held off Richards, Ian Lowry and Cup winner Mason who was comfortably clear of his rivals Peter Hickman and Martin Jessopp.

BSB Championship Positions

1	CAMIER	117
2	ELLISON	89
3	EASTON	78
4	GUINTOLI	77
5	RICHARDS	76
6	HARRIS	60

Cup Championship Positions

1	MASON	150
2	JESSOPP	112
3	HICKMAN	97
4	TUNSTALL	59
5	FAGAN	43
6	GILBERTSON	34

EXIDE
HITACHI
HONDA
EXIDE
BATTERIES
HITACHI
Construction Machinery
HM plant
Arai
HONDA

ROUND
04
Thruxton
31st May

Castrol
25
Castrol
HONDA

Airwaves
7
JEWSON JEWSON
GSE-GROUP.COM
YAMAHA

Left: Brookes was on a charge at Thruxton

Below right: Gary Mason made history by putting his privateer bike on the front row of a BSB grid

ROLL FOR POLE
BSB
BSB
60
KPH
Castrol
Castrol
HONDA

HJC
SHOEI
BUILDBASE
PROBIKE
VENHILL
CYTRA
WGG
ARROW
WebCreationUK
motorbike sport
4

SHOEI
St-Andrews.com
RST
17
PIRELLI
touch 4
ROCK OIL
ROCK OIL
touch 4
JBL
PIRELLI
PIRELLI
Kawasaki

Far right: The pit lane was almost as crowded as the spectator areas as everyone enjoyed the early season Hampshire sunshine

Right: Black lines are the order of the day at Thruxton as the 200bhp machines struggle for grip over the bumps

Bottom left: Brookes leads Richards as the HM Plant boys run in formation

THINK!
THINK!
THINK!

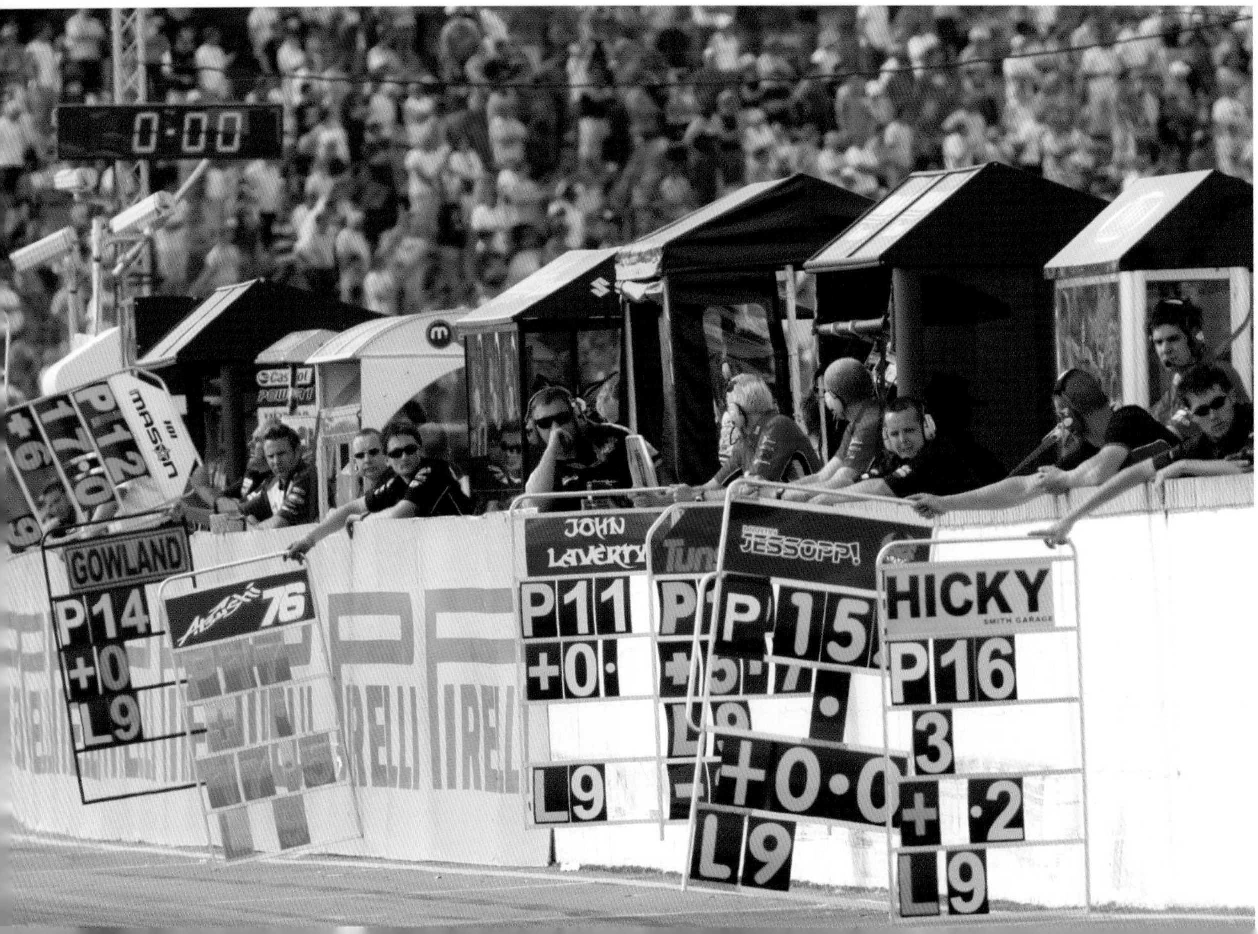
0:00
GOWLAND
P14
+0
L9
JOHN LAVERTY
P11
+0·
L9
JESSOPP!
P15
+0·0
L9
HICKY
SMITH GARAGE
P16
3
+ ·2
L9

Round 04

Thruxton

31st May

THE CAMIER SHOW ROLLS ON…

Michael Rutter, not having settled aboard the North West 200 Yamaha, quit that team but was rapidly snapped up by Worx Crescent Suzuki to deputise for their injured Sylvain Guintoli. Rutter showed well in qualifying securing a front row start.

Leon Camier completed a hat trick of pole starts, out-qualifying his Airwaves Yamaha team-mate James Ellison with Cup runner Gary Mason a stunning third fastest on the Quay Garage Honda to become the first privateer to start from the front row.

In glorious conditions, Ellison led race one but was hard pressed by Hydrex Honda's Stuart Easton before Camier upped his game to take the lead on the fourth lap, running out front to secure the victory by a little over a second, though it was far from easy. "It was hard work as the front tyre was moving around because of the heat and I was lacking grip," explained the race winner.

Ellison had to settle for second best again from Easton, Simon Andrews and Rutter while Josh Brookes, running seventh, had learned quickly to be in a position to pose questions next time out on the HM Plant Honda.

Camier took the lead on the first lap of race two as Ellison ran off line at Club and that was the way it stayed, with Camier taking his second double of the campaign with a victory margin of over three seconds. Brookes meanwhile, showing the speed and style that had seen him a regular podium finisher in World Supersport, was up to third, and missed out on second by only a tenth.

"That was like the old me and I had my flair back," reflected Brookes, adding: "I want to say sorry to Sylvain and I hope that it is now behind us."

Easton took fourth ahead of Rutter, who in between races was sorting out the Suzuki he was running himself in the forthcoming Isle of Man TT races. Andrews completed the top six while Mason completed his clean sweep in the Mirror.co.uk Cup with a fourth winning double to remain unbeaten. Tom Tunstall and Martin Jessopp took second places to him, with Peter Hickman twice third.

BSB Championship Positions

1	CAMIER	167
2	ELLISON	129
3	EASTON	107
4	RICHARDS	95
5	GUINTOLI	77
6	HARRIS	72

Cup Championship Positions

1	MASON	200
2	JESSOPP	145
3	HICKMAN	129
4	TUNSTALL	92
5	FAGAN	64
6	GILBERTSON	42

ROUND

05
Snetterton

21st June

MSS
Colchester Kawasaki
series

SHOEI
SUZUKI
CRESCENT
Bartlett
EXPRESS
34

Left: A packed crowd turned out to watch the action at Snetterton

HM plant
HITACHI
Construction Machinery
Arai
HM plant
racing
HONDA
HONDA

Right: Harris, on the Hydrex Honda, leads Brookes who was getting to grips with the HM Plant Honda

Below: Ian Lowry gets the better of Simon Andrews on the MSS Colchester Kawasaki

45
Castrol
EXIDE

RED TORPEDO
HYDREX

TRIS
BUILDBASE
Kawasaki
SCOTT
LEATHERS
BUILDBASE

THINK!
THINK!
THINK!
3
HYDREX
25
4
9

Round 05

Snetterton

21st June

NO LIVING WITH LEON...

Leon Camier continued his and his team's domination of the series with a fourth consecutive pole start and then a third winning double as he extended his lead in the title stakes over his Airwaves Yamaha team-mate James Ellison while the rest simply struggled to match their pace.

The changeable weather had curtailed qualifying, with only two of the three knockout qualifying sessions completed, leaving Camier half a second faster than the rest. Not that he made the most of it in the opening race, however, with a slow start that gave Stuart Easton the initiative, running his Hydrex Honda ahead of Ellison and Josh Brookes before the action was red-flagged as Michael Rutter tipped off the Worx Suzuki and both Tom Tunstall and Matt Bond also tumbled.

Easton again made the running on the resumption with Ellison and Brookes in close contention while Camier was back in eighth place on the opening lap, but enjoying a fast moving game of catch-up. He was running second at half distance and, piling the pressure on Easton, took the lead with five laps remaining to claim win number seven of the season.

Brookes was third from Ellison, Ian Lowry and Chris Walker while in the Cup category, after Gary Mason had been sidelined by machine problems there was an emotional success for Tommy Bridewell who was returning to the domestic series two years on from the tragic crash that had cost the life of his brother Ollie. "It was hard fought and didn't come easily," said Bridewell, adding "this is dedicated to my brother."

Easton, not happy with being second best earlier, made a flying start in race two at the Norfolk track and was soon hunted down by Brookes, but the growing threat of Camier was soon apparent as he eased ahead of Ellison and Walker and then set about the leading duo.

Camier made the telling move at Russells on the fifth lap, and soon afterwards Ellison was running in formation behind him, with Brookes third from Easton and John Laverty aboard the Buildbase Kawasaki with Julien Da Costa sixth on the MSS Colchester Kawasaki.

Mason avenged his earlier problems by winning the Cup class ahead of Peter Hickman, Tom Tunstall and Bridewell.

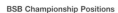

BSB Championship Positions

1	CAMIER	217
2	ELLISON	162
3	EASTON	140
4	RICHARDS	103
5	HARRIS	87
6	GUINTOLI	77

Cup Championship Positions

1	MASON	225
2	HICKMAN	169
3	JESSOPP	145
4	TUNSTALL	108
5	FAGAN	74
6	BOND	68

86
Kawasaki
Kawasaki
RST

ROUND
06
Knockhill
5th July

SUZUKI
PIRELLI
MOTUL
Bendix
SUZUKI
SHARK
Beacon

25
Castrol
HM plant
Arai
HONDA

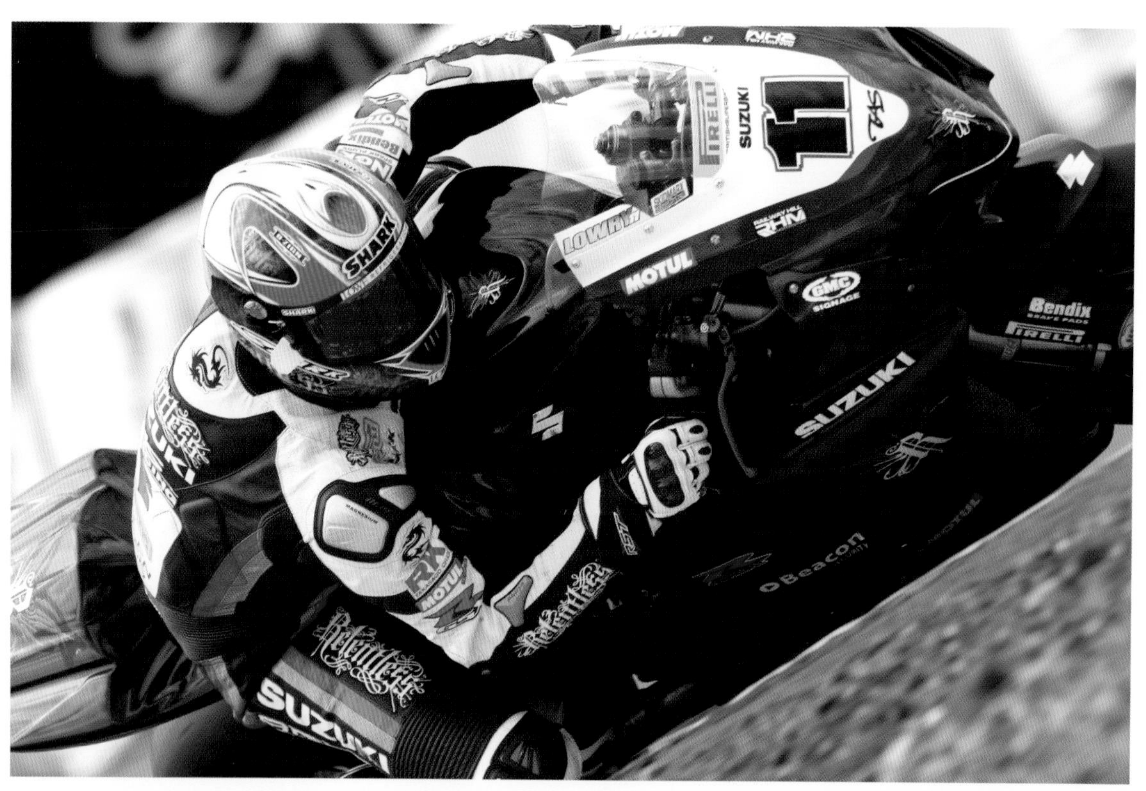

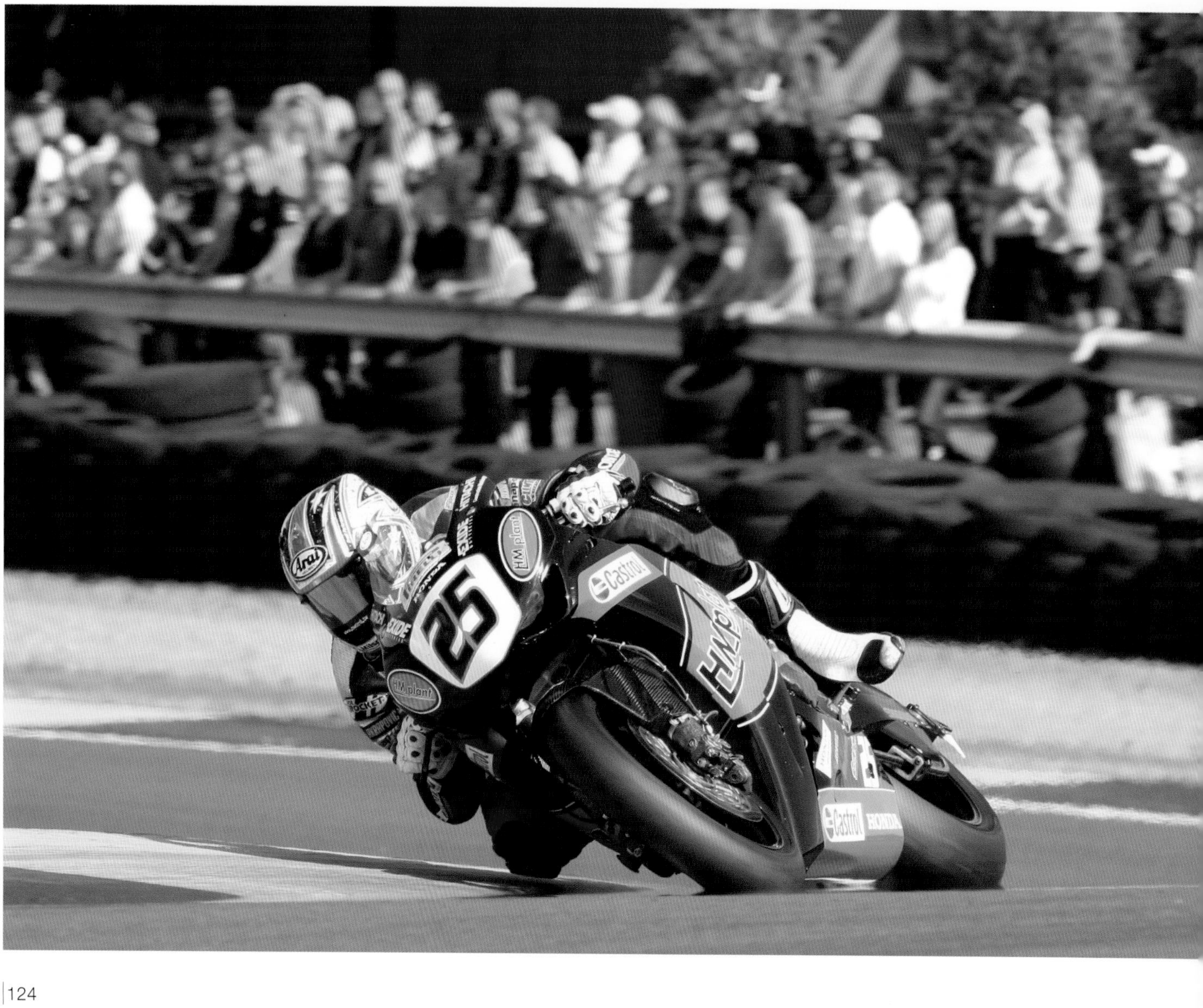

Above: Simon Andrews wrestles with his ZX-10R Kawasaki

Left: Brookes pushes Camier hard, but once again it was Camier who took a double win

Above: Karl Harris uses all the track and a little more

Left: Michael Rutter can only spectate as he is stranded inside the hairpin gravel trap

Right: Chris Walker on the Motorpoint Henderson Yamaha races almost in the shadow of the glorious Forth Road Bridge

YAMAHA
JEWSON
SHOEI
RESPRO.COM
PIRELLI
Castrol
HM plant
hondaracing

SHOEI
2

Arai
HITACHI
3
mcgill

SHOEI
Airwaves
GSE-GROUP.COM

Round 06

Knockhill

5th July

HIGHLAND FLING AT LAST FOR GSE...

The GSE team had never enjoyed a Scottish victory but Leon Camier quickly rectified that as he powered their Airwaves Yamaha to double glory, tightening his grip on the title stakes.

Josh Brookes took his first ever BSB pole for HM Plant Honda in what was a bittersweet time for them as their other rider, Glen Richards, crashed heavily in the Roll for Pole sustaining a broken leg.

On home soil, Stuart Easton was intent on a strong performance, but although he made a great start, he was unable to hold off the rampant Camier who snatched the lead on the second lap with Brookes running third from Simon Andrews who was showing little concerns despite the wrist injury he had sustained during testing for the previous round.

Camier took the victory by a couple of seconds from his Hydrex Honda rival who only just held off the hard charging Brookes while Andrews was ahead of James Ellison and Ian Lowry with Tommy Bridewell bringing his four-year-old Suzuki home in ninth to take the Cup victory from Peter Hickman as Gary Mason crashed out.

Brookes made a fast break in the second race but Camier was chasing hard while Easton ran third from Michael Rutter. Camier nosed ahead on the seventh lap, but Brookes snapped back, briefly regaining the advantage before the Yamaha rider took charge, going on to win with ease.

"Doing the double here is very special for the team," reflected Camier. "It was difficult to concentrate at certain points, but it is a great result and I don't intend slowing down any time soon."

Easton crucially ran wide at the Hairpin at two thirds distance and that allowed Ellison through to take the final podium position, and with it some relief. "The Airwaves Yamaha should not be finishing fifth as it did in the first race. I was ready for my P45 after that, but we worked hard and progressed," said Ellison.

Chris Walker ran a distant fifth from Andrews while Graeme Gowland showed well on the second Motorpoint Henderson Yamaha to be seventh up from Julien Da Costa and Bridewell who completed a Cup double as he held off Mason by half a second.

BSB Championship Positions

1	CAMIER	267
2	ELLISON	189
3	EASTON	173
4	RICHARDS	103
5	BROOKES	99
6	ANDREWS	92

Cup Championship Positions

1	MASON	245
2	HICKMAN	205
3	JESSOPP	145
4	TUNSTALL	137
5	BRIDEWELL	88
6	FAGAN	74

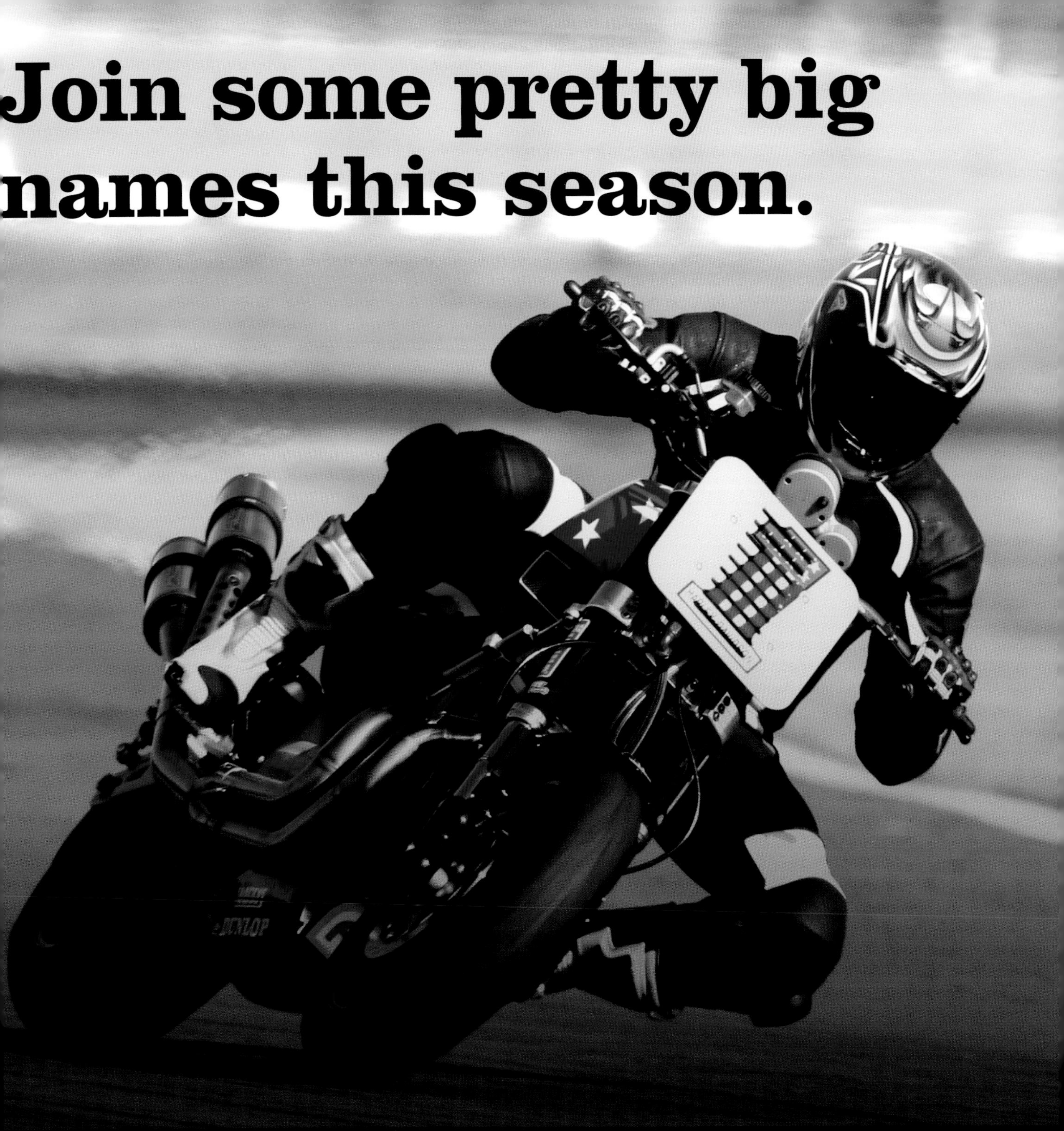

MOTOR
HARLEY-DAVIDSON
CYCLES

ROUND 07 Mallory Park

19th July

JEWSON
SHOEI
JEWSON

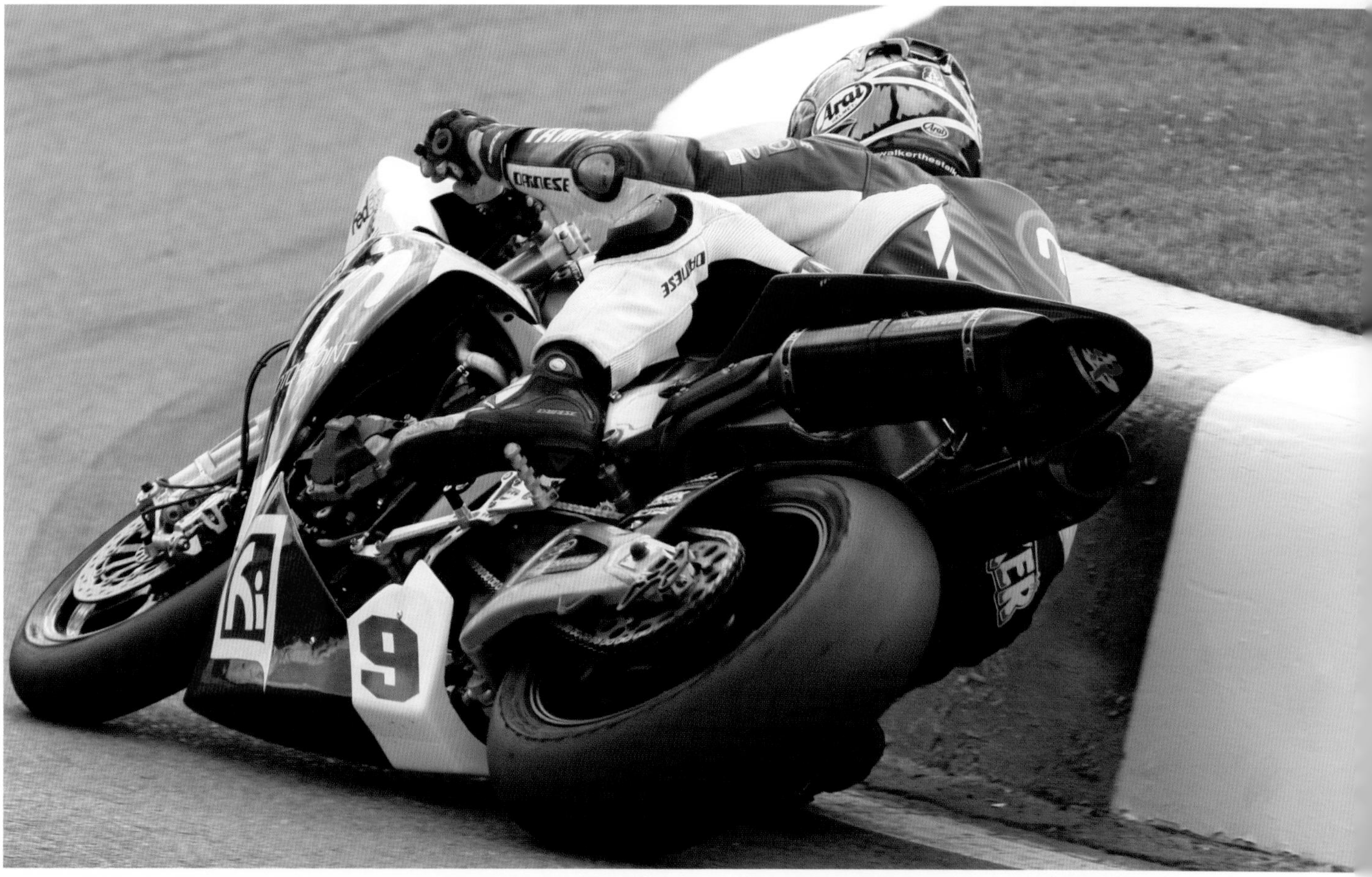
Arai
9

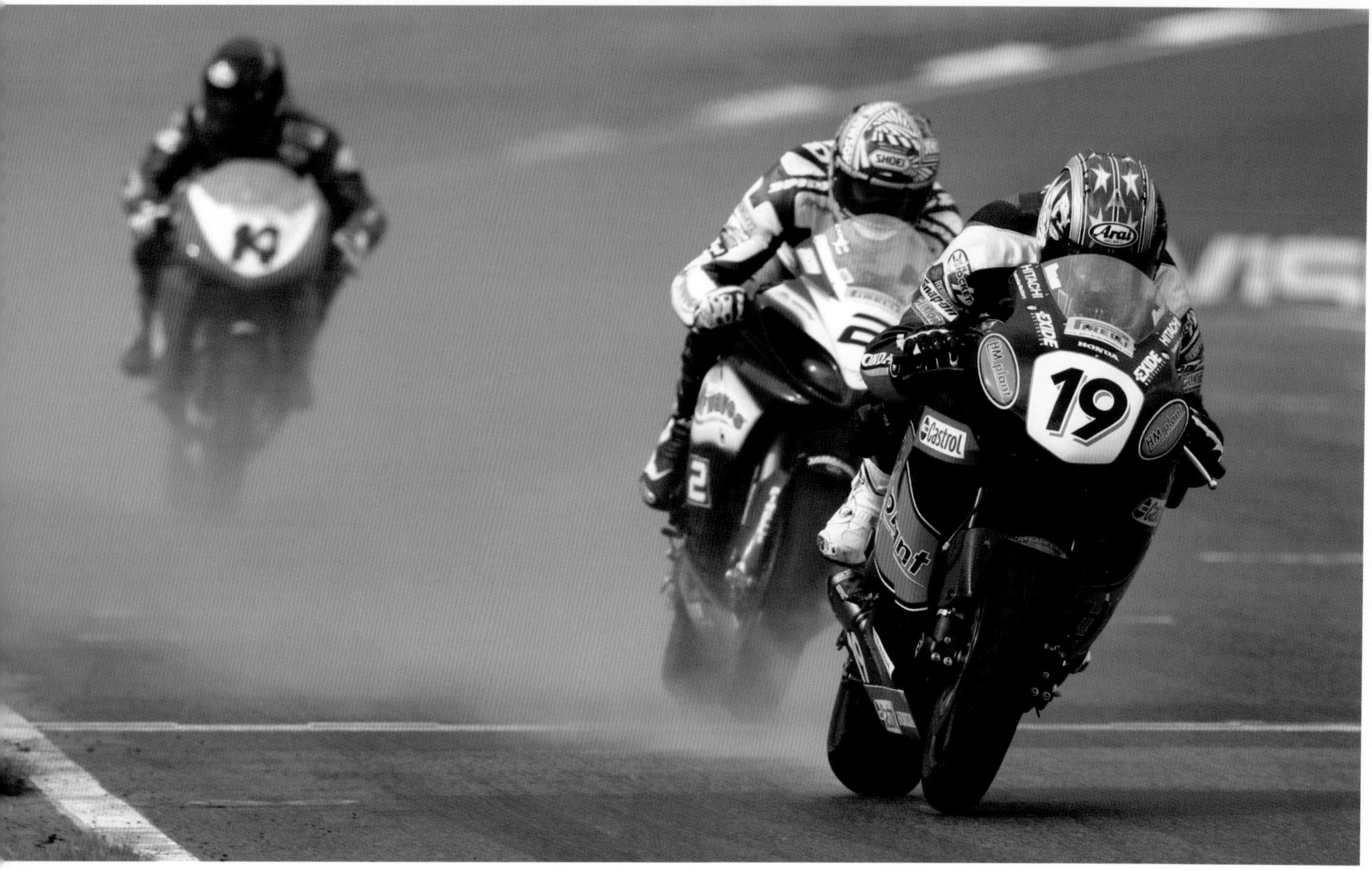
19
Arai
SHOEI
Castrol
EXIDE
HITACHI

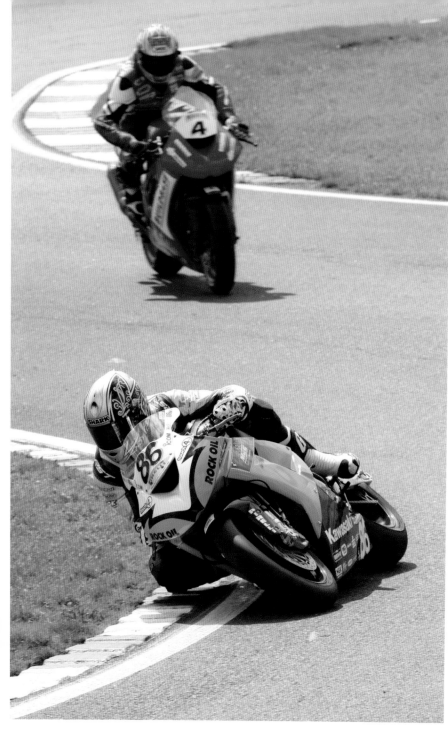

This page, left: Julien Da Costa carried on his steady progress

Below: Tommy Hill took Michael Rutter's place deputising for the injured Guintoli on the WORX Suzuki and proceeded to demonstrate his undoubted class, while **bottom left:** Steve Brogan had a busy weekend deputising for Richards as well as riding his Superstock bike

MALLORY PARK

The dramatic scenes as Josh Brookes lost control of his bike on the bumps entering the hairpin, taking out unlucky race leader Simon Andrews with the ensuing chaos taking out at least half a dozen riders

This page, centre: Brookes has time to contemplate his actions during the long lonely walk back to the pits

Far left: Walker had another strong showing but after being involved in the first race melee, never got back on the pace

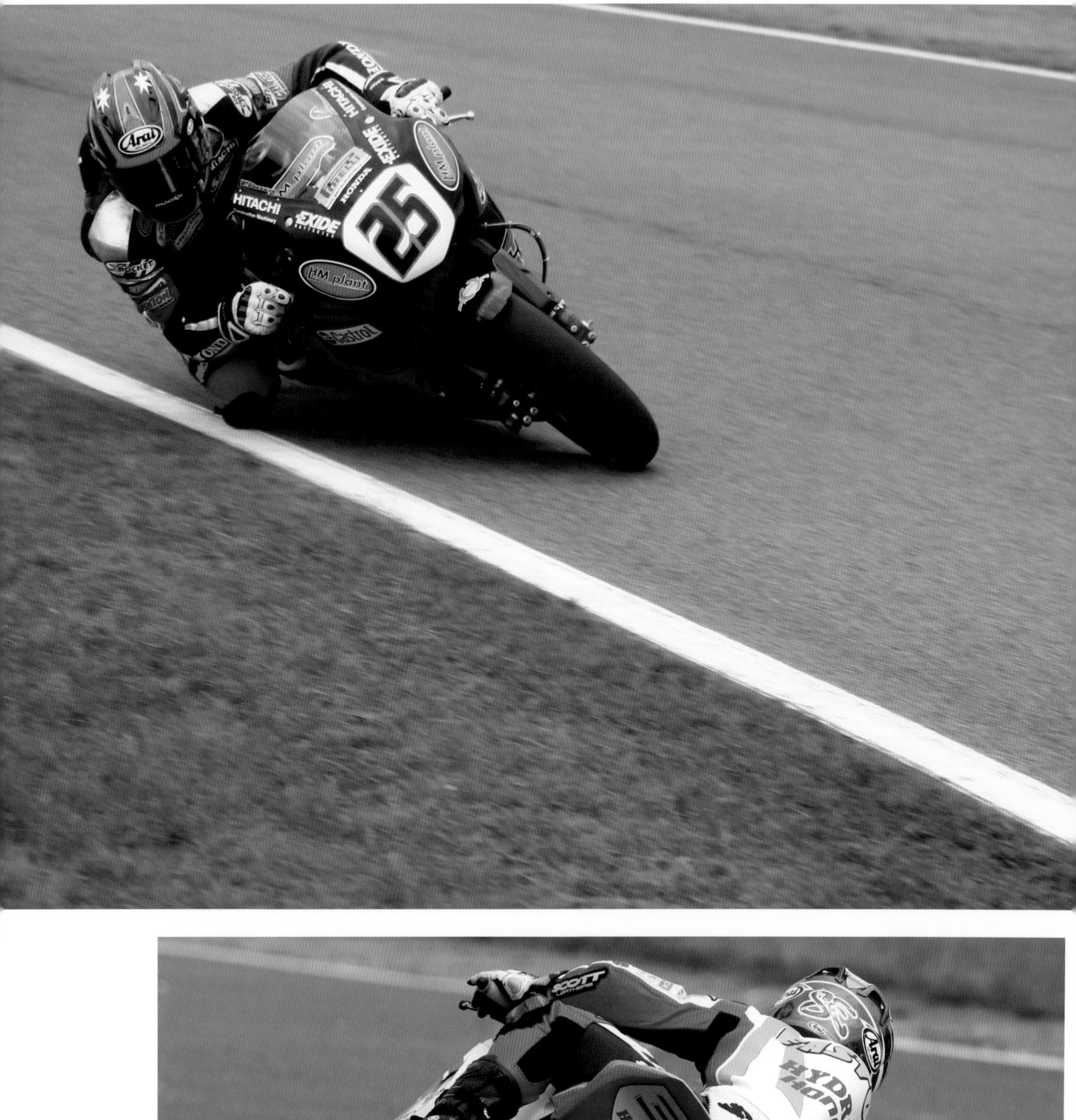

HYDREX
Honda
SCOTT
LEATHERS

agv
YAMALUBE
PIRELLI
YAMAHA
MOTORPOI

SHOEI
JEWSON
PIRELLI

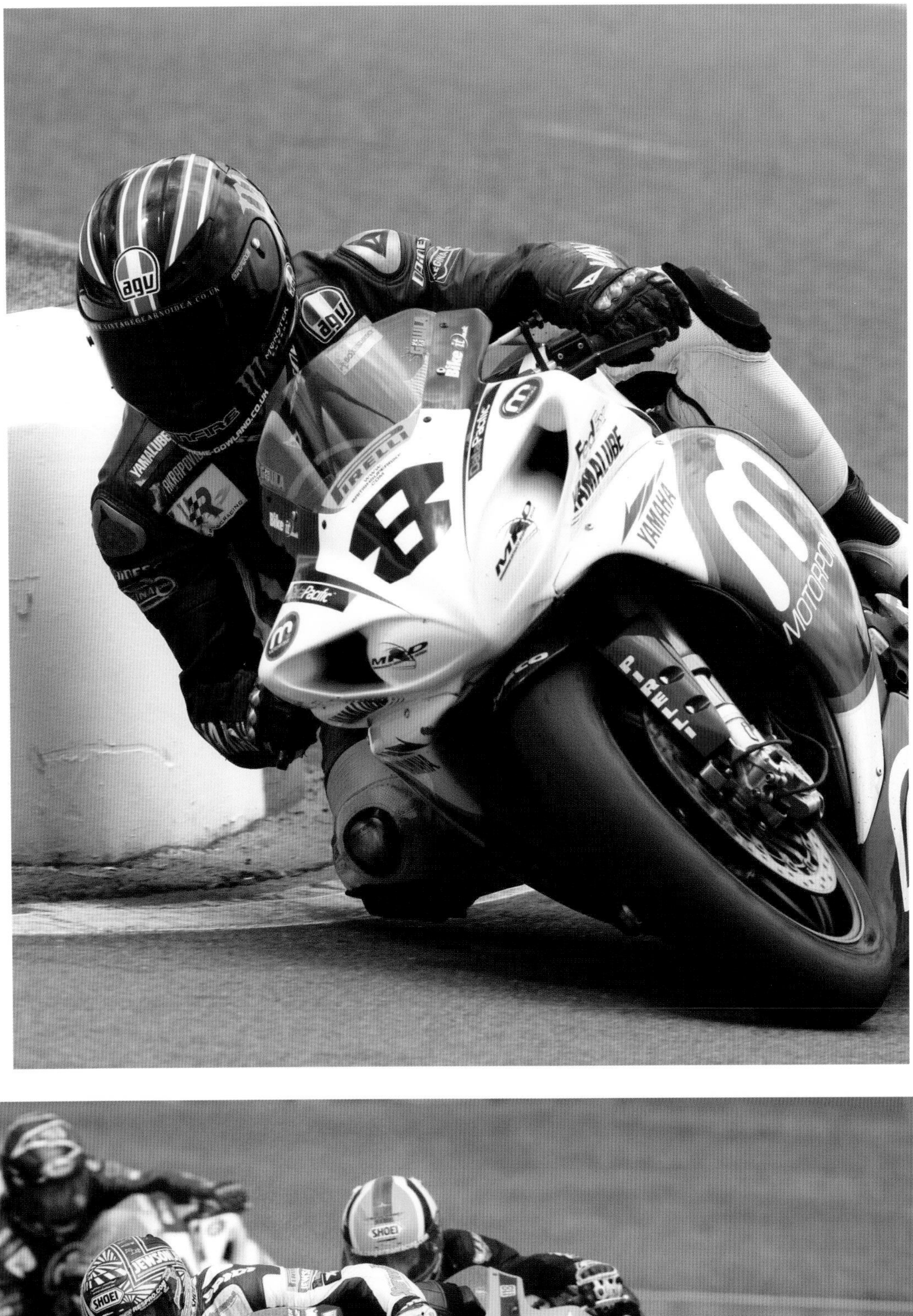

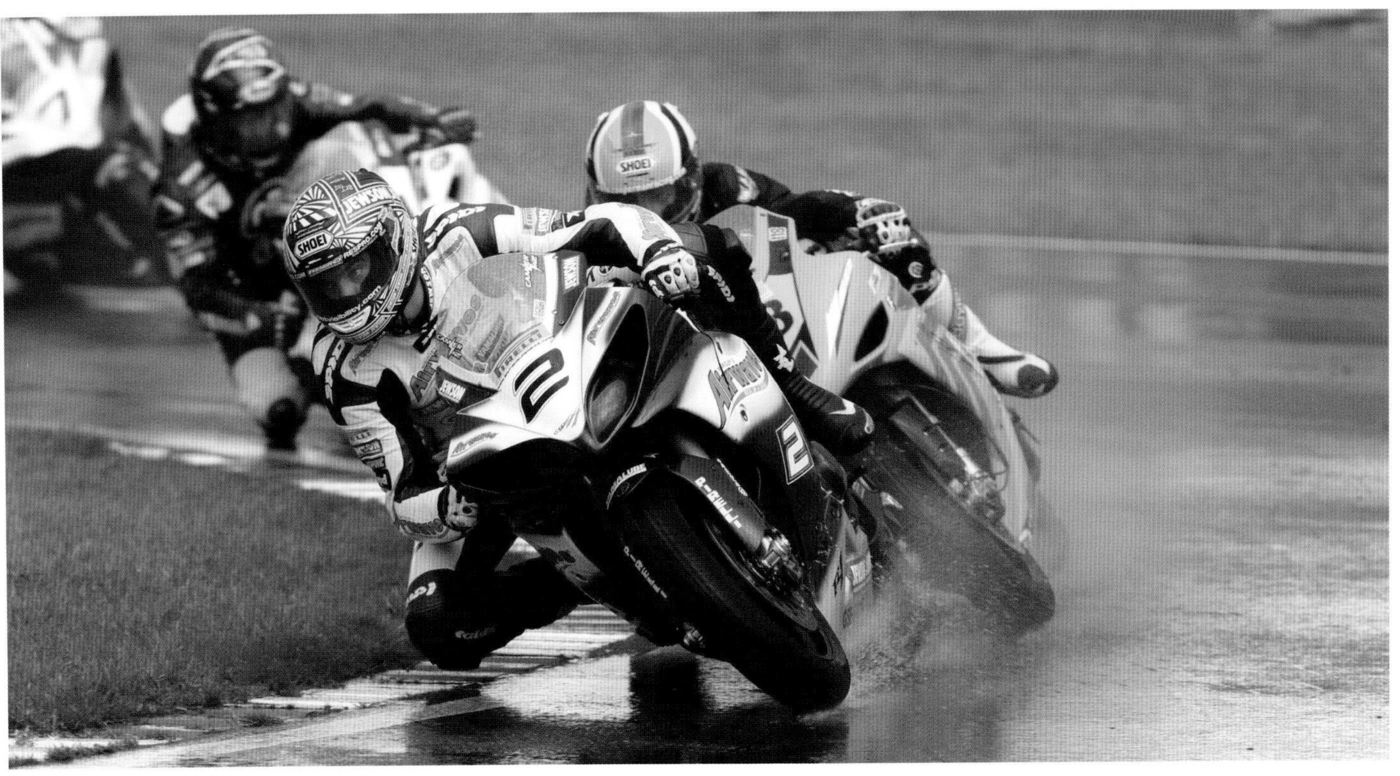

Round 07

Mallory Park

19th July

THEN CAME MALLORY...

The record books will show race victories for James Ellison and Leon Camier but behind those facts lay scenes of anger, sheer frustration and controversy, the like of which had not been seen in BSB before.

Simon Andrews had overcome tough challenges from Chris Walker to be leading the opening race, though Tommy Hill, who had taken over the reins as deputy to the injured Sylvain Guintoli aboard the Worx Suzuki, was closing in as the race entered its final third.

Josh Brookes was in fourth and riding hard when, with eight laps remaining, he ran too fast into the hairpin, and it all went wrong. He lost control of his HM Plant Honda, and that smashed into the luckless Andrews. In the following melee a further five riders went down.

The red flags came out with the slow starting Ellison now in the lead and pole setter Camier, who had all but stopped on the opening lap to avoid the tumbling Richard Cooper and come from last, credited with second from Graeme Gowland and Michael Rutter who had replaced Jason O'Halloran for this round on the SMT Honda.

Jack Valentine, the Suzuki team boss pointed the finger at Brookes: "It was a similar incident to Donington; the rider was out of control of his motorcycle." Nick Morgan of MSS Colchester Kawasaki weighed in: "I'm disgusted with the behaviour of Brookes. He took my rider out and I've lost a bike." Others were more philosophical.

What had been developing into the best race of the year had been ruined and for his part Brookes picked up a two event ban, with a further one event ban suspended for two events. And, he suffered a nasty thumb injury.

Hopes of a straightforward second race were dashed by rain, it was to be one of those afternoons, but Walker was quick off the mark to lead from Co-ordit Yamaha's Cooper, Camier and Ellison. Privateer Cooper was revelling in the difficult conditions to lead for three laps before Camier took him, but as the rain intensified, with water standing on the track, the race was red-flagged and half points awarded.

Ellison was second from Walker, John Laverty, Cup class winner Cooper and Rutter to end a miserable day all round.

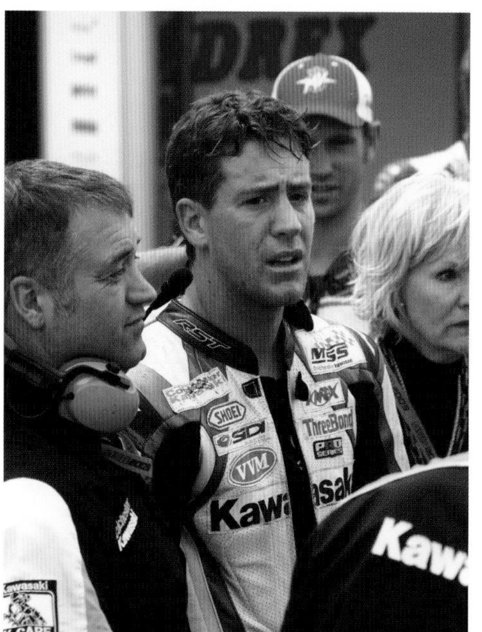

BSB Championship Positions

1	CAMIER	299.5
2	ELLISON	224
3	EASTON	173
4	RICHARDS	103
5	BROOKES	99
6	ANDREWS	92.5

Cup Championship Positions

1	MASON	275.5
2	HICKMAN	231
3	JESSOPP	160
4	TUNSTALL	156.5
5	BRIDEWELL	108
6	GILBERTSON	85

Arai
3

ROUND

08

Brands Hatch GP

9th August

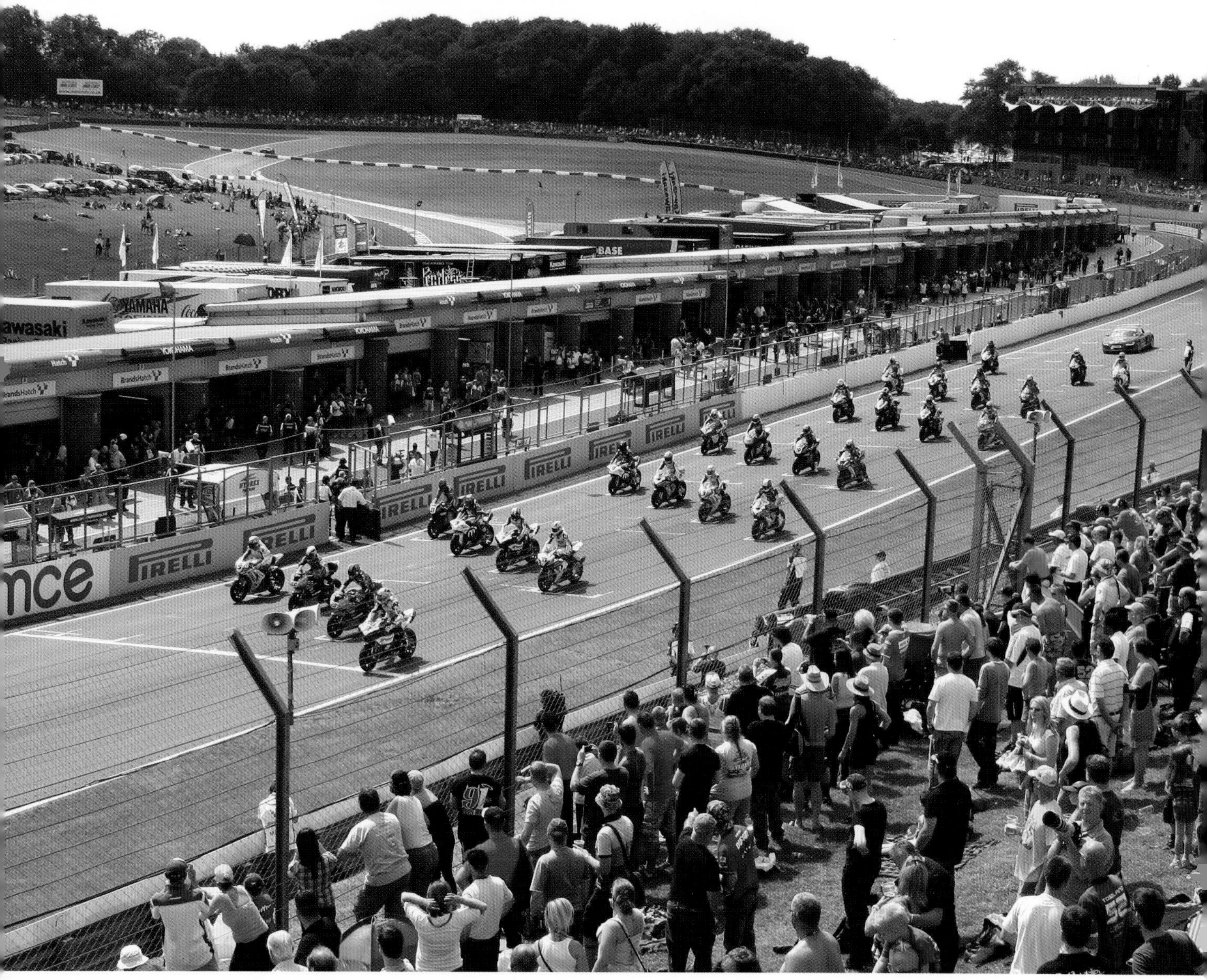
PIRELLI
YAMAHA
kawasaki
YOKOHAMA

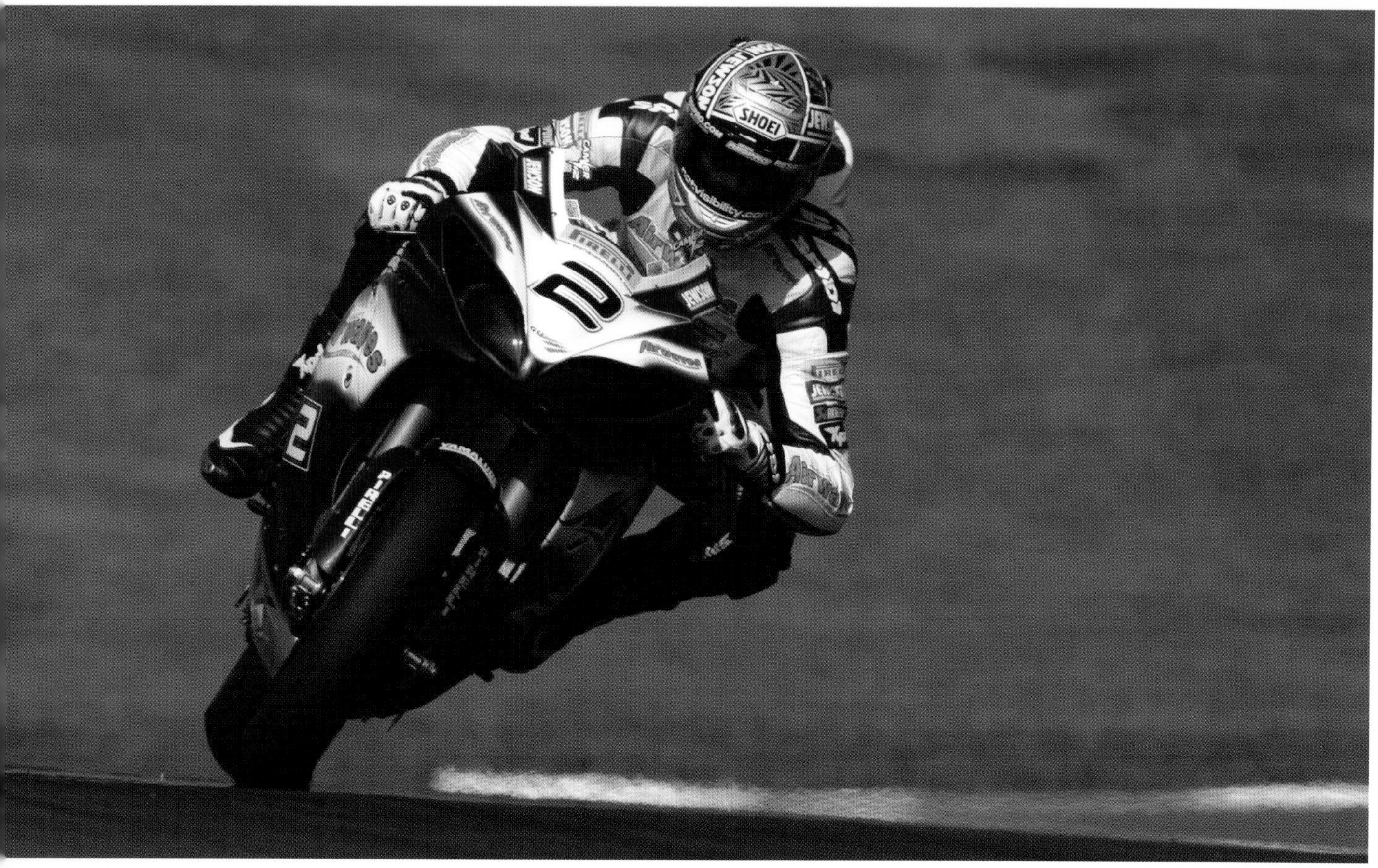
SHOEI
PIRELLI

Left: Another sun-drenched crowd enjoyed BSB's first 'triple-header'

Below: Paul Bird brought his World Superbike team to play and discusses progress with MSS Kawasaki boss, Nick Morgan

Bottom right: James Ellison keeps his Yamaha tight through Sheene Curve

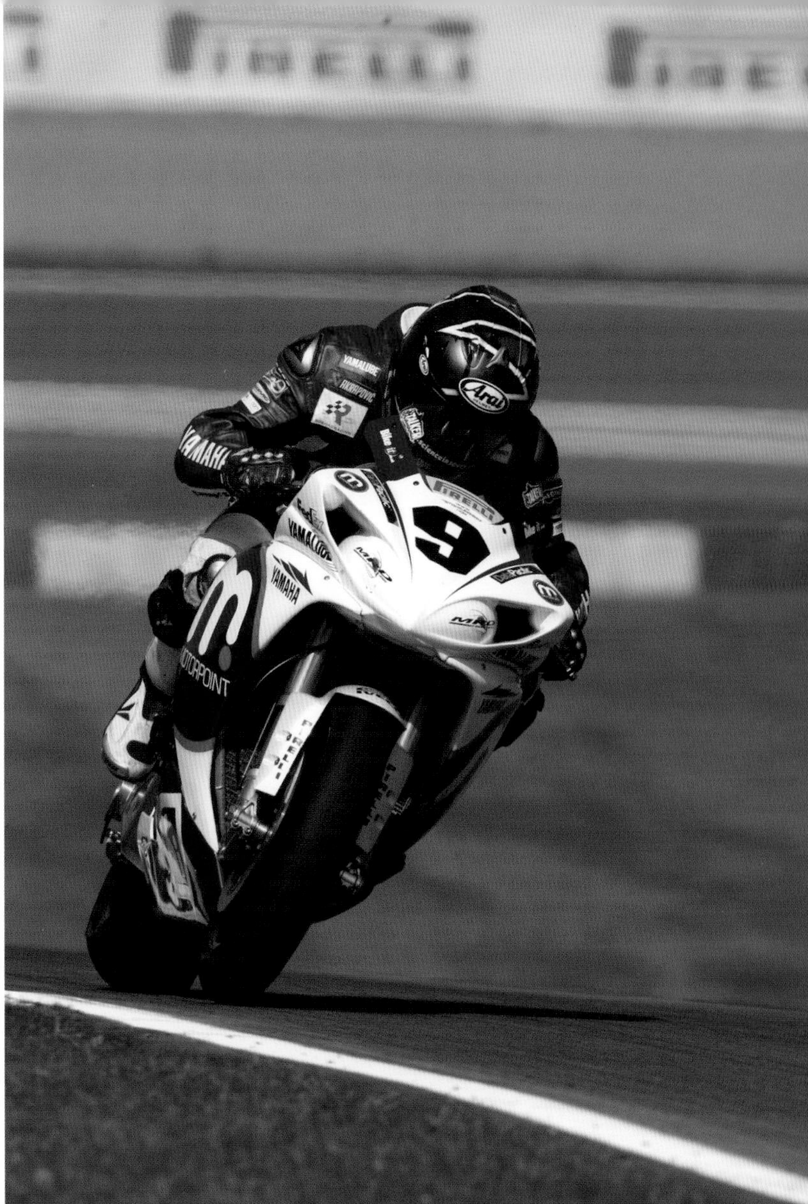

Arai
3
Putoline
PIRELLI

Arai
gbmuk
netvisibility.com
19
HM plant
Castrol
HONDA

SHARK
Kawasaki
touch 4
ROCK OIL
ICOM

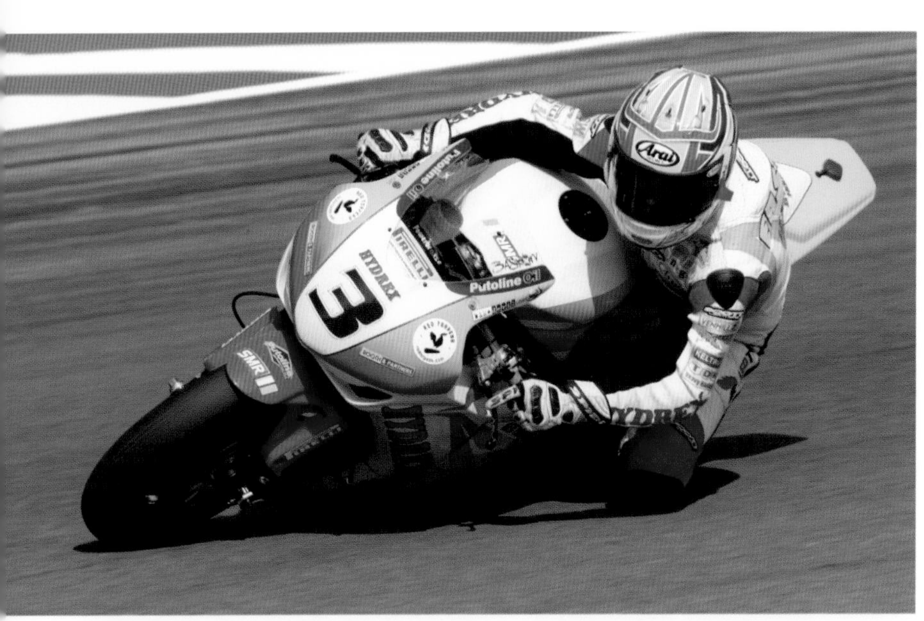

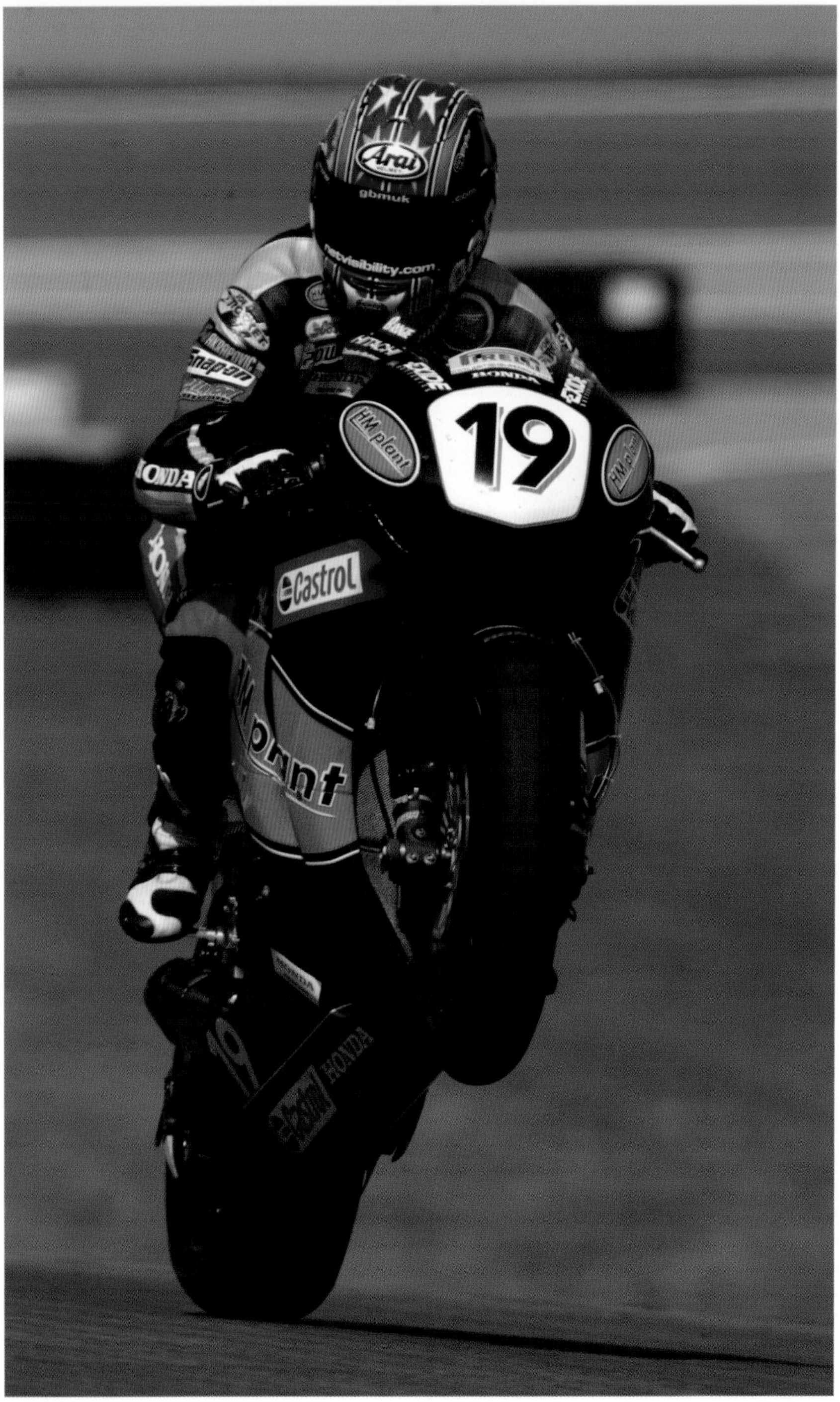

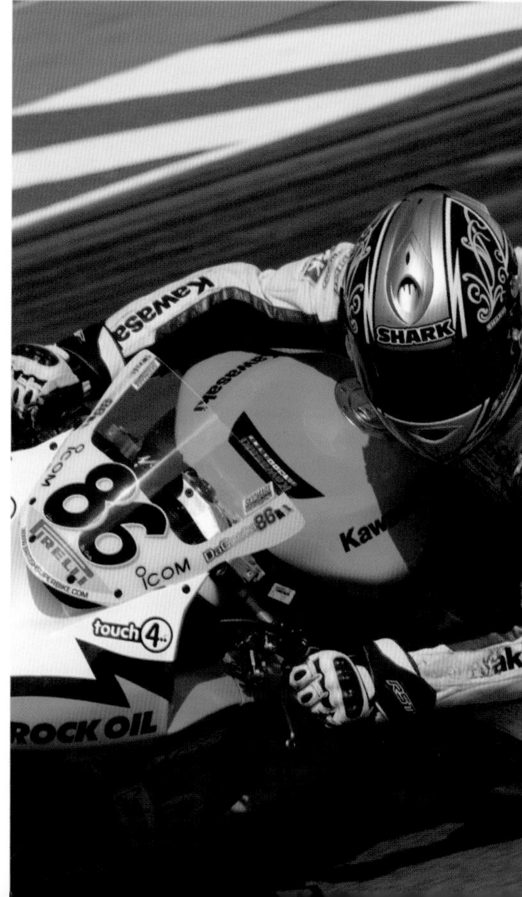

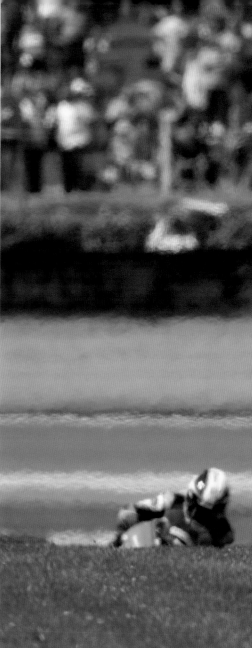

Bottom left: Steve Brogan was out on Glen Richards' Honda while top right: Karl Muggeridge threw a spanner in the works on Josh Brookes' bike

Right: The HM Plant boys do their PR bit as Coronation Street's 'Dev' joins in the fun

SHOEI
2
Airwaves
2
PIRELLI

Far left: Camier was stylish all weekend - as usual

Top: Michael Rutter took over from Simon Andrews as he recovered from an op to his wrist

Left: John Laverty took three points scoring finishes from Brands

Round 08

Brands Hatch GP

9th August

RECORDS TUMBLE AT BRANDS FOR CAMIER...

The 'Big Brands Bash' brought a milestone in BSB history with the first triple header round held amid a festival of the sport that saw legends, among them multiple world champions Giacomo Agostini and Phil Read parading machines, exotic and iconic, around the Kent circuit that enjoyed a weekend attendance of some 53,000.

The on-track action was further spiced by the decision of Paul Bird to run his Kawasaki World Superbike team in a guest appearance in a bid to gain valuable track time during the long summer break in their series. It also gave the BSB regulars a yardstick by which to assess themselves.

Leon Camier took full advantage, underlining his qualities and hopes of graduation to the world stage, as he made it six of the best in terms of pole starts, running a split second from Broc Parkes and Sheridan Morais on the two Kawasakis.

Parkes made a brilliant start to the Saturday afternoon race, while Morais crashed heavily, luckily without injury and another WSB star, Karl Muggeridge, in for the suspended Josh Brookes, ran second from Camier and Chris Walker. Camier was poised to strike, and at half distance he took the lead winning by two seconds from Parkes with Stuart Easton third.

Michael Rutter, by now the sport's super-sub, took eleventh as he rode the MSS Colchester Kawasaki in place of Simon Andrews, not fully fit following surgery on his broken scaphoid.

In race two on Sunday, the perfect getaway put Camier in the clear with Parkes in hot pursuit from Hydrex Honda duo Stuart Easton and Karl Harris while Tommy Hill, continuing for a second round on the Worx Suzuki was well in contention. Camier was gradually easing clear of the rest, eventually taking victory by over four seconds from Parkes, Easton, Hill and Ellison while Walker's hopes were dashed by an engine problem.

That victory brought Camier onto level terms with the record thirteen race wins in a season set by triple champion Niall Mackenzie back in 1996 but good as that was, the Airwaves Yamaha rider had no time to celebrate, rather, he wanted more of the same.

Parkes made life difficult for Camier, running out front, at one point, three seconds clear, but, he could not maintain the pace and the Yamaha rider caught him, and with six laps remaining was in the lead and taking the victory with ease. Ellison took third from Easton, John Laverty and Muggeridge.

Gary Mason completed a hat trick of victories in the Cup class, leading Martin Jessopp, now fully recovered from injury, and Tom Tunstall in each of the races.

BSB Championship Positions

1	CAMIER	374.5
2	ELLISON	261
3	EASTON	218
4	HARRIS	111.5
5	RICHARDS	103
6	LOWRY	101

Cup Championship Positions

1	MASON	350.5
2	HICKMAN	257
3	JESSOPP	220
4	TUNSTALL	204.5
5	BRIDEWELL	108
6	GILBERTSON	85

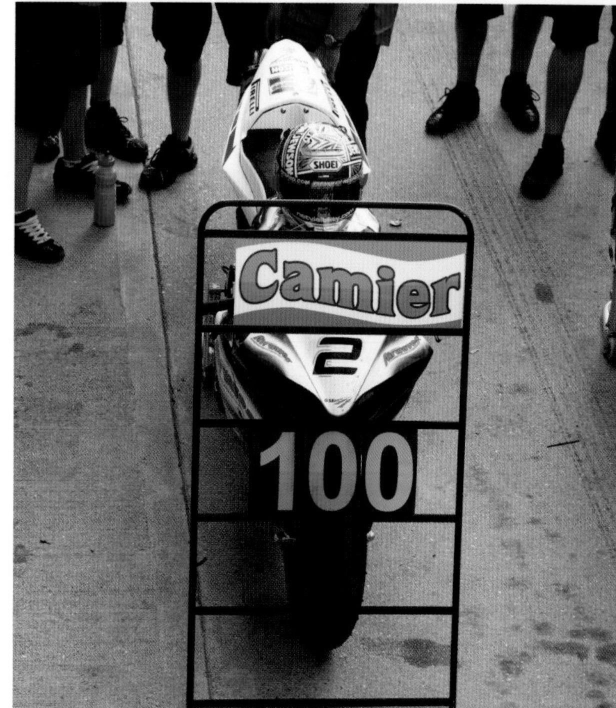

YAMAHA
RACING
AIRWAVES-YAMAHA.CO.UK
WRIGLEY'S
Airwaves®
KICK UP A GEAR®
JEWSON
YAMAHA
PIRELLI

ROUND
09
Cadwell Park
31st August

JEWSON
GSE-GROUP
JEWSON
JEWSON
Airwaves
PIRELLI
2
JEWSON
Airwaves
YAMALUBE

SUZUKI

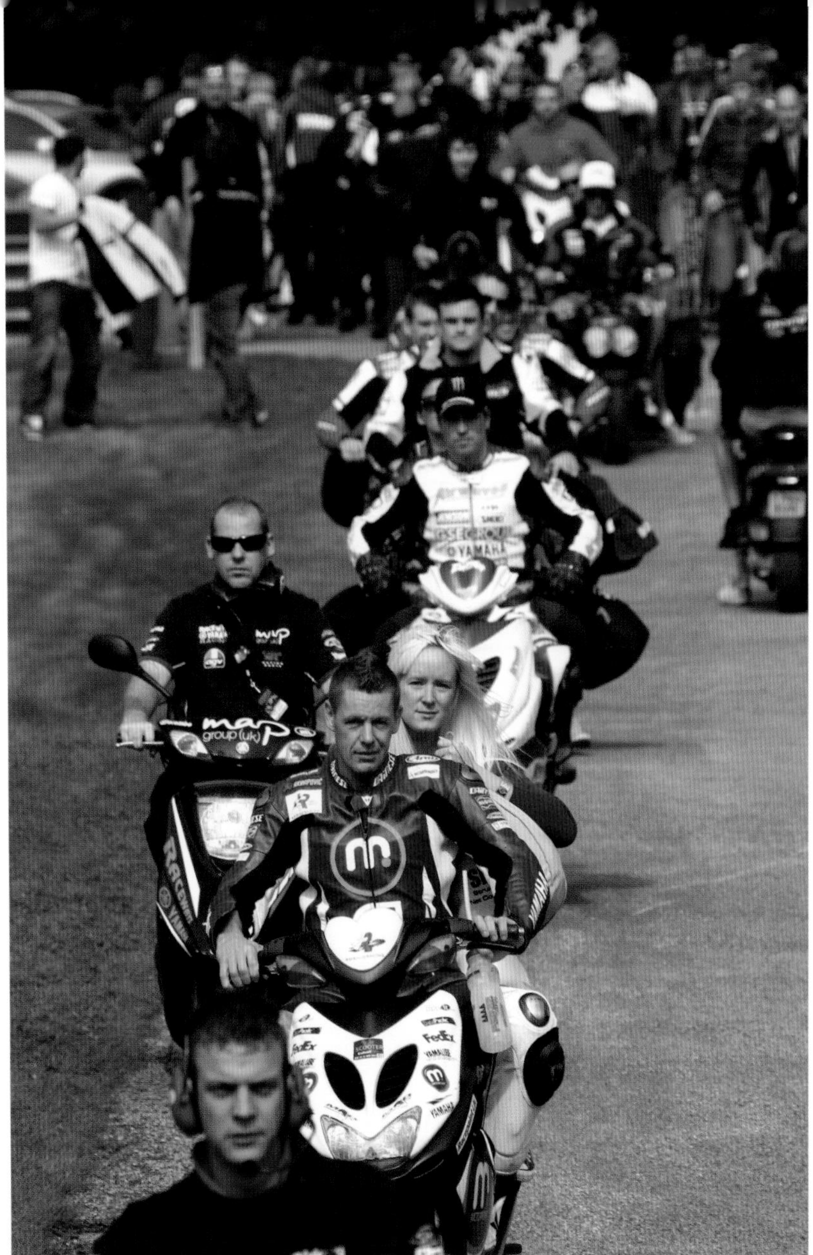

Far left: Stuart Easton heads the pack through Hall Bends

Bottom left: An unusual view of Ian Lowry through Barn Corner

Right: Guintoli made a stylish return at Cadwell but struggled with overall fitness on a demanding track

Bottom left: Karl Harris leads the HM Plant Honda - this time ridden by TT Legend John McGuinness

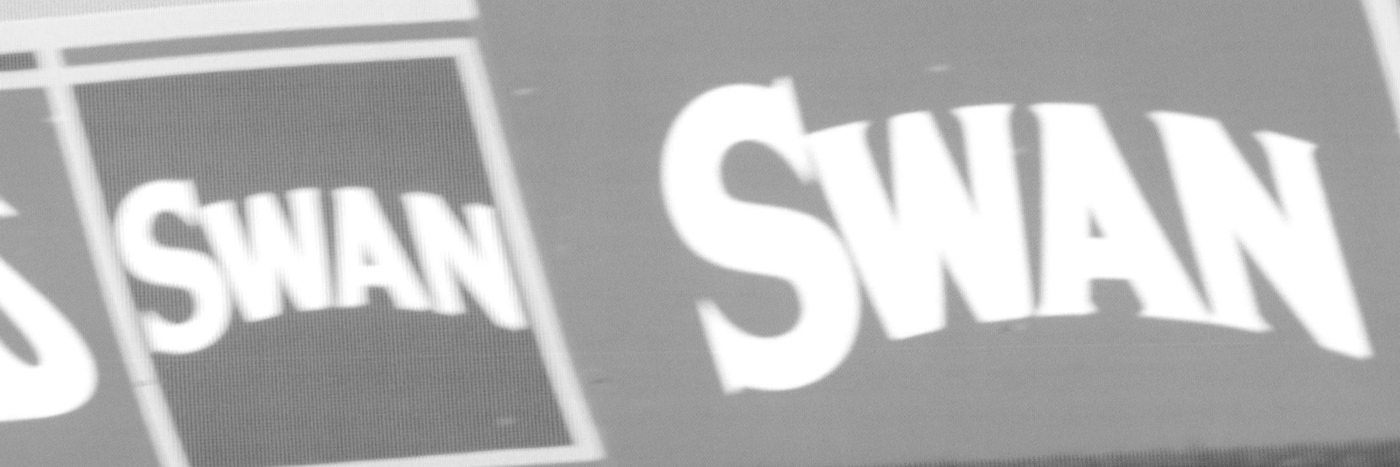
SWAN
SWAN

50
WORX SUZUKI
SUZUKI
SHARK
CRESCENT
Bartlett
WORX
SUZUKI

Top right: Julien Da Costa sweeps through Hall Bends as Karl Harris launches over the infamous Mountain in his own inimitable style

HYDREX
RED TORPEDO

Round 09

Cadwell Park

31st August

CAMIER KICKED OUT…!

Runaway series leader Leon Camier crossed the line comfortably clear of the pack at the end of the second race believing that he had completed yet another daily double victory in his relentless charge to the title, but this time he was left bitterly disappointed, disqualified for non-observance of a flag signal.

The Airwaves Yamaha rider, building up a useful lead, had been ahead when the Safety Car intervened to allow marshals to deal with an oil spill, and then done it all again as the action resumed for real, running six seconds clear of the pack on the penultimate lap when race officials spotted smoke emitting from his bike.

Camier was shown the black and orange flag, requiring him to pull in immediately, but he finished the last lap explaining afterwards: "I misinterpreted the rules! It's just one of those things and I am really disappointed as I felt more comfortable on the bike in that race and my lap times were better."

The consolation for the team was that their other rider James Ellison, who had been second behind his team-mate, took his third victory of the season and his second to be decided by the rule book although the controversy wasn't over as the returning Sylvain Guintoli was later penalised a place for overtaking during the Safety Car intervention.

Stuart Easton, strong all weekend aboard the Hydrex Honda, took second place from Simon Andrews riding the MSS Confused.com Kawasaki. They had also featured in the front-running mix in the earlier race which had been won by the stylish Camier.

In that opening encounter Easton was fast away at the start, but was soon reeled in by Camier who had started from his seventh pole position of the campaign and once in front the Airwaves rider controlled the action. Ellison tried everything he knew to find a way past the determined Easton, but had to settle for third ahead of Ian Lowry who was having one of his best rides of the season on the Relentless Suzuki while team-mates Simon Andrews and Julien Da Costa squabbled for fifth.

Sylvain Guintoli returning from injury aboard the Worx Crescent Suzuki finished eighth and seventh but at their local circuit there was disappointment for the HM Plant Honda team, double winners the previous year, but this time around struggling with Karl Muggeridge their best in seventh and thirteenth.

Gary Mason continued his charge toward the Cup crown with another winning double ahead of Tommy Bridewell and Peter Hickman.

BSB Championship Positions

1	CAMIER	399.5
2	ELLISON	302
3	EASTON	258
4	HARRIS	120.5
5	ANDREWS	119.5
6	LOWRY	114
	DA COSTA	114

Cup Championship Positions

1	MASON	400.5
2	HICKMAN	289
3	JESSOPP	244
4	TUNSTALL	217.5
5	BRIDEWELL	148
6	GILBERTSON	85

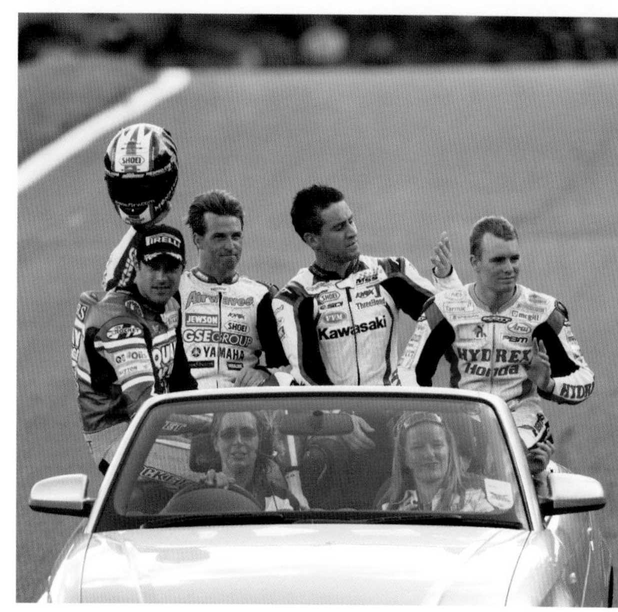

EATON
LAFARGE
BSW
AKRAPOVIC

ROUND

10

Croft

13th September

HYDREX
SHOEI
BKS
33

Arai
9

Above: Camier takes a lesson in flag meanings following his failure to obey a flag signal at Cadwell

Far left: Tommy Hill took over from Karl Harris on the Hydrex Honda

Below: Brookes was on a charge

Arai
Arai
PIRELLI
HYDREX
3
RED TORPEDO
redtorpedo.com
BOOTH & PARTNERS
BOOTH & PARTNERS
HYDREX
RED TORPEDO
PIRELLI
Pectel
Control
Systems
Putoline
Tarmac
MSW
3

Above: Walker crashed out in spectacular style

Below: John Laverty's fire breathing Buildbase Kawasaki dices with James Ellison's Airwaves Yamaha

Airwaves
AIRWAVES-YAMAHA.CO.UK
Kawasaki
GSEGROUP
YAMAHA
JEWSON
SHOEI

SHOEI

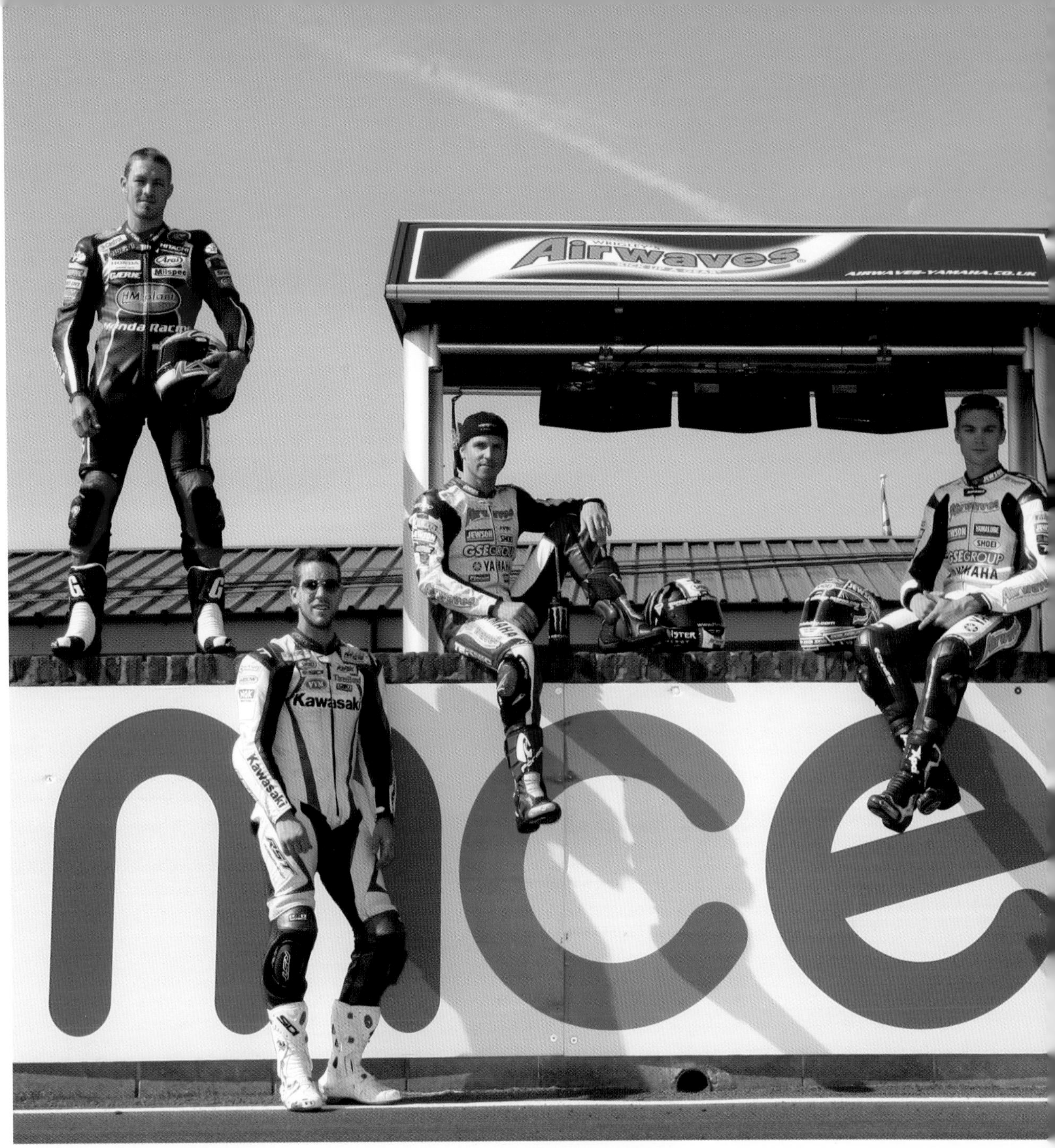

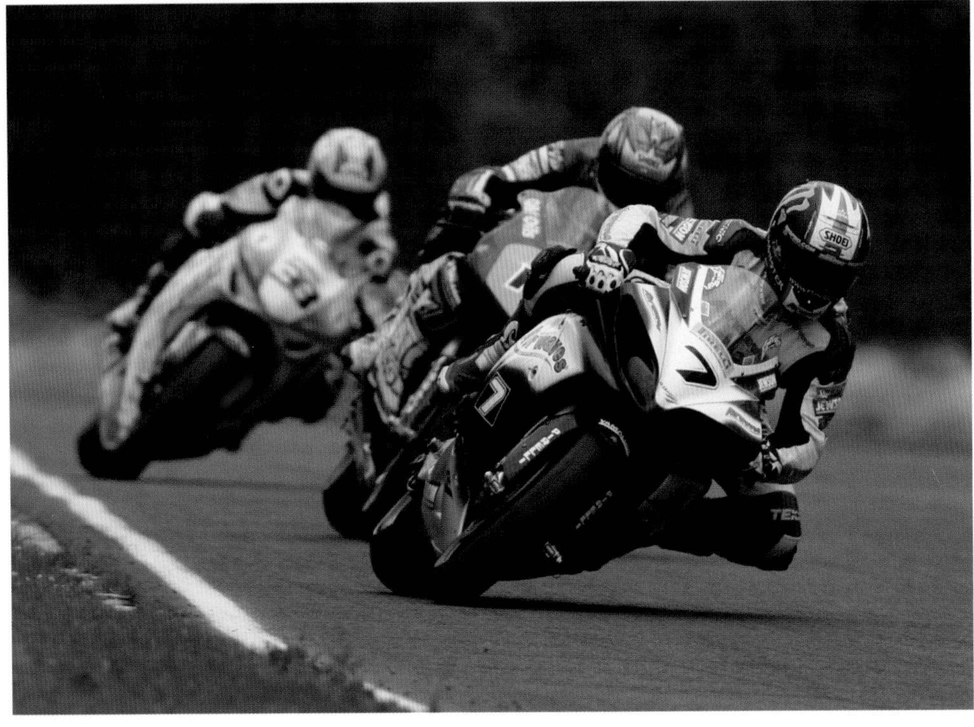

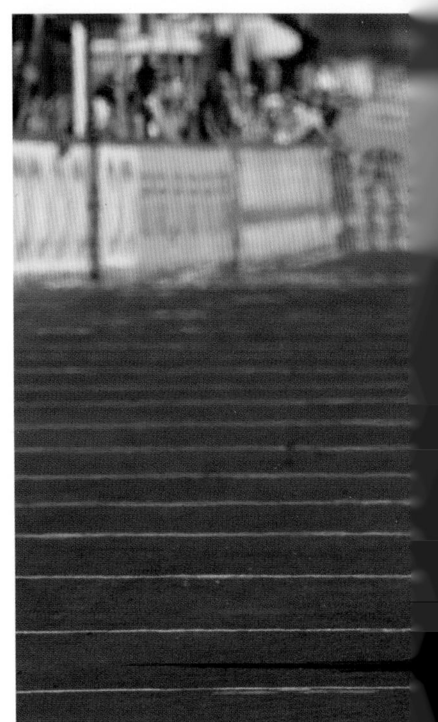

Top left: The main BSB Championship contenders line up for a PR photo

Round 10

Croft

13th September

EASTON IS THE DADDY…

Stuart Easton enjoyed his maiden victory in a dramatic opening race in which the pole-starting title favourite Leon Camier recovered well from a costly early error and then ensured business as usual with a comfortable victory in race two.

In the opening encounter, Camier was running fifth on his Airwaves Yamaha but he overshot Tower Bend early on, ploughing across grass and gravel but managing to keep the bike going before rejoining last, and then charging through the pack in a damage limitation exercise that earned him valuable points with sixth place.

Flying Scot Easton, whose wife Claire was expecting their first child over the weekend, led throughout and held off the close attentions of James Ellison to take his and the locally-based Hydrex Honda team's first victory in the top flight. "It's great for me and for the team who have given me a race package that enables me to go for these results," enthused Easton while team owner Shaun Muir added: "It couldn't be better, our first win, five years in the making, here on our local circuit. It is just rewards for all of our hard work and makes it all worthwhile."

Easton was well in the mix next time out, running second to Camier who was keen to make amends for what his team boss Colin Wright described as a 'schoolboy error'. He did just that by comfortably completing victory number sixteen of a dominant campaign and reflected: "I got too excited in the first race and made a disappointing mistake but this time I was 100% careful and when I made the pass, I made it stick. It is awesome to win, and get the team championship, now I have to get myself the title next time out."

Josh Brookes, returning to action on the HM Plant Honda having served his two-event suspension, showed his real riding qualities with determined performances that twice took him onto the bottom step of the podium but his team-mate for the day, former twice champion Ryuichi Kiyonari made a lacklustre return to the series.

For Gary Mason and the Quay Garage Honda team it was celebration time with another winning double ensuring that they were the Mirror.co.uk Cup Champions.

BSB Championship Positions

1	CAMIER	434.5
2	ELLISON	335
3	EASTON	303
4	LOWRY	134
5	BROOKES	131
6	ANDREWS	130.5

Cup Championship Positions

1	MASON	475.5 (CHAMPION)
2	HICKMAN	341
3	JESSOPP	266
4	TUNSTALL	243.5
5	BRIDEWELL	184
6	GILBERTSON	85

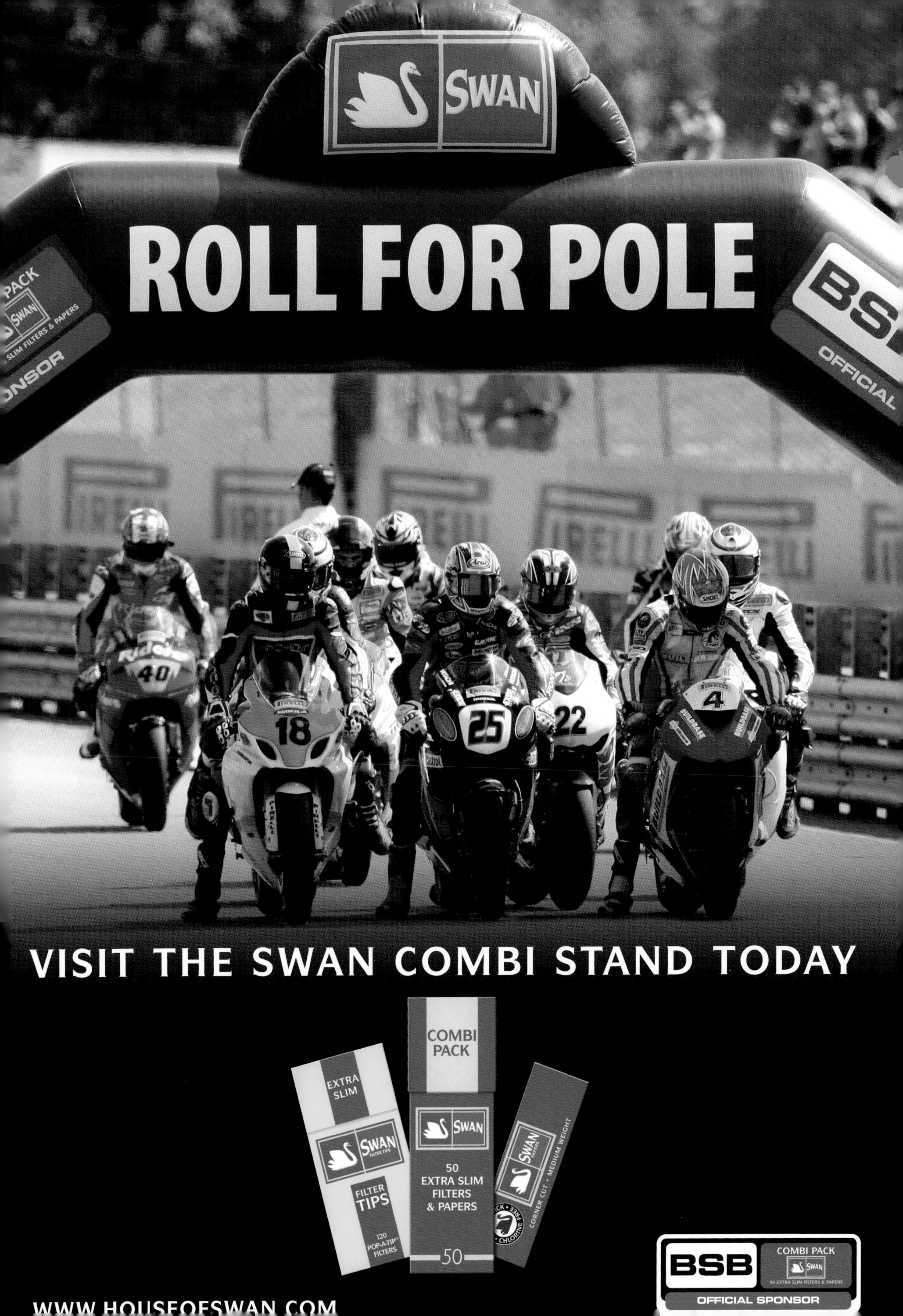
SWAN
ROLL FOR POLE
BSB
OFFICIAL
VISIT THE SWAN COMBI STAND TODAY
COMBI PACK
EXTRA SLIM
SWAN
FILTER TIPS
120 POP-A-TIP™ FILTERS
50 EXTRA SLIM FILTERS & PAPERS
50
CORNER CUT • MEDIUM WEIGHT
CHLORINE FREE
BSB
COMBI PACK
SWAN
50 EXTRA SLIM FILTERS & PAPERS
OFFICIAL SPONSOR
WWW.HOUSEOFSWAN.COM

SHOEI
JEWSON
RESPRO
netvisibility.com
PIRELLI
www.britishsuperbike.com
2
Airwaves
YAMALUBE
PIRELLI
PIRELLI

ROUND
11
Silverstone
27th September

mce mce mce SILVERSTONE

METZELE
HYDREX
Castrol
Castrol
HONDA

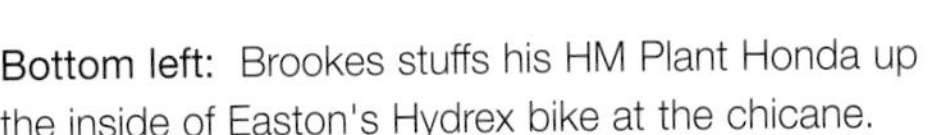

Bottom left: Brookes stuffs his HM Plant Honda up the inside of Easton's Hydrex bike at the chicane.

Top right: Richards returned from his injury still in pain and despite wringing the neck of his HM Plant Honda, the pain proved too much and he sat out race two

Above: Leon Camier shares a joke with Seeing Red's editor Larry 'Scoop' Carter

Right: Karl Harris had a strong showing on the SMT Honda

JEWSON
SHOEI
RESPRO.COM
SPIDI
PIRELLI
Xpd
YAMALUBE
Airwaves
WRIGLEY'S
Airwaves
KICK UP A GEAR
2
2
PIRELLI
brembo

Left: Camier took the win and the Championship title, but he was made to work hard for it by his team-mate, James Ellison

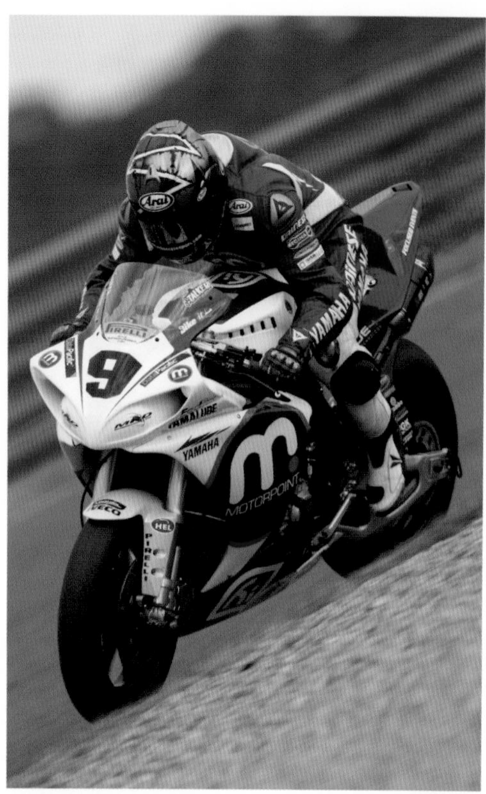

SHOEI
HJC
BUILDBASE
Kawasaki
TSUBAKI
bitubo
WebCreationUK
WGG
4

SHOEI
7
2

Round 11

Silverstone

27th September

LEON LANDS IT...

Leon Camier overcame his hard-riding Airwaves Yamaha team-mate James Ellison to win the opening race of the penultimate round and with it the crown.

The two riders had duelled fiercely for supremacy, but it was Ellison who held the upper hand (just) for much of the race as he battled to keep his outside hope of the title alive. Camier however had the little bit extra in reserve, keeping his cool and taking the chance when it came.

"I thought it [winning the title at Silverstone] was not going to happen as I was trying so hard, trying not to make any mistakes, but always looking for a way through. I knew that James would go well but I didn't expect him to be that strong," Camier explained after taking the 17th victory of a dominant season, though by only 0.244secs from the determined Ellison.

"That was the hardest race of the whole season, it was ridiculous as I was out of shape at times, and the front end of the bike was going out of line. I was pushing so hard because I wanted to get the thing sorted out in that first race," explained Camier who having been thwarted twice as he nosed in front at the chicane finally made the decisive, if audacious move, at Bridge with less than two laps remaining.

"James was so difficult to pass. He was braking late and I couldn't get him. It was a case of trying to work out where I could take him and going into Bridge I just kept on the gas, lunged for it, and it came off. Job done and I'm over the moon, this is a dream come true," added a delighted Camier who then made life difficult for himself in race two, running wide and dropping to ninth before charging back through the pack to take second place to Ellison.

Behind them in each of the races there was the ever-present threat of Josh Brookes on the HM Plant Honda with Stuart Easton reinforcing his third place in the overall standings with a pair of fourths on his Hydrex Honda.

Tommy Bridewell completed a double on the NB Suzuki in the Mirror.co.uk Cup while Superstock champion Alastair Seeley made his debut into the top flight, taking tenth place in the second race aboard a Relentless Suzuki built to the new Evolution specification. This Evolution class is an initiative introduced for 2010 by the series promoter aimed at cutting costs and going back to basics.

BSB Championship Positions

1	CAMIER	479.5 (CHAMPION)
2	ELLISON	380
3	EASTON	329
4	BROOKES	163
5	LOWRY	149
6	ANDREWS	146.5

Cup Championship Positions

1	MASON	470.5 (CHAMPION)
2	HICKMAN	361
3	JESSOPP	289
4	TUNSTALL	259.5
5	BRIDEWELL	234
6	GILBERTSON	85

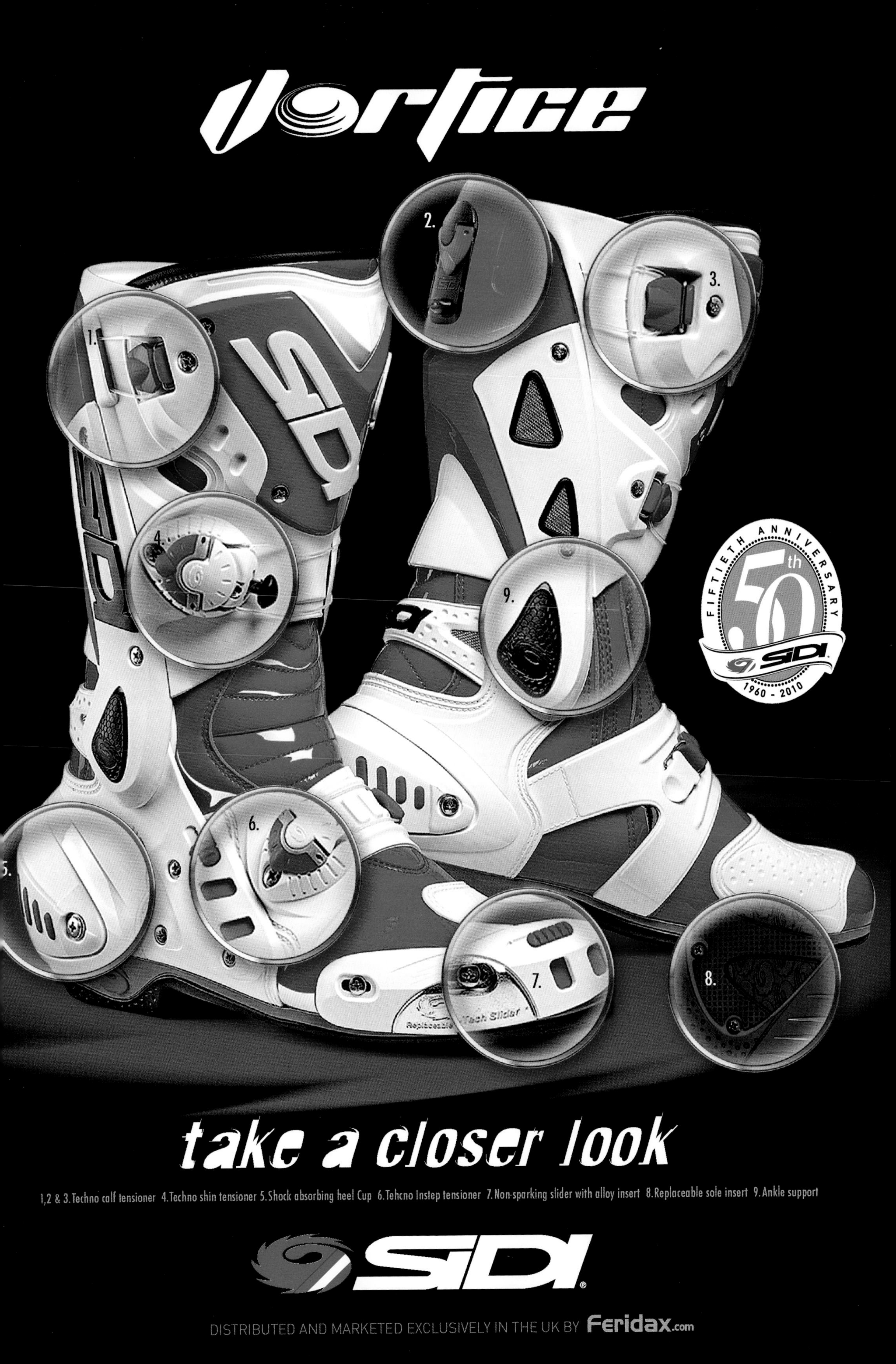
Vortice
1.
2.
3.
4.
5.
6.
7.
8.
9.
FIFTIETH ANNIVERSARY
50th
SIDI
1960 - 2010
Replaceable Tech Slider
take a closer look
1,2 & 3. Techno calf tensioner 4. Techno shin tensioner 5. Shock absorbing heel Cup 6. Tehcno Instep tensioner 7. Non-sparking slider with alloy insert 8. Replaceable sole insert 9. Ankle support
SIDI
DISTRIBUTED AND MARKETED EXCLUSIVELY IN THE UK BY Feridax.com

ROUND

12

Oulton Park

11th October

SHOEI
TOM
SHOEI
GROUP
GSEGROUP
MONSTER
ENERGY

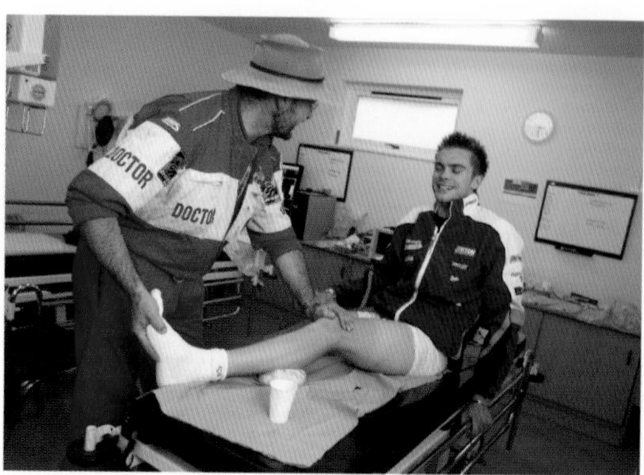

Above: Camier has his damaged knee assessed by chief medical officer, Toby Branfoot

Bottom right: The view the other riders saw of Leon Camier for most of the season

Above: Ellison and Easton still had a score to settle for second place

Left: Poor old Graeme Gowland had to go back to Rob Mac's pit and explain this! It's not starting Rob... I think it might be flooded?

3
SHOEI
JEWSON
SPIDI
2
PIRELLI
YAMALUBE

Right: Brookes shows his usual flamboyant style

Bottom right: Camier and his team celebrate yet another win

SHOEI
Airwaves
7
JEWSON
GSE-GROUP.COM

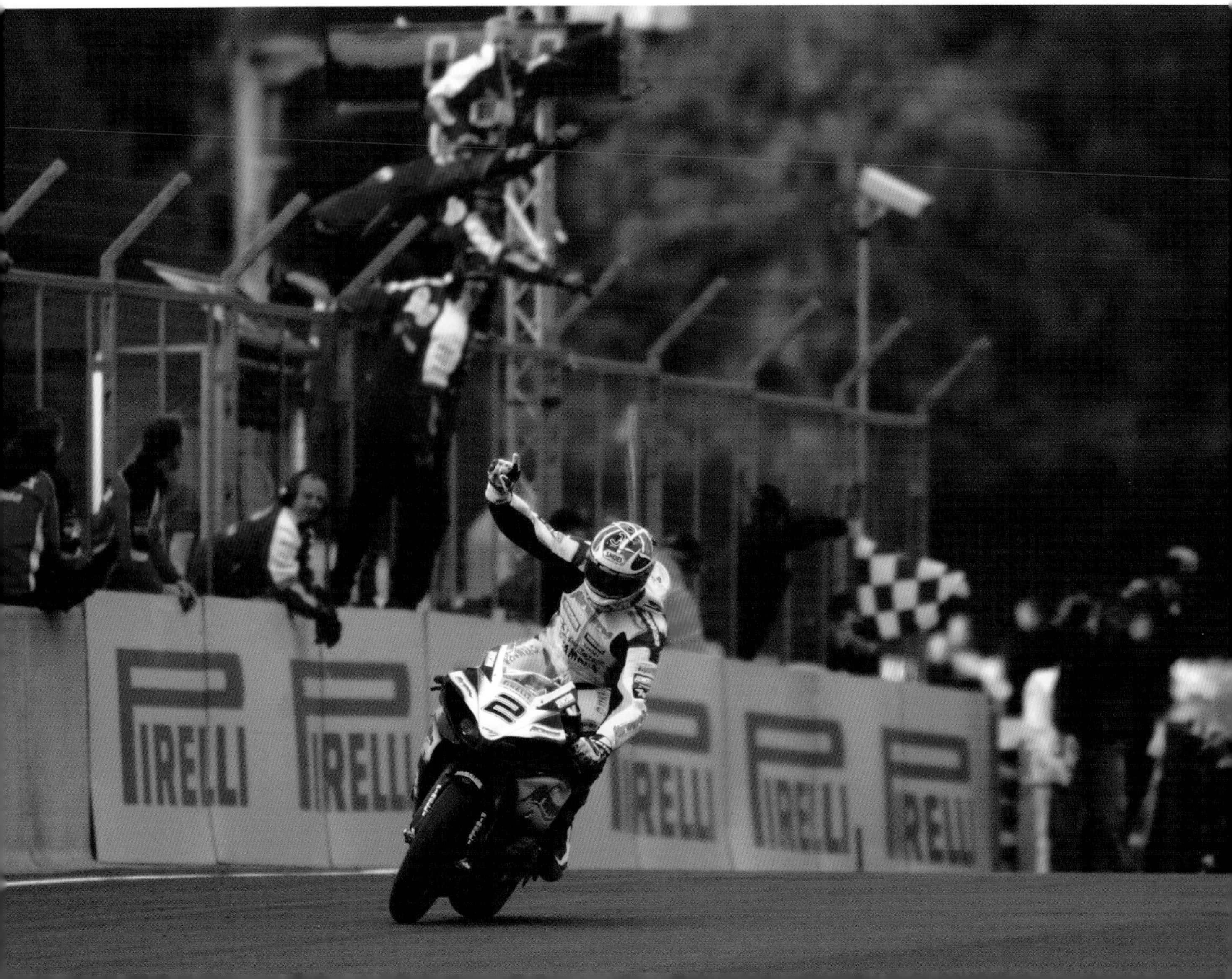
PIRELLI
PIRELLI
PIRELLI
PIRELLI
PIRELLI
2

Round 12

Oulton Park

11th October

SIGNED, SEALED AND DELIVERED...

For Leon Camier, it was almost the perfect ending to his title winning campaign. There was a fifth double victory to extend his record winning spree in the championship to 19 races, though there was a little disappointment that he had missed out on a second winning triple.

That had been denied the Airwaves Yamaha rider by the hard riding, determined Stuart Easton in the Saturday afternoon race when, appropriately at Hizzy's Chicane on the last lap, the young Scot pulled off a superb overtaking move that his mentor, the late Steve Hislop, would have been so proud of.

That gave Easton, who had started from his first ever Superbike pole, his second victory of the campaign, and the satisfaction of a job well done as he explained: "That was a proper win, I beat Leon fair and square, it was hard fought and difficult."

Camier had missed out by barely a quarter of a second and stung by that, he was all out for revenge with another polished performance on the final afternoon of the championship.

The first race was equally hard fought, and again on the last lap at Hizzy's Chicane, Easton menaced, but this time Camier held the upper hand, keeping his line and with it the race result. "I wanted that one," said the champion as he crossed the line a split second ahead.

Camier was made to wait for his final glory as the last race of the season was halted on the opening lap as Simon Andrews crashed heavily at Cascades, but on the restart, the champion showed his speed and style, moving ahead, and taking charge of the race.

Easton crashed out in his vain pursuit with Tommy Hill running second, but there was no way that Camier was to be denied. "That's the job done, the perfect way to end the season... with another victory," he said with a winning smile.

"That was an awesome way to finish the season," said Camier afterwards. "It really has been a dream season for me, I could not have asked for anything more. I've had a strong team around me, and I owe so much to those guys for what they've done to help make this all possible for me," he added as he received the Arthur Price Queen's Golden Jubilee Trophy, which he won with a record points haul.

In the Mirror.co.uk Cup, Gary Mason, already crowned champion, won the opener, but had to settle for second best to Tommy Bridewell in the final two races.

BSB Final Championship Positions

1	CAMIER	549.5
2	ELLISON	413
3	EASTON	374
4	BROOKES	188
5	LOWRY	170
6	ANDREWS	163.5

Cup Final Championship Positions

1	MASON	535.5
2	HICKMAN	381
3	JESSOPP	326
4	TUNSTALL	315.5
5	BRIDEWELL	300
6	GILBERTSON	85

Mirror.co.uk Cup

GARY GLITTERS...

Having joined the series a third of the way through 2008, Gary Mason came into 2009 very much as the man to beat in the Mirror.co.uk BSB Privateers Cup, and the Lichfield rider didn't disappoint, dominating the series from the word go.

The 30 year old once again lined up on the Quay Garage Honda, a machine dating back to 2007, and won the opening eight races to forge clear in the title race, a lead he was never to relinquish or to come under real threat. Indeed, Mason's dominance mirrored that of Leon Camier and he ended the year with no less than 18 wins from the 26 races and it was only the Knockhill and Silverstone rounds where he didn't record a win. Such was his pace, he was also a major player in the championship proper, often finishing in the top ten as he hassled and harried the 'factory' teams, eventually ending the season in 13th place overall.

Taking runner-up spot was Peter Hickman who rejoined the Superbike class on one of the new R1 Yamahas, after a successful year back in the Superstock division. His small team, led by father Dave, put together a strong package that allowed him to finish on the podium in all bar three of the races he finished and it was that consistent run of podiums that meant Mason was unable to clinch the title until the Croft round in mid-September.

It was a similar story for Martin Jessopp (Riders Honda) and Tom Tunstall (Doodson/Hardinge Honda) who were almost always ever present in the top four at each and every round, alternating positions throughout with Hickman. Jessopp was forced to miss the Snetterton and Knockhill rounds due to injury but he bounced back to edge out Tunstall in the race for third by just 11.5 points.

Although he only finished fifth in the final championship table, the man who arguably challenged Mason the most was Team NB's Tommy Bridewell. The 21 year old only joined the series at the fifth round, after splitting from the Lorenzini by Leoni Italian European Superstock team he had started the year with, but he was immediately on the pace. Riding his late brother Ollie's 2006-spec Suzuki, Bridewell took seven wins and six podiums whilst, like Mason, he was a regular thorn in the side of the works' riders, taking a number of top ten finishes along the way.

The only other rider to win a race all season was Team Co-Ordit's Richard Cooper, who qualified on the front row at Mallory in a guest ride, before finishing fifth in the race itself, the highest result attained by any of the Cup competitors.

It was a tough year for the Privateers as the credit crunch kicked in with a vengeance, but organisers announced in September that a new BSB 'Evolution' class will be introduced for 2010. The class, which will see 'stock' engines slotted into a BSB rolling chassis, will also see the elimination of electronic rider aids and should save teams in the region of up to £200,000 in tuning, engine rebuilds and complex electronic packages. Superstock 1000cc champion Alastair Seeley debuted an 'Evo' bike at Silverstone and finished in the top ten, also lapping within 1.5 seconds of race winner Leon Camier.

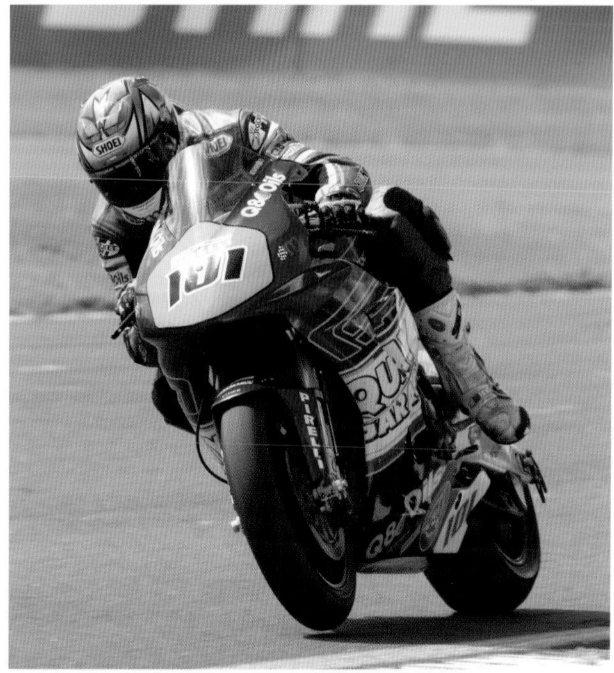

Championship Positions

1	Gary MASON (Honda)	535.5
2	Peter HICKMAN (Yamaha)	381
3	Martin JESSOP (Honda)	326
4	Tom TUNSTALL (Honda)	315.5
5	Tommy BRIDEWELL (Suzuki)	300
6	Kenny GILBERTSON (Kawasaki)	85

Arai
21
Mirror.co.uk
ICEVALLEY
doodson
MOTORSPORT
EXCEPTIONAL INSURANCE
brembo
64

THINK! THINK!
SHOEI
101
PIRELLI
Q8 Oils
101
7

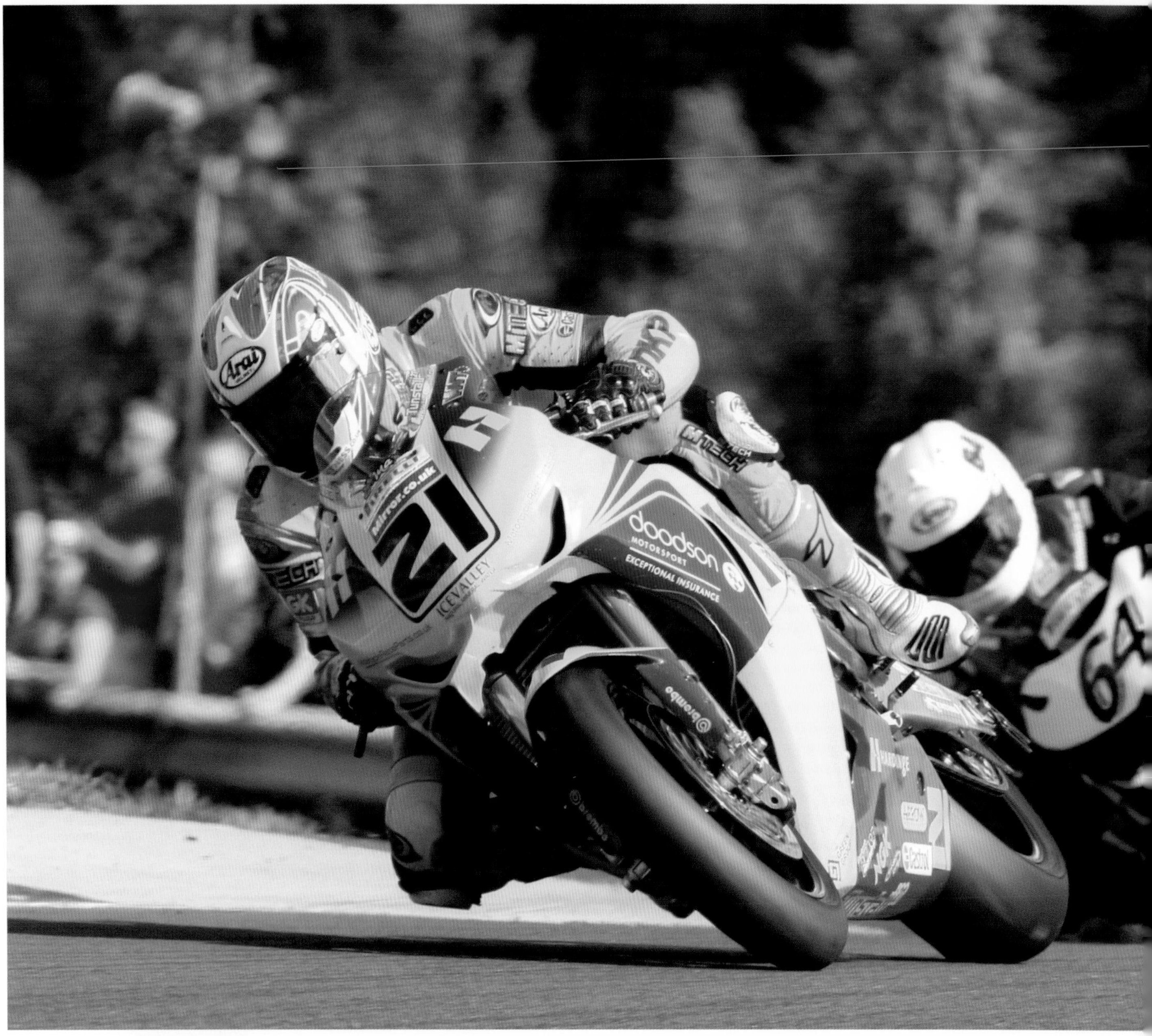

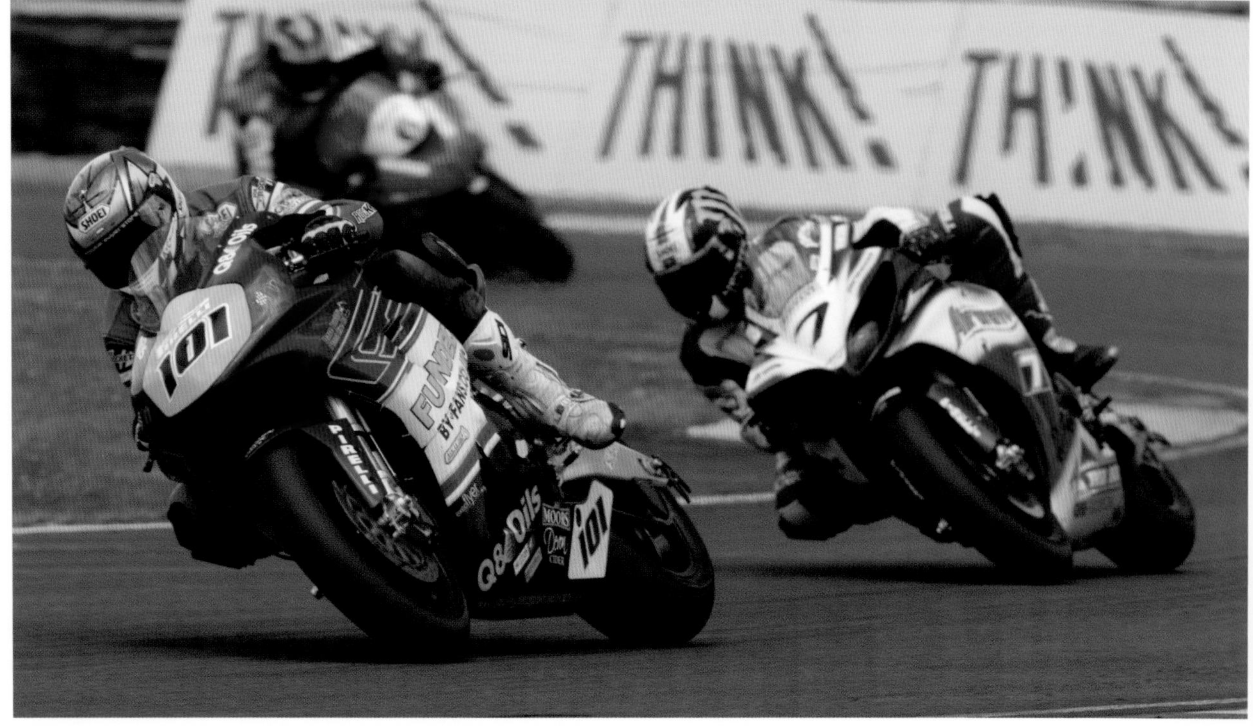

SHOEI
ROCK OIL
Arai
14

18
SHOEI

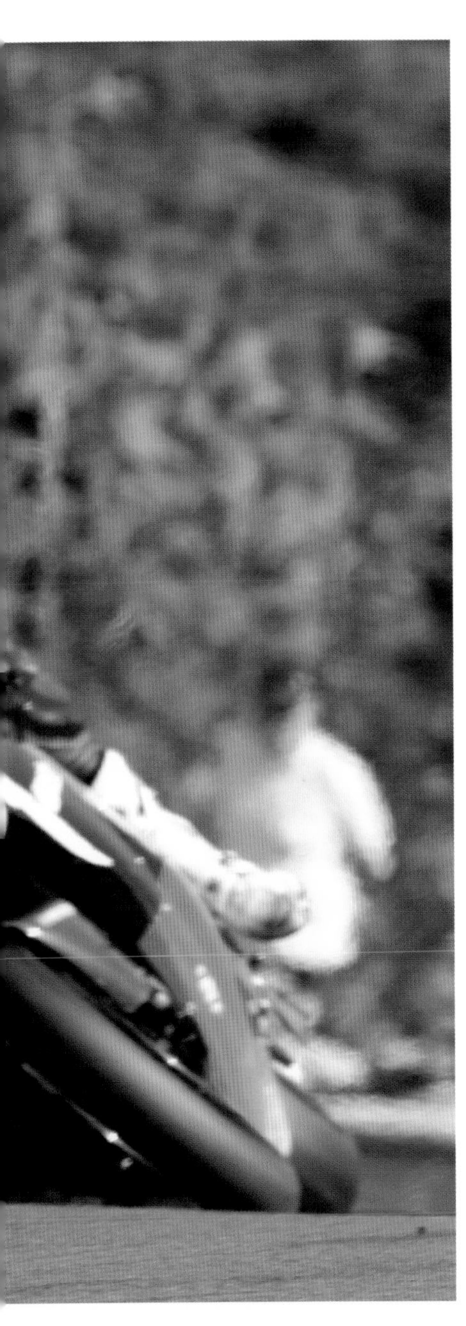

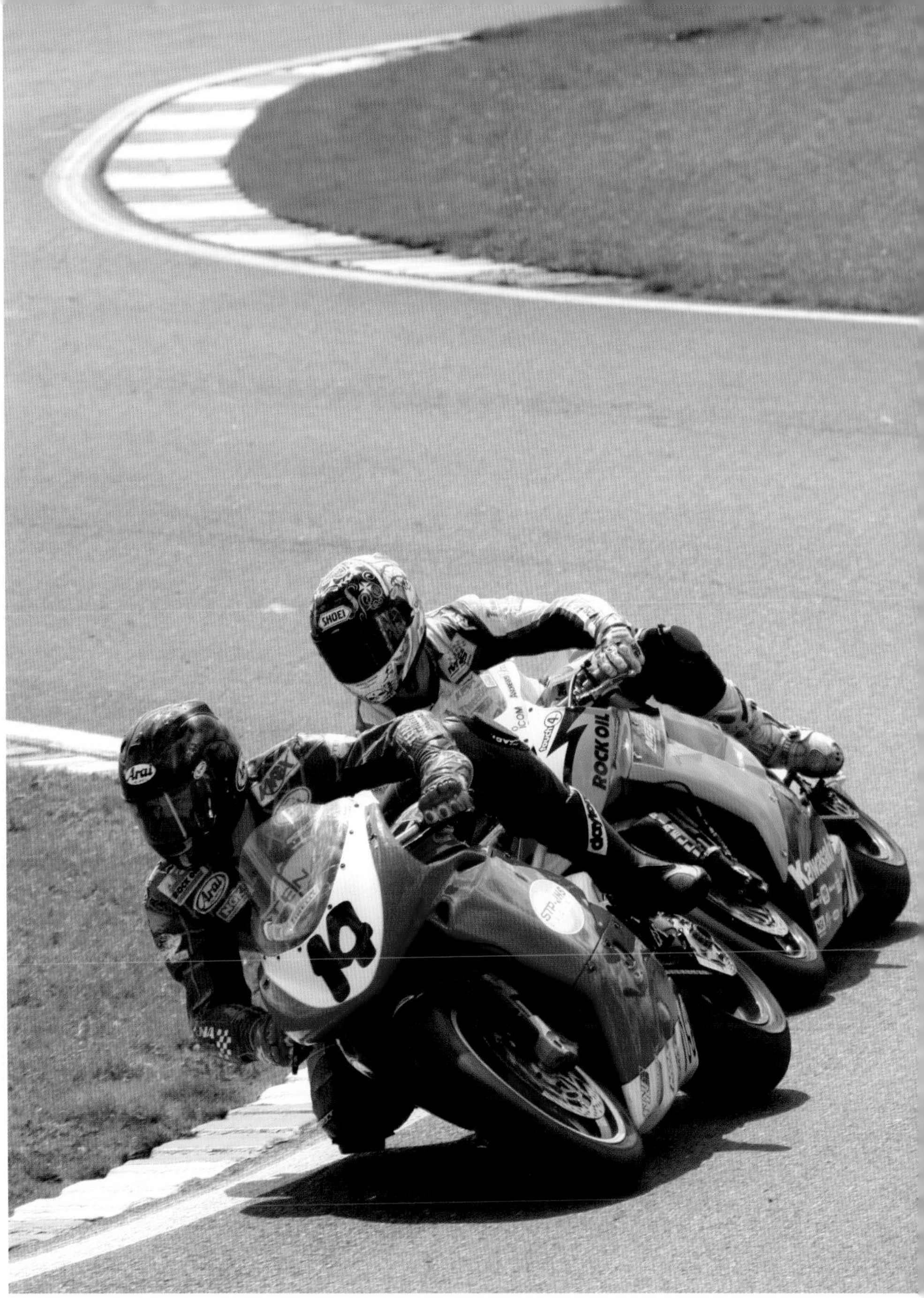

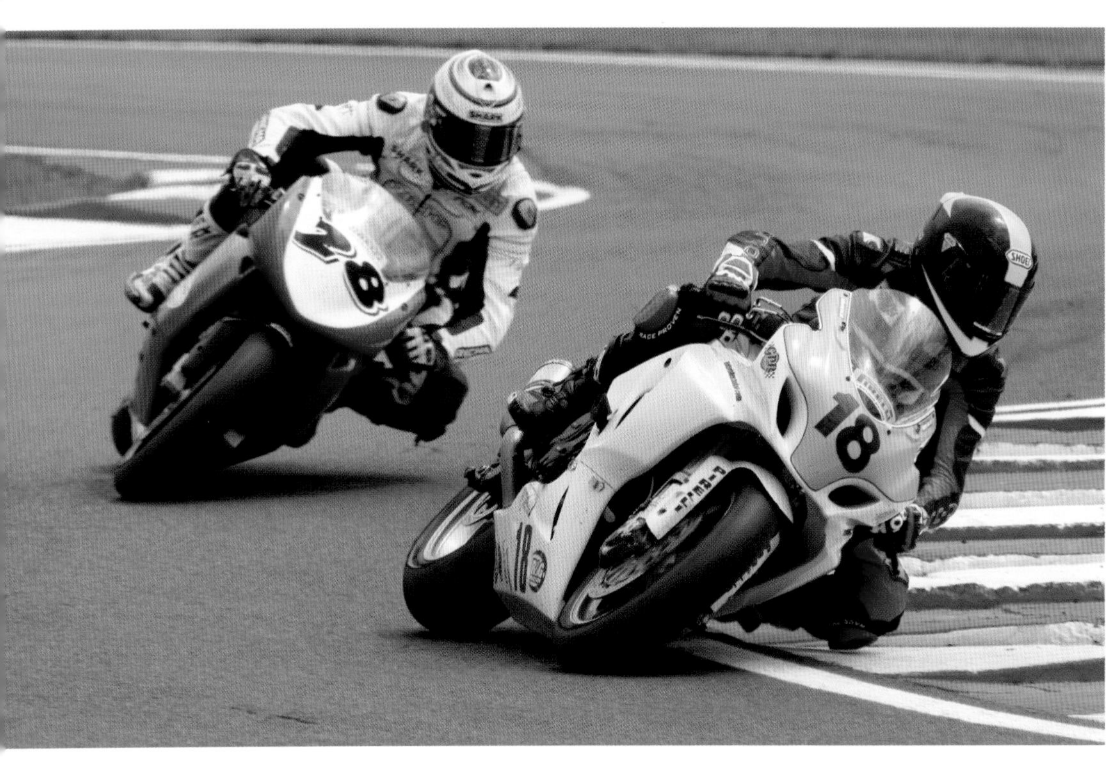

60
46

118

101

IRELLI
64
68
21
28

Relentless
Relentless
21
Riders
40
SHOEI

21
76
Arai
111
megabikes
Arai
64

Fuchs-Silkolene British Supersport Championship

PLATER DOES IT AT LAST!

Thirteen years after entering the class for the first time, Lincolnshire's Steve Plater finally claimed the British Supersport Championship and after suffering a slight lull mid-season, he bounced back in the style of a true champion. Lowly finishes at Knockhill and Mallory allowed season-long rival Billy McConnell to close to within a handful of points but five rostrums in the last five rounds, including wins at both Croft and Oulton saw the title deservedly go the way of the HM Plant Honda rider. The success also went some way to easing the pain of the 1999 season when he finished level on points with Suzuki's John Crawford only to lose the title on countback.

Australian ace McConnell, back in the class after a year in Superbikes, never let up in his quest for title success on the MAP Raceways Yamaha and three wins put him right on the back wheel of Plater as the series headed in to its final third of the season. However, a DNF at Snetterton in June ultimately proved costly and, after clashing fairings with Plater at Silverstone's penultimate round, he came in to the final race 11 points adrift of his arch rival. A soft tyre choice backfired towards the end of the race and he ended up 19th, not at all what the 22-year-old deserved.

Best of the rest was undoubtedly James Westmoreland on his privately-run Triumph and had it not been for a sluggish start to the year, the Hull youngster would almost certainly have made it a three-way fight for the championship. Clearly the most in-form rider in the second half of the season, 'Westy' took dominant wins at both Brands Hatch and Silverstone whilst he also took four more podiums.

Ben Wilson (Gearlink Kawasaki) got the green meanies back on the Supersport map with victory at Knockhill, also scoring a number of podiums during the year, whilst Daniel Cooper (Centurion Honda) and Chris Martin on the second Gearlink Kawasaki were also race winners. Double TT winner Ian Hutchinson was another to impress and despite only joining the series at the fifth round he ended the season in sixth place overall.

In the Supersport Cup, Sam Lowes wrapped up the title at the final round with Dean Hipwell and Robbie Brown completing the top three.

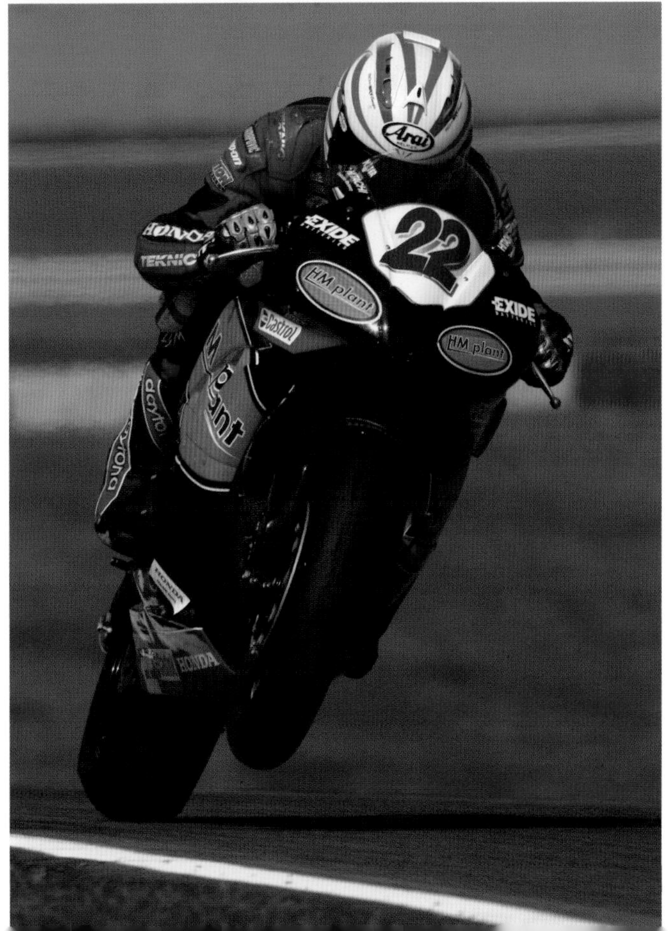

Championship Positions

1	Steve PLATER (Honda)	215
2	Billy MCCONNELL (Yamaha)	179
3	James WESTMORELAND (Honda)	171
4	Ben WILSON (Kawasaki)	137
5	Daniel COOPER (Honda)	104
6	Ian HUTCHINSON (Honda)	78

7
6
ROCK OIL
IFS
PRIDGETT'S

14
48
48

20
CLOWES
95
YAMAHA
70
CLOWES

96
48
A.S. TAYLOR
INTERNATIONAL

22
HONDA
EXIDE
YAMAHA

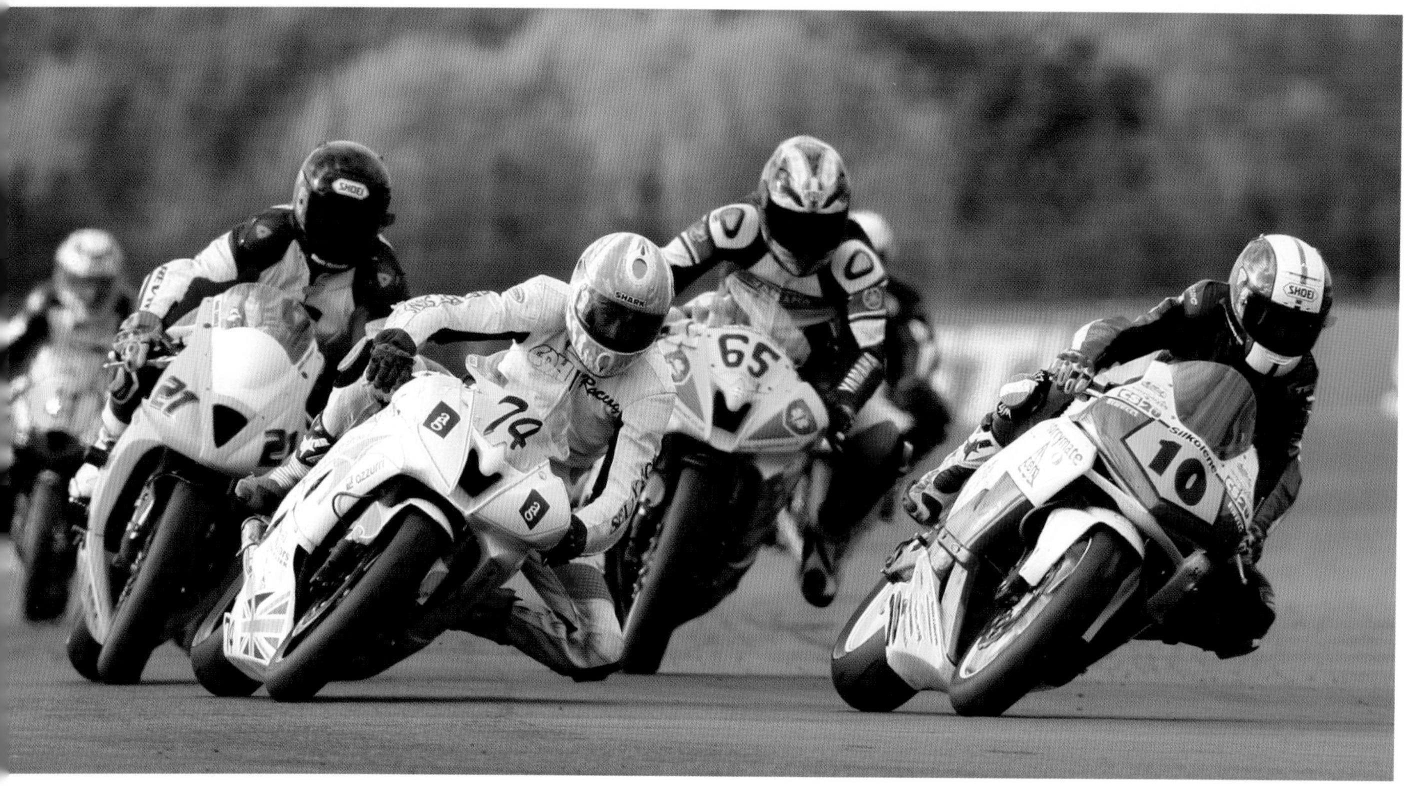

Metzeler National Superstock 1000 Championship

SEELEY DOMINATES...

The 1000cc Superstock series was all about one man and that was Northern Ireland's Alastair Seeley. The 'Wee Wizard' from Carrickfergus dominated the championship on the Relentless by TAS Suzuki winning all nine of the first nine rounds and that dominance allowed him to wrap up the title with three rounds remaining, an incredible season for the 29-year-old.

Seeley started the year on board the JMF/Millsport Racing Yamaha R1 and duly won the opening round at Brands Hatch but just days afterwards he split with the team and was left searching for a ride for the rest of the season. Philip Neill stepped in and initially offered Seeley a three-race deal but when he won the next two rounds at Oulton Park and Donington Park, as well as the Superstock race at the North West 200, the Moneymore businessman had little option other than to retain the services of Seeley for the rest of the year.

Whilst those nine wins may have looked like he had it easy, it was anything but, with last year's champion Steve Brogan and Padgetts Honda team-mate John McGuinness, as well as the Co-Ordit Yamaha of Richard Cooper making him work for each and every victory. Brogan amazingly ended the year without a win despite riding the wheels off his Honda but he was without doubt the hardest, and most entertaining, rider of the class, finishing the season in second overall and with seven podiums to his name.

McGuinness, meanwhile, proved a number of doubters (who had suggested his short circuit career was over), wrong, and he got his first British Championship win since 2001 with victory at Croft. This was undoubtedly the race of the year and was also the final round Seeley contested before heading to the premier Superbike class.

Adam Jenkinson won the penultimate round at Silverstone for the hard-working SMT Honda squad and clinched fourth place overall after Cooper crashed out of the final round whilst Luke Quigley took sixth place and was the only rider to score points in every race.

Championship Positions

1	Alastair SEELEY (Yamaha / Suzuki)	241
2	Steve BROGAN (Honda)	173
3	John MCGUINNESS (Honda)	154
4	Adam JENKINSON (Honda)	139
5	Richard COOPER (Yamaha)	136
6	Luke QUIGLEY (Honda / Suzuki)	109

PIRELLI
PIRELLI
PADGETTS
118
88

103

11
2

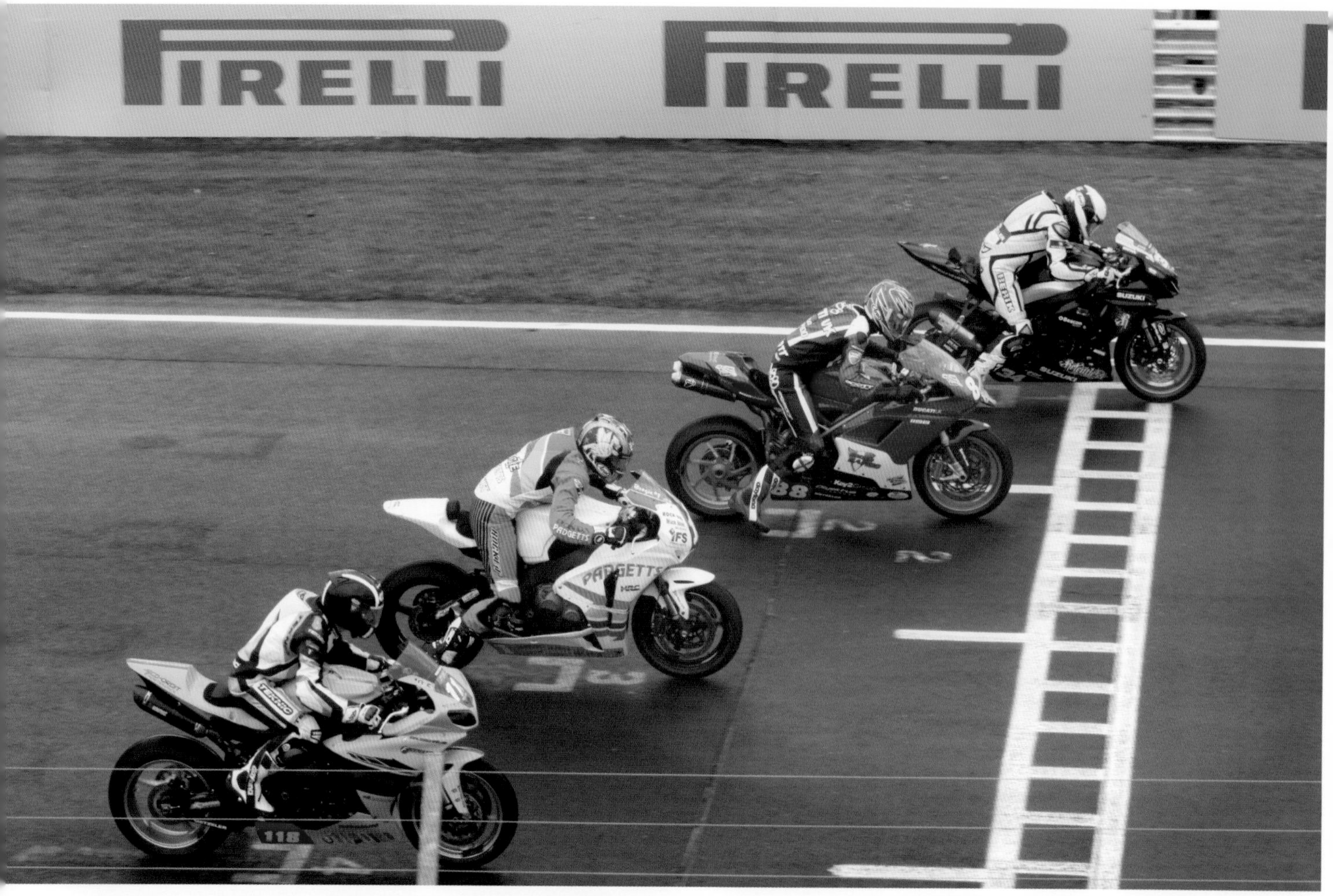

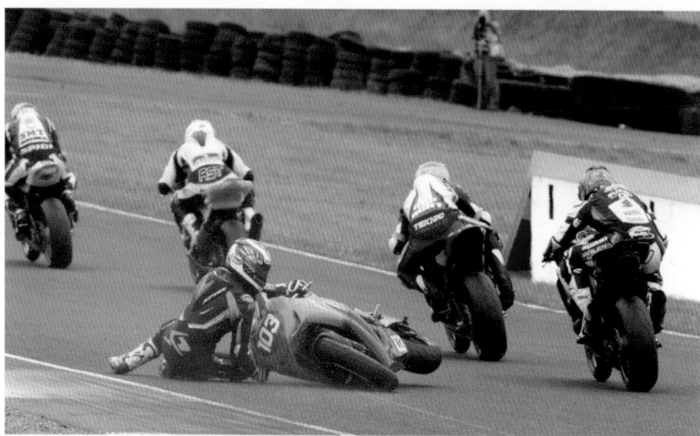

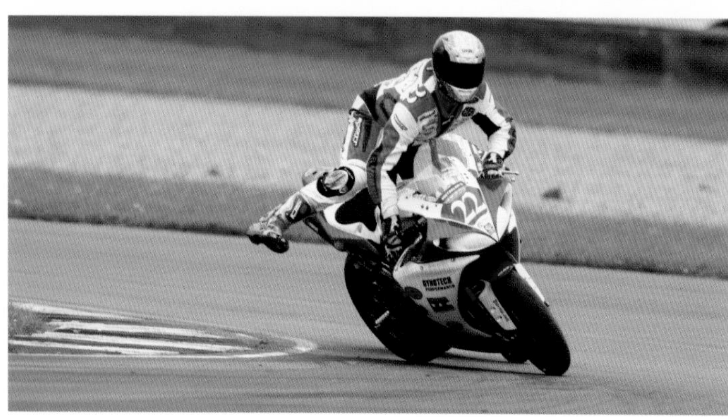

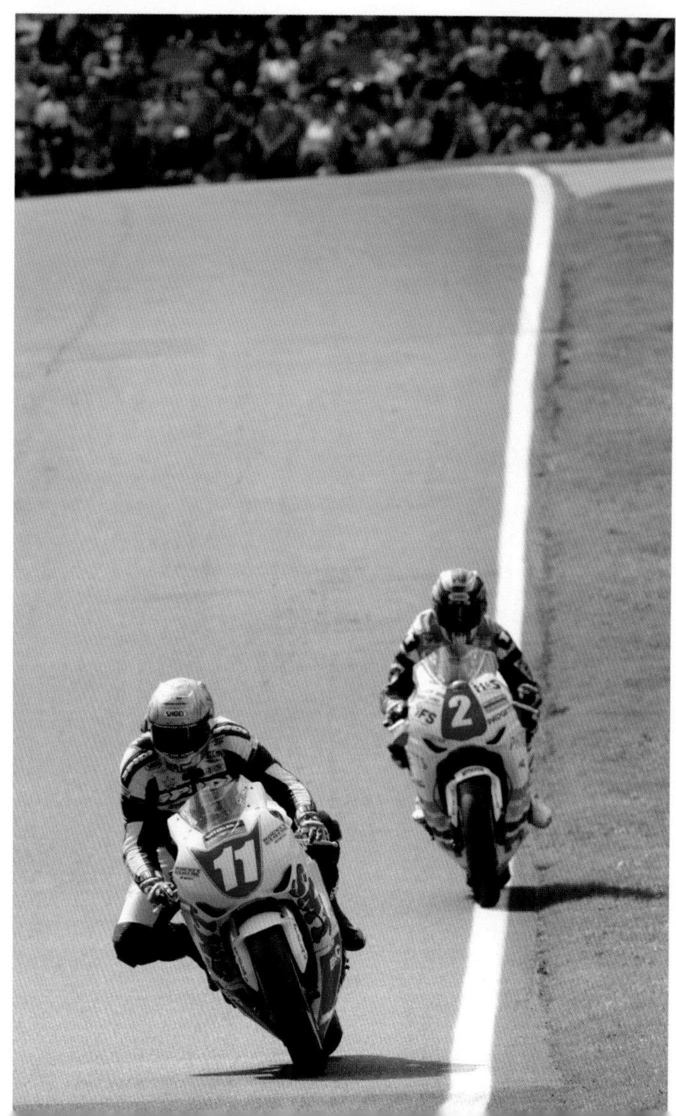

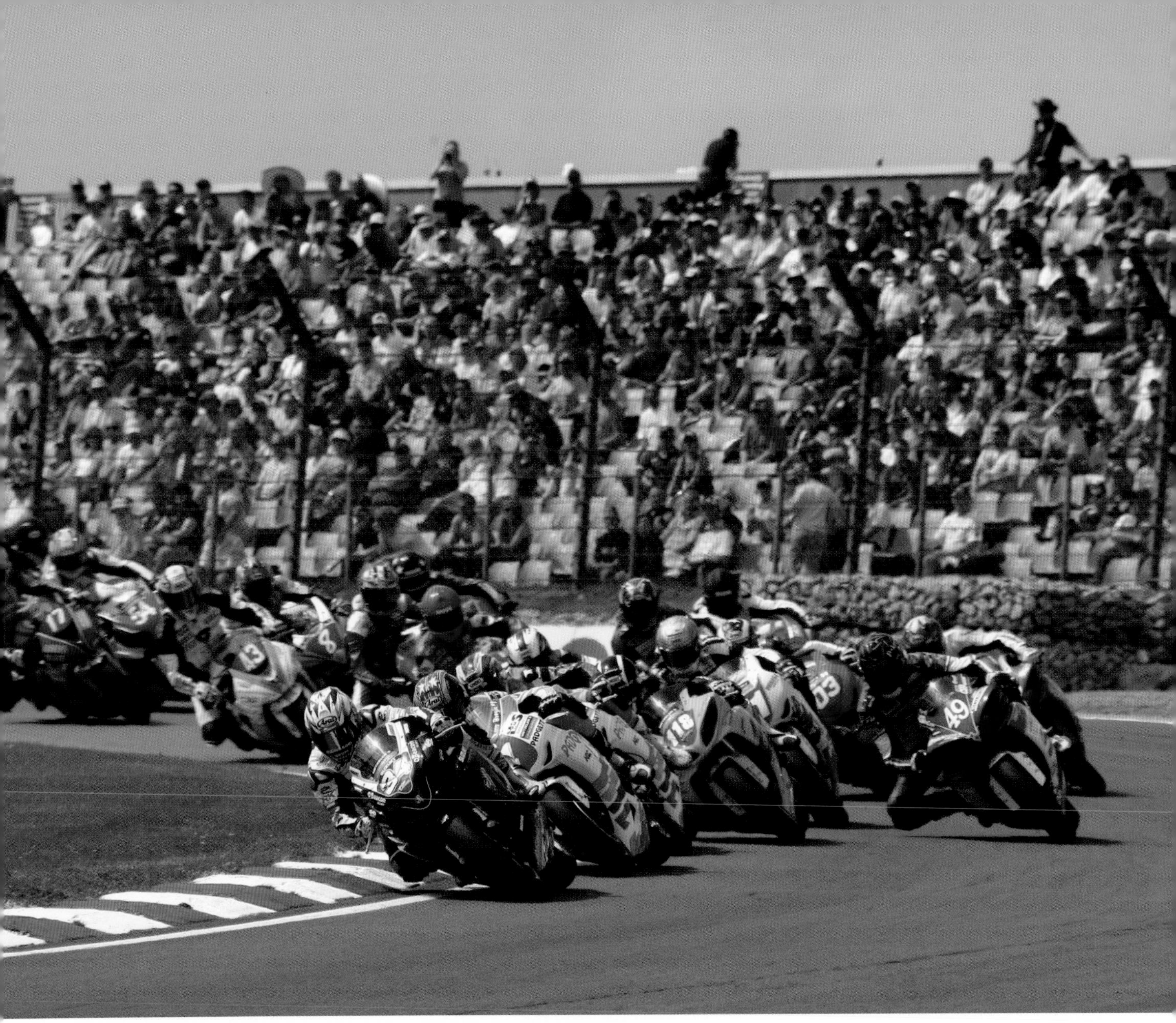
17
13
8
Arai
118
03
49

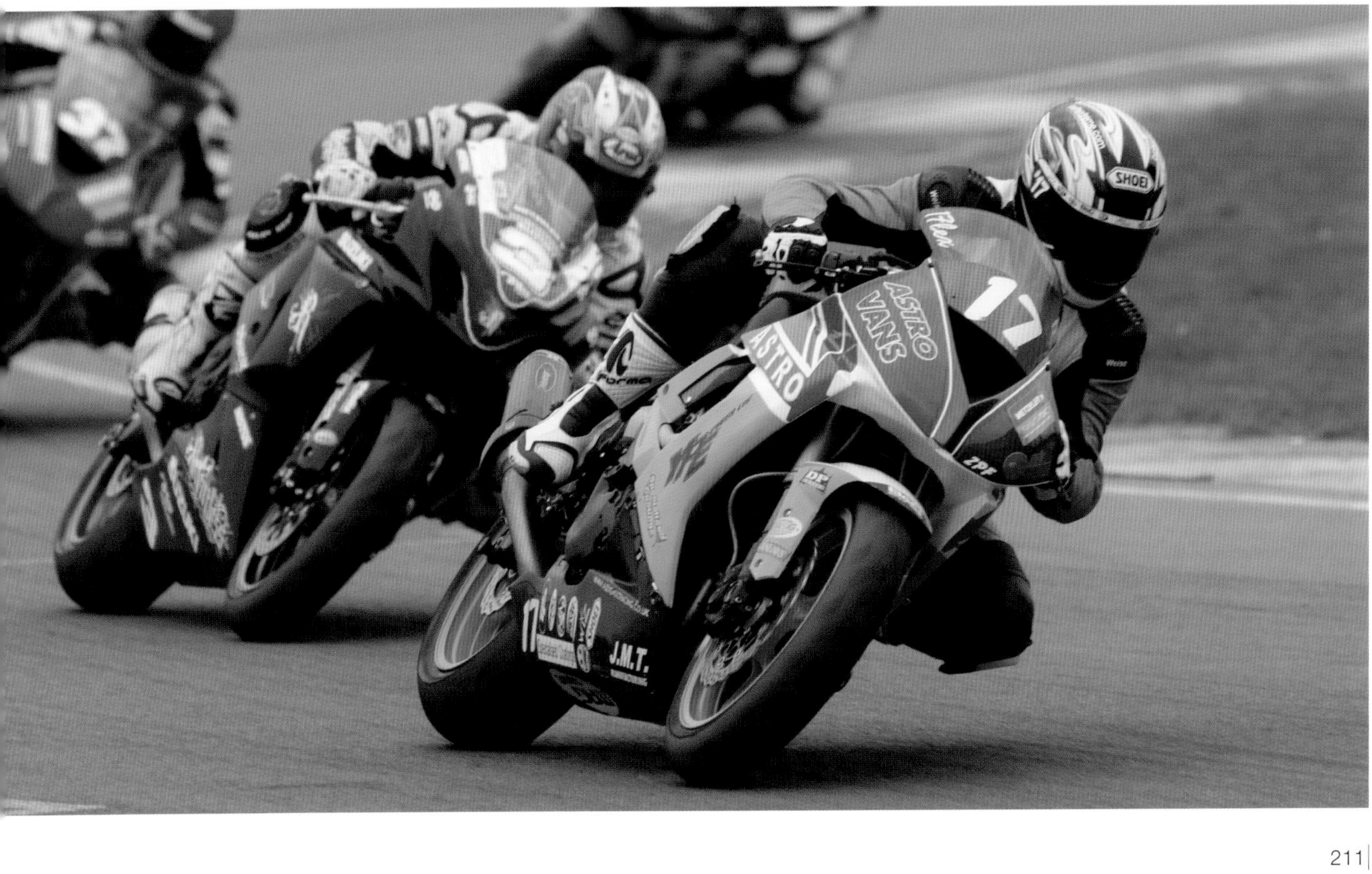
SHOEI
17
ASTRO
VANS
ASTRO
J.M.T.

Arai
ROCK OIL
IFS
HRC
HiS
PADGETTS
PADGETTS
HONDA

Arai
Beacon
SUZUKI
SUZUKI
Beacon
MOTUL

black
YAMAHA
ROCKET
SPIDI

34
SUZUKI
Arai
2
PADGETTS
118
103
13
37
49
17

Arai
10

SHOEI
4

103
90
49
118
9

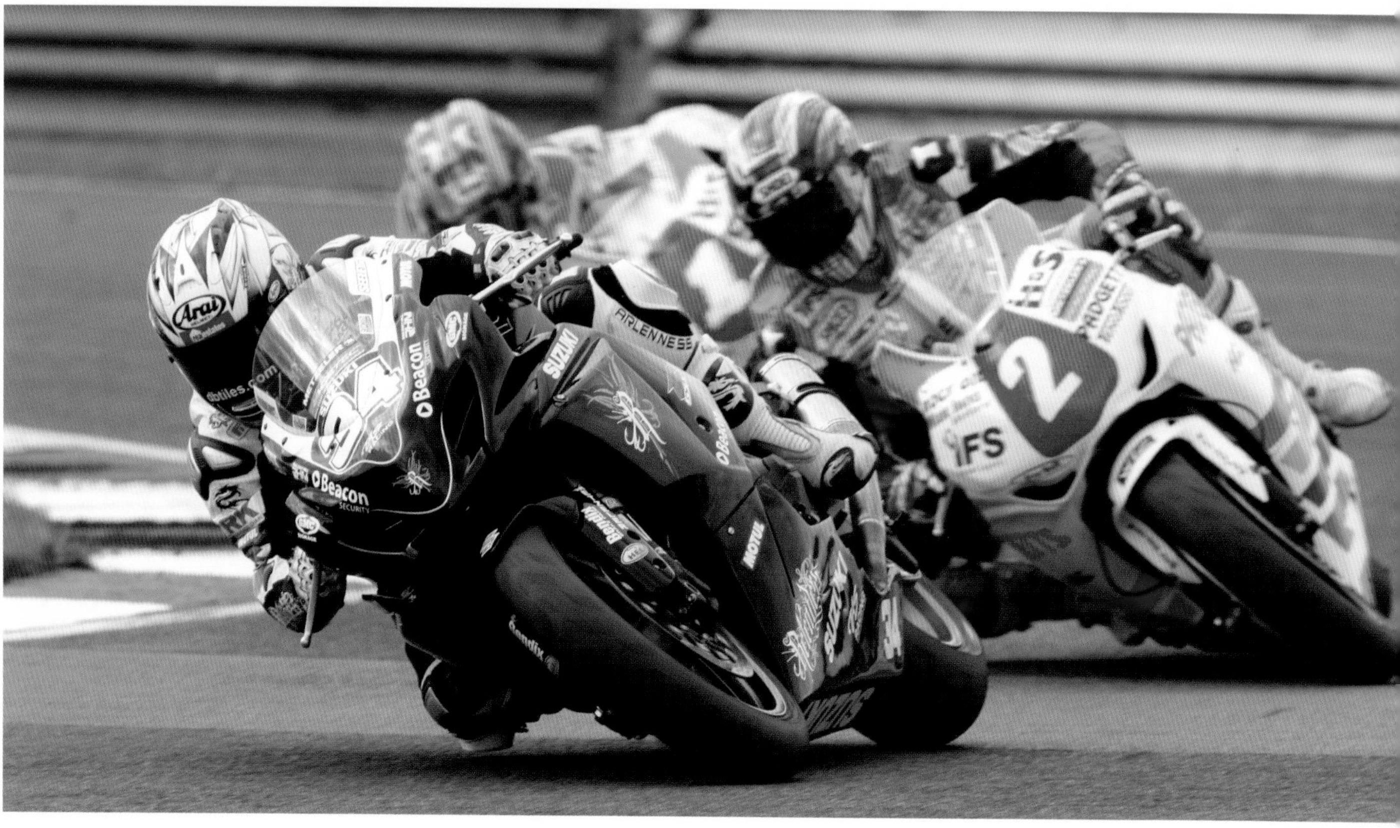

51
88

88
43

Arai
SUZUKI
3

Metzeler National Superstock 600 Championship

ACADEMICAL FOR HAMILTON

Eighteen-year-old Jamie Hamilton followed in the footsteps of his fellow Ulsterman Lee Johnston, and strung together the most consistent season of anyone in the 600cc Superstock series, taking the title at the penultimate round.

The Gearlink Kawasaki rider missed the Brands opener and only took two points from the following Oulton round where he had to qualify via the 'Shoot-Out' race. He then embarked on a superb run of seven podiums from eight races, including two race wins, to forge clear of the chasing pack and follow in the footsteps of Tom Sykes, Craig Jones, Tommy Hill and co, all of whom emerged from the 'junior' series.

The chasing pack was, as always, considerable and the championship was once again the most fiercely fought of them all but it was Luke Mossey who proved to be the best of the rest in second overall. Like Hamilton, the Sabre Sport rider had a slow start to the year and although he took five wins, considerably more than any other rider, four non-scores and a disqualification at Silverstone was ultimately what cost him the title.

Former 125cc British Champion Luke Jones took two wins during the course of the year and was a consistent front-runner throughout as was Manxman Daniel Kneen. The 21-year-old won at Oulton in May and recorded five podiums in the eight races he finished and had it not been for missing three races, the legacy of leg injuries sustained in a spill at the Isle of Man TT Races (where he also excelled), he too would have pushed Hamilton all the way.

Other winners included Patrick McDougall and Irishman John Simpson but it was Matt Bilton, the only rider to score points in every race, who ended the year in fifth overall just ahead of Jesse Trayler.

Championship Positions

1	Jamie HAMILTON (Kawasaki)	165
2	Luke MOSSEY (Yamaha)	143
3	Luke JONES (Yamaha)	143
4	Daniel KNEEN (Yamaha)	128
5	Matt BILTON (Yamaha)	114
6	Jesse TRAYLER (Kawasaki)	113

VISK
FOCUSED EVENTS

VISK

Relentless British 125GP Championship

Championship Positions

1	James LODGE (Honda)	182
2	Rob GUIVER (Honda)	170
3	Martin GLOSSOP (Honda)	155
4	Brian CLARK (Honda)	138
5	Paul JORDAN (Honda)	104
6	Timmy HASTINGS (Honda)	103

LODGE COMES OUT ON TOP...

Once again, the 125cc series was one of the closest championships during 2009 and just like 2008, it went down to the final round as James Lodge, Rob Guiver and Martin Glossop all went to Oulton Park in with a shout of title success.

Six rostrums in the first eight races, including a debut win at Knockhill, had seen Lodge surge clear but a DNF at Cadwell and sixth at Croft meant it was a nervy end to the year for the Holmfirth rider. The title was his until the very last lap at Silverstone when he got pushed back to third but he made sure at Oulton with a solid seventh place, shepherded home by KRP team-mates Paul Jordan and Tom Hayward.

Guiver, the elder statesman at 24, made his return to the class after a three-year absence and he showed he'd lost none of his flair with victories at Mallory, Brands and Silverstone but three lowly sevenths in the first four rounds played a significant part in his charge for glory coming up short and he had to settle for second in the title table.

It was Glossop who made all the running at the beginning of the year and three straight victories looked like he was going to run away with proceedings. Three non-scores blunted his charge and saw him drop off the pace slightly but he fought back well and another victory at Cadwell hauled him back into title contention until Lodge delivered the goods at Oulton.

Brian Clark made a successful return to the sport after a year's enforced retirement and two wins saw him rewarded with a fine fourth place overall ahead of Snetterton winner Jordan and Timmy Hastings, who at least had the satisfaction of taking the ACU Academy Cup for the second successive year. Connor Behan was the only other rider to taste the winners' champagne as he took the victory at Croft.

Deane Brown overcame a wretched start to the season to become a front runner in the second half of the season as did Adam Blacklock on the Repli-Cast Honda whilst Taylor Mackenzie, son of GP star and former multiple BSB Champion Niall, made significant strides forward over the course of the twelve rounds. Catherine Green also impressed ending the year in 14th overall after posting an impressive nine points scoring finishes.

13
2

77
19
FedEx

53
11
46
SHARK
SHOEI

SHOEI
6
TIVA
Silkolene

SHOEI
Arai
29
TIVA
KRP

VISK VISK VISK VISK
PIRELLI PIRELLI
VISK

Relentless

Focused Events KTM RC8 Super Cup Championship

WOODY AT IT AGAIN...

For 2009, the KTM series saw the Austrian manufacturer showcase its RC8 Superbike machine but it was still the same end result with former British Superbike Championship rider David Wood again ending the year as champion.

The season got off to the worst possible start for 'Woody' when he was disqualified from the opening two races and a DNF in the third race left him with an awful lot of catching up to do. However, seven wins from the final ten races elevated him to the top of the table and he was able to clinch the series with a round to spare.

It was Kelvin Reilly who set the early season pace taking four of the first five race victories but a series of results in the bottom half of the top ten saw him fall away and that allowed Finnish rider Pauli Pekkanen to secure second overall. Pekkanen, who spent 2008 contesting the World Supersport series, ended the year with two wins and nine podiums to his name to finish 14 points clear of Reilly.

Wood's former British Superbike sparring partner Francis Williamson had another consistent year finishing fourth overall just ahead of James Edmeades, Ed Smith and 1996 British Supersport Champion Dave Heal, all of whom featured heavily during an entertaining year.

The only other winner in the 14-race series was Sam Bishop who was also able to take the Under-25 Championship after a year-long battle with Jonathan Railton.

Championship Positions

1	David WOOD	243
2	Pauli PEKKANEN	212
3	Kelvin REILLY	198
4	Francis WILLIAMSON	177
5	James EDMEADES	158
6	Ed SMITH	139

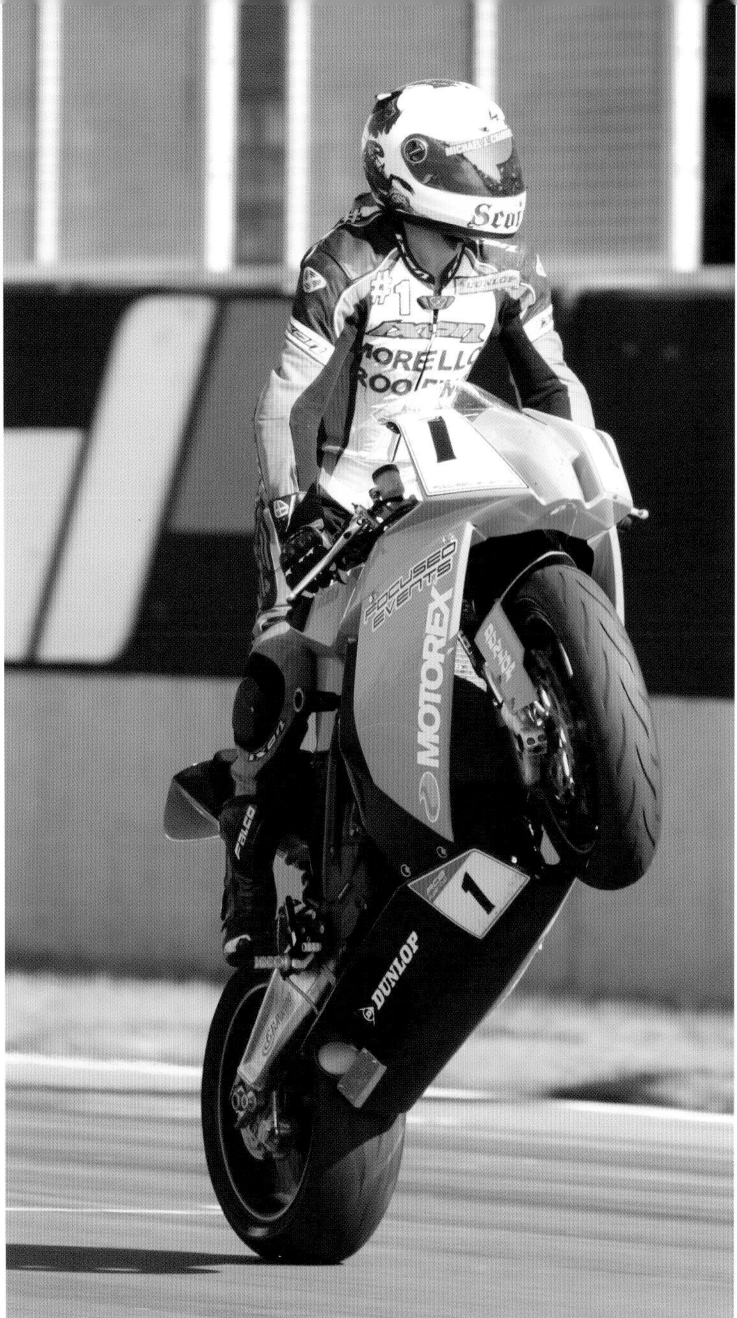

mce mce mce
Santander

brands

eni

Behind the scenes

PIRELLI

mce insurance
Canon

mce
BIG ED
mce insurance

METZELER
RACETEC

WORX
SUZUKI
CRESCENT

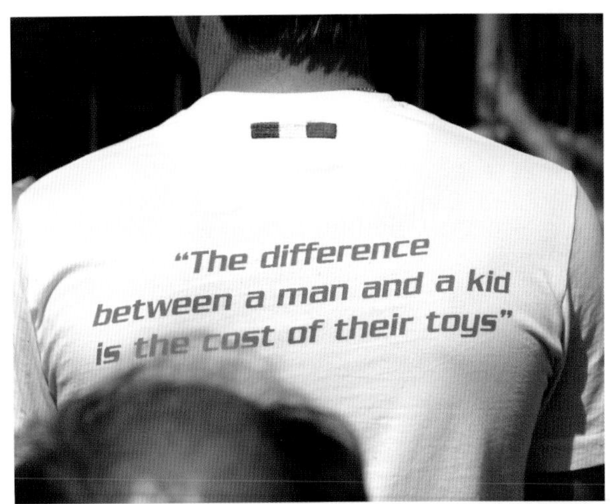
"The difference
between a man and a kid
is the cost of their toys"

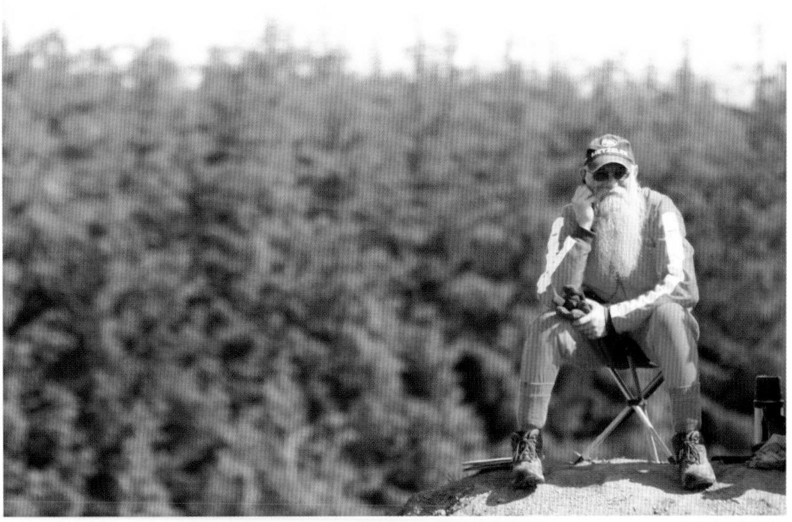

FAT
BIKERS
BOUNCE
BETTER

FAN
CLUB
SYLVAIN
GUINTOLI
ALLEZ
SYLVAIN
50

The Power of Dreams

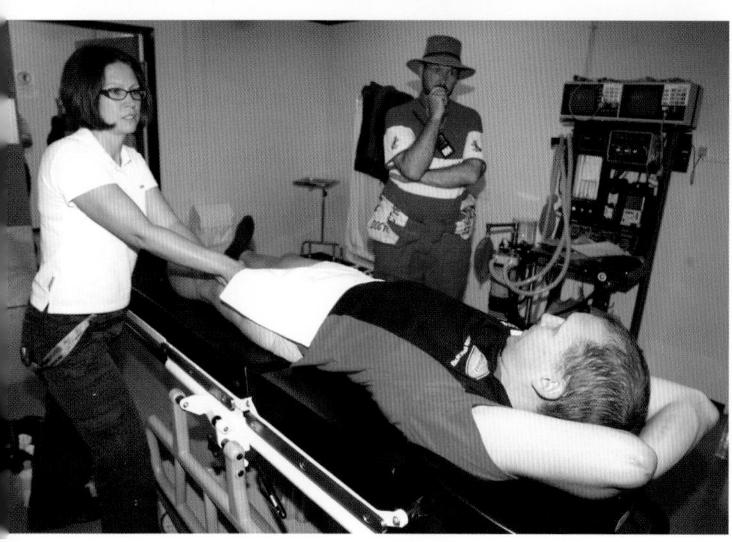

WORX
SUZUKI
CRESCENT
HONDA

SWAN
ROLL FOR POLE
COMBI PACK

Bavaria
RC8
BSB
Bavaria

Super
WILDCATS
MAXX
maxxis.c
s.co.uk
SHARK
METZELER
TEKNIC
SPONSOR!!!
SPONSOR!!!
Al-MURAD
TILES
HB
Motorcycles
RACE TEAM

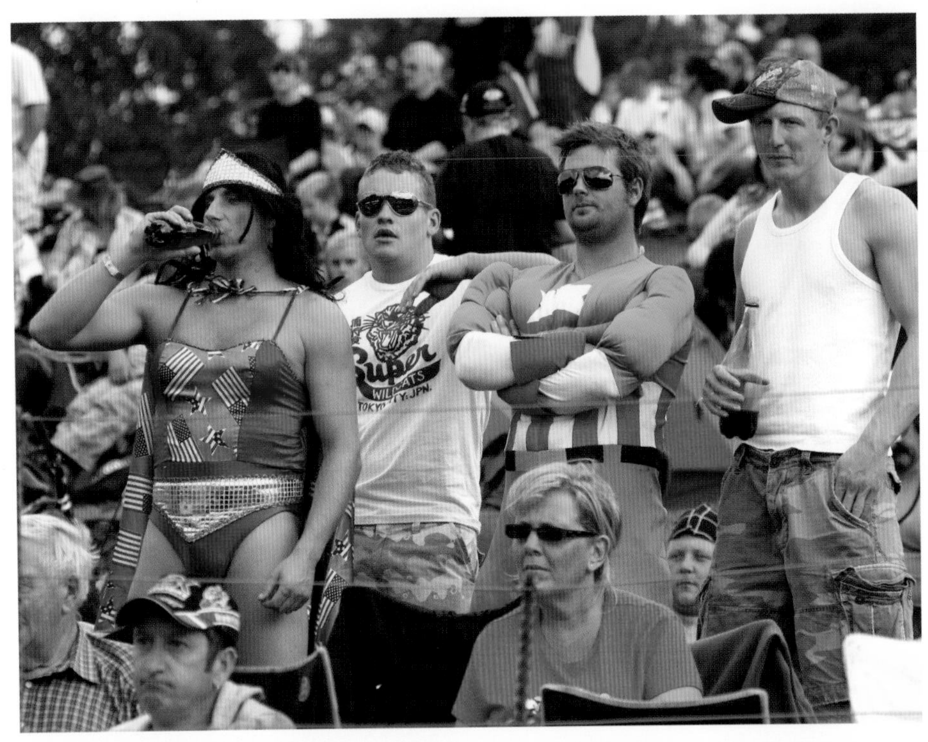

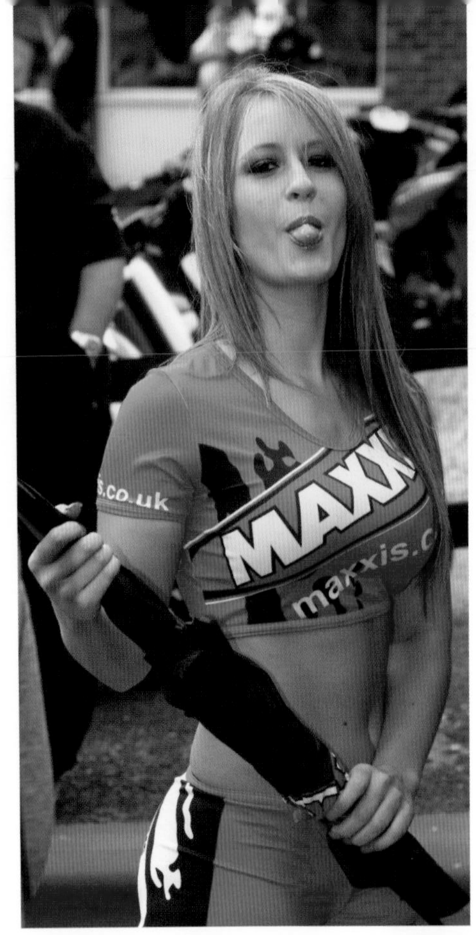

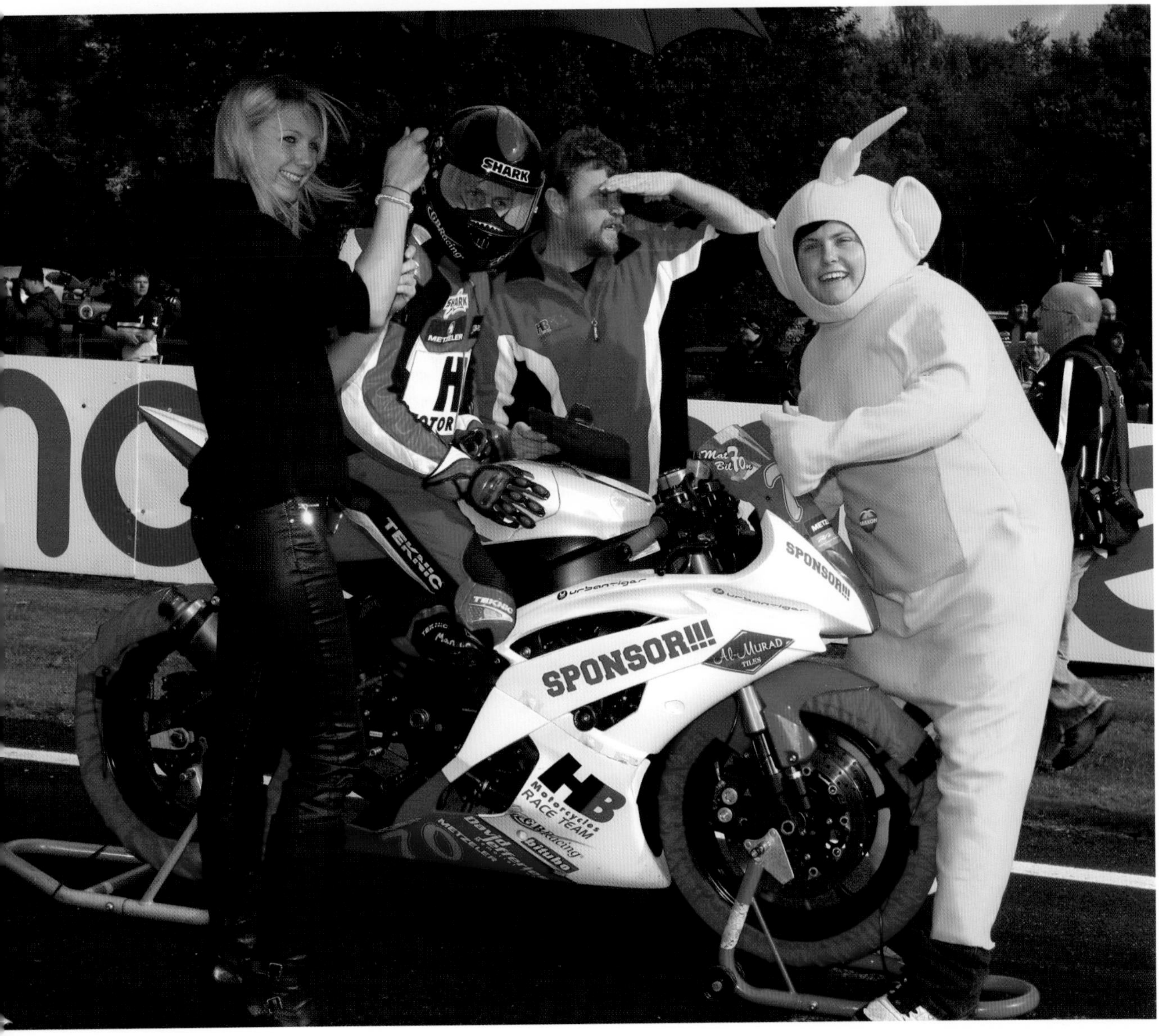

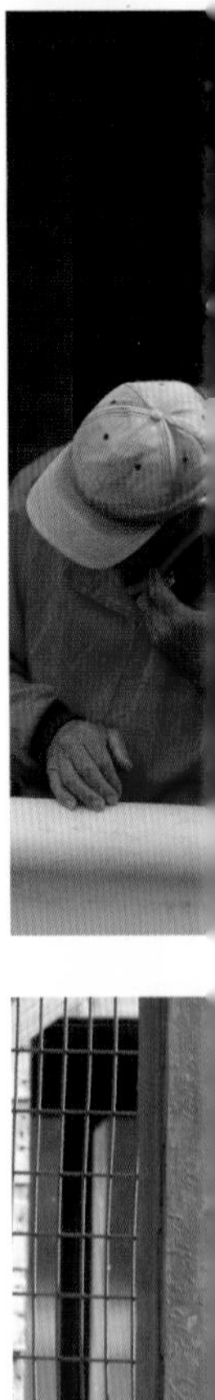

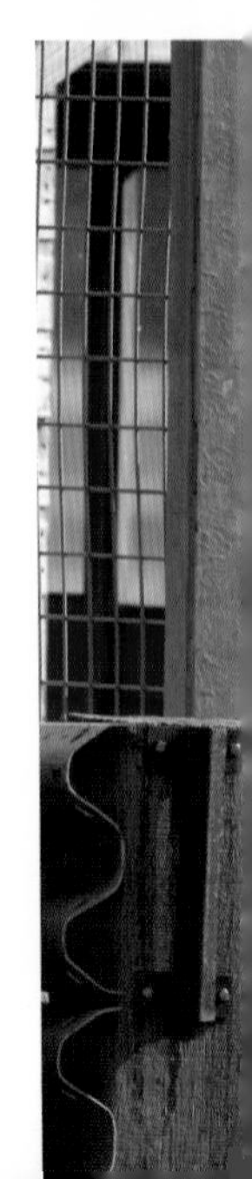

2009 MCE Insurance British Superbike Championship

Points after final round

Name	Total	Round 01 Brands Hatch Indy 13 April 2009		Round 02 Oulton Park 4 May 2009		Round 03 Donington Park 25 May 2009		Round 04 Thruxton 31 May 2009		Round 05 Snetterton 21 June 2009		Round 06 Knockhill 5 July 2009		Round 07 Mallory Park 19 July 2009		Round 08 Brands Hatch GP 9 August 2009			Round 09 Cadwell Park 31 August 2009		Round 10 Croft 13 September 2009		Round 11 Silverstone 27 September 2009		Round 12 Oulton Park 11 October 2009		
Name	Total	R1	R2	R3	R4	R5	R6	R7	R8	R9	R10	R11	R12	R13	R14	R15	R16	R17	R18	R19	R20	R21	R22	R23	R24	R25	R26
Leon CAMIER *(Yamaha)*	549.5	13	25	25	25	25	4	25	25	25	25	25	25	20	12.5	25	25	25	25		10	25	25	20	20	25	25
James ELLISON *(Yamaha)*	413	11	9	11	13	20	25	20	20	13	20	11	16	25	10	10	11	16	16	25	20	13	20	25	13	16	4
Stuart EASTON *(Honda)*	374	16	13	13		16	20	16	13	20	13	20	13			16	16	13	20	20	25	20	13	13	25	20	
Josh BROOKES *(Honda)*	188			6				9	16	16	16	16	20								16	16	16	16		9	16
Ian LOWRY *(Suzuki)*	170	3		9	10	8	10		8	11	9	10		8		4	4	7	13		11	9	8	7	8		13
Simon ANDREWS *(Kawasaki)*	163.5	9	5		8		13	13	10	6	5	13	10		0.5				11	16		11	7	9	10	7	
Julien DA COSTA *(Kawasaki)*	163	5	6	4		9	5	6	6	7	10		8	11	3	6	5		10	13	7	7	6	10	9		10
Sylvain GUINTOLI *(Suzuki)*	147	25	20	16	16														8	9		3	9	8	11	11	11
Chris WALKER *(Yamaha)*	141	2	8	5	7	11	16			10		9	11		8	7		4	5	10		5		5	7	2	9
John LAVERTY *(Kawasaki)*	130.5	4	3			7	7	8	5	3	11				6.5	9	3	11	7	11	3	6	10		6	10	
Tommy HILL *(Honda)*	127														4	11	13	9			9	10	11	11	16	13	20
Glen RICHARDS *(Honda)*	125	20	11	10	11	13	11	10	9		8												3		5	6	8
Gary MASON *(Honda)*	125	10	7	7	9	4	9	7	4		2		6	10		3	2	1	6	7	8	8	2		3	4	6
Karl HARRIS *(Honda)*	124.5		10	20	20	10		5	7	8	7				4.5	8	10	2	1	8	2			2			
Graeme GOWLAND *(Yamaha)*	101.5	7	1			6	6	4	3	5	4	8	9	16	1.5		7	3			6	4	5			1	5
Michael RUTTER *(Ducati)*	78							11	11	9		5		13	5	5		6						1	4	8	
Broc PARKES *(Kawasaki)*	60															20	20	20									
Tommy BRIDEWELL *(Suzuki)*	56									1		7	7	5					3	6	4	2	4	4	1	5	7
Jason O'HALLORAN *(Honda)*	54	8	4	8	6	5		3		4	6	6	4														
Karl MUGGERIDGE *(Honda)*	44															13	9	10	9	3							
Tristan PALMER *(Kawasaki)*	35	6	2	1			8						5	6	2	1				4							
Peter HICKMAN *(Yamaha)*	35				1		2		1		1	4	2	4	1				2	5	5	1	1	3	2		
Steve BROGAN *(Honda)*	27.5													9	3.5	2	8	5									
Jon KIRKHAM *(Yamaha)*	21	1		3	5	3	3			2	3									1							
Steve PLATER *(Honda)*	16		16																								
David JOHNSON *(Yamaha)*	14.5				2								3	7	2.5												
Sheridan MORAIS *(Kawasaki)*	14																6	8									
Atsushi WATANABE *(Suzuki)*	14			2	4			2				2	1	2			1										
Ryuichi KIYONARI *(Honda)*	13																				13						
Tom TUNSTALL *(Honda)*	12					2		1				3		3													3
Alastair SEELEY *(Suzuki)*	9																							6		3	
Martin JESSOPP *(Honda)*	7				3	1	1		2																		
Richard COOPER *(Yamaha)*	5.5														5.5												
Howie MAINWARING *(Yamaha)*	5																			2	1						2
John McGUINNESS *(Honda)*	4																		4								
Aaron ZANOTTI *(Honda)*	1											1															
Kenny GILBERTSON *(Kawasaki)*	1													1													
Dan LINFOOT *(Yamaha)*	1																										1

2009 Mirror.co.uk Cup

Points after final round

Name	Total	R1	R2	R3	R4	R5	R6	R7	R8	R9	R10	R11	R12	R13	R14	R15	R16	R17	R18	R19	R20	R21	R22	R23	R24	R25	R26
Gary MASON *(Honda)*	535.5	25	25	25	25	25	25	25	25		25		20	25	5.5	25	25	25	25	25	25	25	20		25	20	20
Peter HICKMAN *(Yamaha)*	381	16	16	16	16	13	20	16	16	20	20	20	16	16	10		13	13	16	16	20	16	16	20	20		
Martin JESSOPP *(Honda)*	326	20	20	20	20	16	16	13	20					10	5	20	20	20	13	11	11	11	10	13	11	13	13
Tom TUNSTALL *(Honda)*	315.5			13	13	20	13	20	13		16	16	13	13	6.5	16	16	16		13	13	13	11	16	13	16	16
Tommy BRIDEWELL *(Suzuki)*	300									25	13	25	25	20					20	20	16	20	25	25	16	25	25
Kenny GILBERTSON *(Kawasaki)*	85	10	13	11				8		13			11	11	8												
Alastair FAGAN *(Honda)*	74	13			11	9	10	10	11		10																
Matt BOND *(Suzuki)*	68					11	11	9	10	16	11																
Brian McCORMACK *(Kawasaki)*	30	11		9		10																					
Richard COOPER *(Yamaha)*	25.5														12.5								13				
David HAIRE *(Kawasaki)*	23											13	10														
Malcolm ASHLEY *(Kawasaki)*	11							11																			
Dan STEWART *(Honda)*	10			10																							

2009 Manufacturers Championship

Points after final round

Name	Total	R1	R2	R3	R4	R5	R6	R7	R8	R9	R10	R11	R12	R13	R14	R15	R16	R17	R18	R19	R20	R21	R22	R23	R24	R25	R26
Yamaha	615.5	13	25	25	25	25	25	25	25	25	25	25	25	25	12.5	25	25	25	25	25	20	25	25	25	20	25	25
Honda	465	20	16	20	20	16	20	16	16	20	16	20	20	13	5	16	16	13	20	20	25	20	16	16	25	20	20
Suzuki	293	25	20	16	16	8	10	11	11	11	9	10	7	8	4	11	13	9	13	9	11	9	9	8	11	11	13
Kawasaki	285.5	9	6	4	8	9	13	13	10	7	11	13	10	11	6.5	20	20	20	11	16	7	11	10	10	10	10	10
Ducati	13																							1	4	8	

2009 Fuchs-Silkolene British Supersport Championship

Points after final round

Name	Total	R1	R2	R3	R4	R5	R6	R7	R8	R9	R10	R11	R12
Steve PLATER	215	20	5	25	20	25	5	9	16	20	25	20	25
Billy McCONNELL	179	25	6	16	25		13	13	20	25	20	16	
James WESTMORELAND	171	8	7	8	13	16	20		25	16	13	25	20
Ben WILSON	137		16	13	10	8	25	20	13		16		16
Daniel COOPER	104	4	25	6	2	20	16	8			10	8	5
Ian HUTCHINSON	78					9	10	16	11	8	11	13	
Dan LINFOOT	72	16		20	16					11	9		
Tom GRANT	65	5	10	10	5		9	5		6	4	11	
Hudson KENNAUGH	58	13		2	8	13	3					6	13
James WEBB	57	10		11	11	11			7	4			3
Jack KENNEDY	54			4	3		4	3	6	9	6	9	10
Lee JOHNSTON	52	11		7	7		11				5		11
Allan Jon VENTER	51			1		6	7		8	13	7		9
Sam LOWES	50	6		3		3	6	7	9	10			6
Craig FITZPATRICK	42	9	11			10	2		10				
Marty NUTT	40		9					1		7	8	7	8
Chris MARTIN	33						8	25					
Joe DICKINSON	33				6	5	1	6			1	10	4
Paul YOUNG	31	7			9	7			4	2			2
BJ TOAL	28							10	2	1	3	5	7
Dean HIPWELL	23	1	13			2		4	1			2	
Dennis HOBBS	20		20										
Lee JACKSON	20			5	1				3	5	2	3	1
Robbie BROWN	20		4		4	4			5	3			
Kev COGHLAN	17		8	9									
Brendan ROBERTS	11							11					
Ross WALTER	9	2	3									4	
Jimmy HILL	3	3											
Mark CRINGLE	2		2										
Chris NORTHOVER	2							2					
Nick MEDD	1		1										
David PATON	1					1							
Aaron WALKER	1											1	

2009 Metzeler National Superstock 1000 Championship

Points after final round

		Brands Hatch Indy 13 April 2009	Oulton Park 4 May 2009	Donington Park 25 May 2009	Thruxton 31 May 2009	Snetterton 21 June 2009	Knockhill - R1 5 July 2009	Knockhill - R2 5 July 2009	Brands Hatch GP 9 August 2009	Cadwell Park 31 August 2009	Croft 13 September 2009	Silverstone 27 September 2009	Oulton Park 11 October 2009
Name	Total	R1	R2	R3	R4	R5	R6	R7	R8	R9	R10	R11	R12
Alastair SEELEY	241	25	25	25	25	25	25	25	25	25	16		
Steve BROGAN	173	16	20	11	20	20	20	20	20		13		13
John McGUINNESS	154	11	16			13	16	11	16	20	25	20	6
Adam JENKINSON	139	10		13	16	11	3	4	11	16	10	25	20
Richard COOPER	136	20		16	9	16	11	16	13	10	9	16	
Luke QUIGLEY	109	9	11	9	8	9	13	13	9	4	5	10	9
Scott SMART	92	8	13	20		10				13	20	8	
Marshall NEILL	83		7	8	2	8	7	7		11	4	13	16
James HILLIER	71	13		10	13	7	5	9	7		2	5	
Conor CUMMINS	68	3	6	6		6	10	10	8	7	6	3	3
Sam WARREN	49			2	10				6	9		11	11
Howie MAINWARING	44		10	7	11		6		10				
Daniel HEGARTY	34				6					8	8	4	8
Alex GAULT	30			5		4	8	8	4	1			
Jimmy STORRAR	29	5				1	4	3		6	3	7	
Victor COX	25									5	7	6	7
Gavin HUNT	25		2	4	7		2	6	2			2	
Ian HUTCHINSON	25												25
Gary JOHNSON	24										11	9	4
BJ TOAL	18	7	8				1	2					
Bob GRANT	14						9	5					
Matt LAYT	12	4		1	4	2		1					
Christian IDDON	10												10
Cameron DONALD	9		9										
Jonathan HOWARTH	9				3					3	1	1	1
Steven NEATE	8		3		5								
Daniel BRILL	6	6											
Sam OWENS	6				1	5							
Dan STEWART	5		5										
Barry BURRELL	5								5				
Tristan PALMER	5												5
Ian MACKMAN	4		4										
Mike EDWARDS	3			3									
Andy WEYMOUTH	3					3							
John CROCKFORD	3								3				
James HURRELL	2	2											
Billy MELLOR	2									2			
Joe BURNS	2												2
Christian ELKIN	1	1											
Grant MALLOY	1		1										
David HAIRE	1								1				

2009 Metzeler National Superstock 600 Championship

Points after final round

		Brands Hatch Indy 13 April 2009	Oulton Park 4 May 2009	Donington Park 25 May 2009	Thruxton 31 May 2009	Snetterton 21 June 2009	Knockhill - R1 5 July 2009	Knockhill - R2 5 July 2009	Brands Hatch GP 9 August 2009	Cadwell Park 31 August 2009	Croft 13 September 2009	Silverstone 27 September 2009	Oulton Park 11 October 2009
Name	Total	R1	R2	R3	R4	R5	R6	R7	R8	R9	R10	R11	R12
Jamie HAMILTON	165		2	25	20	20	20	25	13	20	20		
Luke MOSSEY	143		9	9	25		25		25		25		25
Luke JONES	143	20		5	16	25	16		10	13	7	25	6
Daniel KNEEN	128		25	16	11				20	6	10	20	20
Matt BILTON	114	6	8	13	7	7	13	20	3	9	6	13	9
Jesse TRAYLER	113	9	10	20	8	4		16	16	7	11	2	10
Patrick McDOUGALL	106	25	13	6	10	2	10	11		5		11	13
Luke STAPLEFORD	86	11	20					13	9	8	16	9	
Leon HUNT	71			11			7	7	8	10	5	7	16
Nikki COATES	62				9	13			11		13	16	
Joe BURNS	53	16	11	10	6	10							
Michael BOOTH	44	8	4	4	13		5	10					
Daniel FREAR	35	4	7			8				16			
Jonathan DICKSON	35	7	3		1			1		11	8		4
Jack GROVES	34			3	3		8	8		1	3	8	
John SIMPSON	33									25		5	3
Nick CLARK	33		16		2	9	6						
Jordan THOMPSON	29			7	4		11		6			1	
Johnny BLACKSHAW	27	13							2	3	9		
Joshua DAY	27	3		8						2	4	10	
Ashley MIDWOOD	22		6			16							
Adam LYON	21					11	3		7				
Freddie RUSSO	21	1				5	1					6	8
Liam LYON	20	10				6	4						
Brad ANDERSON	20			1		1	9	9					
Bruce WINFIELD	18				5						2		11
Josh WAINWRIGHT	14									4		3	7
Josh CAYGILL	8		5						1				2
Michael ROBERTSON	7						2	5					
Niall WADDELL	6							6					
James DYE	5	5											
Danny BUCHAN	5								5				
Stanley GAMBLE	5												5
Anthony ROGERS	5										1	4	
James EAST	5	2				3							
G HOGTON-RUSLING	4							4					
Mike McLEAN	4								4				
Dominic USHER	4		1					3					
Grant WHITAKER	3							2					1
Sam NEATE	2			2									

2009 Relentless British 125GP Championship

Points after final round

Name	Total	Brands Hatch Indy 13 April 2009	Oulton Park 4 May 2009	Donington Park 25 May 2009	Thruxton 31 May 2009	Snetterton 21 June 2009	Knockhill 5 July 2009	Mallory Park 19 July 2009	Brands Hatch GP 9 August 2009	Cadwell Park 31 August 2009	Croft 13 September 2009	Silverstone 27 September 2009	Oulton Park 11 October 2009
James LODGE	182	13	16	20	13	20	25	20	20		10	16	9
Rob GUIVER	170	9	20		9	9	20	25	25	8		25	20
Martin GLOSSOP	155	25	25	25		11	11		13	25		20	
Brian CLARK	138			16	25	10	10	10	11		20	11	25
Paul JORDAN	104	11		8	16	25	4		8	10	6	8	8
Tim HASTINGS	103		10	5	20	16	5	16		9	16	6	
Connor BEHAN	98	10	11		10		16			16	25		10
Tom HAYWARD	90	20	13		7	13	6		6	13		5	7
Deane BROWN	76					4	9		7	20	11	9	16
Adam BLACKLOCK	76			3	8	7		9	16	11	9		13
Taylor MACKENZIE	53	3		13		3	7		4		7	13	3
Shaun HORSMAN	49	16		6	11			11		4		1	
Robbie STEWART	42		4		2		13	13	10				
Catherine GREEN	38	6	8		1	5		2		3	5	4	4
Ryan SAXELBY	36	7	9		5	6	3						6
Lee COSTELLO	33			11	6		8	8					
Matthew HOYLE	28								5		13	10	
Harry STAFFORD	26	8							3		8	7	
Michael HILL	25		2	10	4		2	6	1				
Peter SUTHERLAND	24		6	7		8					3		
Edward RENDELL	19	5			3	2			9				
Philip WAKEFIELD	19	4	5				1			7		2	
Matthew PAULO	13			9				4					
Sam HORNSEY	12		7										5
Danny KENT	11												11
Tom WEEDEN	9							5	2	1	1		
Ross WALKER	9									5	4		
Jon VINCENT	9	1		4						2	2		
Corey LEWIS	7							7					
Jay LEWIS	7									6			1
Shaun WINFIELD	5	2						3					
Rob HODSON	3		3										
Ian LOUGHER	3											3	
Luke HARVEY	2			2									
Andy REID	2												2
John McPHEE	2			1				1					
Ben BARRETT	1		1										
Jamie MOSSEY	1					1							

2009 Focused Events KTM RC8 Super Cup Championship

Points after final round

Name	Total	Brands Hatch Indy - R1 13 April 2009	Brands Hatch Indy - R2 13 April 2009	Oulton Park 4 May 2009	Donington Park - R1 25 May 2009	Donington Park - R2 25 May 2009	Thruxton 31 May 2009	Snetterton - R1 21 June 2009	Snetterton - R2 21 June 2009	Knockhill - R1 5 July 2009	Knockhill - R2 5 July 2009	Brands Hatch GP - R1 9 August 2009	Brands Hatch GP - R2 9 August 2009	Cadwell Park 31 August 2009	Silverstone 27 September 2009
Dave WOOD	243				25	20	25	8	20	25	25	20	25	25	25
Pauli PEKKANEN	212	1	11	20	13	16	16	13	25	16	16	25	20		20
Kelvin REILLY	198	25	25	25		25	13	9	16		9	16	16	11	8
Francis WILLIAMSON	177	16	16	6	11	13	20	20	10	13	10	9	11	9	13
James EDMEADES	158	13	13	16	20		11	16	8	11		11	10	20	9
Ed SMITH	139	20	20	13	16		10			9	8	7	9	16	11
Dave HEAL	132			8	9	11	8	5	9	20	20	13	13		16
Sam BISHOP	124	11	9	7	10	10	6	25	13		11	10	8		4
Jonathan RAILTON	118	10	10	9	8	9	9	11	11	10	13	8			10
Ben TAYLOR	79	9	8	4	7	8	7	6	7		3	6	6	5	3
Adam FOSTER	73	6	6	11	4		5	7	4	7	6	3		7	7
Rikki OWEN	49	2	2	3	5	7	3	2		8	5		4	8	
Richie THORNTON	45		5	1		2	2	4				5	7	13	6
Andy BATTYE	43	7	7	5	6	6				6	4	2			
Taryn SKINNER	41	5	4	10	3		1	3		4	7			4	
Andrew MARRIOTT	32			2					5	3	2	4	5	6	5
Jon PAINE	19	4	1		1	3		10							
Peter GOLDEN	19	8			2	4	4						1		
Rob McNEALY	16							1	6	5		1	3		
Nick HOBDEN	13	3	3			1			2				2		2
Scott ROPER	10													10	
Pete HASLER	8								3	2				3	
Shaun GILBERT	5					5									
Ben BROADWAY	2													2	
Jay SMITH	1														1

JEWSON
WRIGLEY'S
Airwaves
KICK UP A GEAR
JEWSON
YAMALUBE
SHOEI
GSEGROUP
mce

SHOEI
Airwaves
PIRELLI
brembo
2009
2